Bankruption

Bankruption

How Community Banking Can Survive Fintech

John Waupsh

WILEY

Published by John Wiley & Sons, Inc., Hoboken, New Jersey.
Published simultaneously in Canada.

For general information on our other products and services or for technical support, please contact our Customer Care Department within the United States at (800) 762-2974, outside the United States at (317) 572-3993 or fax (317) 572-4002.

Wiley publishes in a variety of print and electronic formats and by print-on-demand. Some material included with standard print versions of this book may not be included in e-books or in print-on-demand. If this book refers to media such as a CD or DVD that is not included in the version you purchased, you may download this material at http://booksupport.wiley.com. For more information about Wiley products, visit www.wiley.com.

Library of Congress Cataloging-in-Publication Data is available:

ISBN 9781119273851 (Hardcover)
ISBN 9781119273868 (ePDF)
ISBN 9781119273882 (ePub)

Cover Design: babarzaman
Cover Image: © Lightspring/Shutterstock

Printed in the United States of America

10 9 8 7 6 5 4 3 2

To Brooke, Lowen, and Jack, for the constant
support and inspiration.

To my parents and family, for the unrelenting encouragement.

Contents

Preface

As battle-scarred survivors of a financial crisis and deep recession, community bankers today confront a frustratingly slow recovery, stiff competition from larger banks and other financial institutions, and the responsibility of complying with new and existing regulations. Some observers have worried that these obstacles—particularly complying with regulations—may prove insurmountable.

—Ben Bernanke, chairman, board of governors
of the Federal Reserve System

We Have Become Enslaved by Fintech Content

Today's bankers get so much help. A constant bombardment of LinkedIn articles, blog posts, tweets, podcasts, books(!), reports from big and small consulting firms, conferences, private discussion forums and tweet-ups, and, of course, an incessant barrage of regulation updates.

The help/noise would overwhelm any banker, if the content of the cacophony hadn't already done so.

Flippant conference panel conjecture, medium expositions on what's happening or what's not happening, limited sample set surveys, and otherwise poorly researched analysis clog the analytical filter of even the most engaged banker.

Figure P.1   The Number of Financial Institutions in the United States by Type

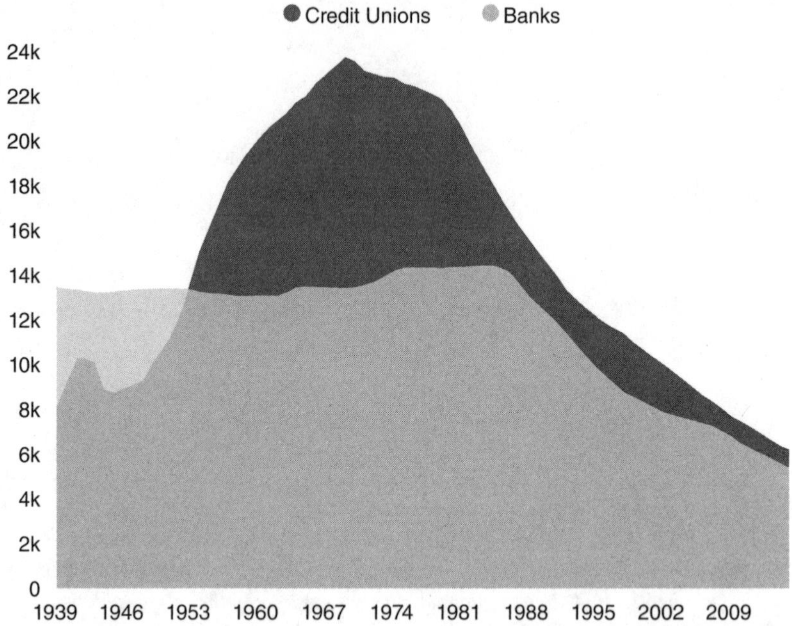

SOURCE: CUNA and FDIC
The number of banks and credit unions has dropped significantly over the past 35 years.

One day, peer to peer (excuse me, *marketplace*) lending is going to transform how someone borrows money, and the next day it is torn apart by the SEC.[1] Then, it's legal and thriving: all unicorns and showboats. Seemingly, a few days later, it's in the Consumer Financial Protection Bureau (CFPB)'s crosshairs (though consumers don't seem to be worried about it).

As my buddy @leimer is fond of saying, "Fintech never sleeps." Perhaps. Or maybe, fintech never shuts up.

According to Mike D King (@bankwide), in April 2016, "#fintech" was seeing 138 unique tweets and 562,000 exposures per hour. That doesn't include all those tweets about fintech that don't contain the word, of course.

This continuous media and pundit churn delivers the consequence of imposed, conscious blindness. Those of us who should know most about what is happening end up knowing the very least, because, to put it simply, keeping track of it all is mind-numbing and defeating.

Maybe the fintech startup hype machine is serving its purpose: beating bankers into submission. Smashing, loud dissonant intimidation puts the silent, introverted banker quants who thrive in the shadows, directly where the STEM experts want them: fetal position, wailing. And, Stockholm syndrome may yet force partnership discussions.

Sexy, boisterous, overcompensating fintech startups extending the partnership olive branch to financial institutions (again). Perhaps the noise is simply a byproduct of the remarkable innovation these guys bring to the table.

So maybe the weight of it all is something other than the noise.

Maybe It's That Community Banking as We Know It Is No Longer Relevant

FDIC-insured institutions dropped from 8,396 at the end of 2007 to 6,210 at the end of 2015, and credit unions fell from 7,284 to 5,410 during the same time period. This has got to be the end of banking as we know it, right?

Buckminster Fuller (inventor of the geodesic dome, a pioneer of sustainable planetary thinking, and one of the greatest comprehensive design minds of the modern era) spent most of his adult life relearning everything he was taught in school.[2]

His rationale for this was quite simple: much of what he learned in school classrooms and texts originated from facts that had been skewed over time by governments, religions, societies, or simply accidents (a byproduct of human-powered recordkeeping).

The banking world of today has more contaminated and more biased reporting than Bucky's of a hundred years ago.

For example, if one bothered to research the data behind the aforementioned stats, one would find that nearly the same number of institutions disappeared the six years preceding 2007 as the six years following.

Does that make the trend more or less alarming? What if there were more sizable declinations of financial institutions at other points in history—would that change the argument? What if, when further analyzing the data, one would find the disappearing FIs were being replaced (via new charters) at a much slower rate than in the past? And what if, in one's quieter moments, one were to consider that artificial intelligence can and should automatically manage money for humans and that blockchains and their enabled technologies such as bidirectional payment channels will be the ultimate arbiters, thereby making banks and credit unions obsolete?

This is the juncture when the preponderance of noise clouds the real data and obscures actionable intelligence.

Futurists, technologists, and others suggest an end to banking as we know it. While today's banking will undergo complete transformation over time, that may not be *today's banking story*. The future of banking is entertaining to read and lots of fun to listen to or to debate at a conference, but it's also not the best use of time for a banker who needs to drag her credit union or bank across the ever-widening chasm between yesterday and today.

> If you want the very end of the banking story: ones and zeroes win. In the future, thousands of existing "financial institutions" will assimilate, our money will be managed for us automatically via artificial intelligence, dumb or smart contracts and learned behaviors, and no banked human anywhere on earth will have to think about bills, managing their money, or rates on insurances, mortgages, or deposits.
>
> I spend a few pages discussing this idea at the end of this book. A few pages out of a couple hundred. The reason is simple: any prediction toward the "big" future will prove itself true at some point in the horizon of time, but we should not confuse that far off world with today's—or even the next 10 years'—reality. And, perhaps if financial institutions make small changes now, they can adapt or, better yet, knock a dent in that trajectory.

Not unlike Bucky's endeavor, today's community banking leaders need a clear baseline—a cleansing of the various myths that have promulgated themselves into mainstream thinking.

Where possible, *Bankruption* will use unadulterated data to distill the myths from the truths, the hypotheses from the facts. Historical evidence and detailed data (rather than daily trends) will inform the practical guidance for short-term and long-term planning contained in the latter two-thirds of this book.

> You'll find this data in the many charts throughout the book, and to round out the analysis, many more charts are available via the book's website for you to download and use in your own presentations.

In an attempt to maintain that focus, we won't spend much time in this book on Ethereum, digital payments, internet of things, artificial intelligence, etc. that are in the midst of evolution today. While these topics must be given mind space as they may foundationally change the future of banking, they are outside the scope of this text—Brett King or Chris Skinner can offer you some great reads on these subjects.

Speaking of stellar industry thinkers, this book contains something that no conference has been able to do: get the absolute best minds in the industry in one place to share their thoughts on near-term, practical guidance for community banking executives.

I'm humbled by the generosity of these thinkers and doers. Over 20 brilliant friends, from community bankers to industry analysts, offer their expert advice to community bankers—exclusively for *Bankruption* readers—and they asked for nothing in return.

So here it is: a project that has taken way too long, and required way too much sacrifice from my wife, co-workers and family. My passion for the community banking industry is no secret, but all the passion in the world isn't enough to return relevance to a dying model. My hope is that by shedding the weight of the noise, you and your team can build a timely, executable business model around a strategy that makes sense for you, with achievable goals and deliberate solutions.

- John

Oh and some notes:

- At times, I can't stand the noise, either. By Chapter 3 of *Bankruption*, you'll find stream-of-consciousness breaks. This is my brain making sense of it all during the extended writing process—the effect of a person living in (and contributing to) the noise 24/7 for 10 years. If it gets too thick, feel free to skip forward. Heaven knows I wish I could have.
- While I use inspiration from around the world for various solutions, *Bankruption* is focused on the U.S. community banking system of credit unions and community banks.
- Unlike other books that casually use the word *bank* to refer to community banks and credit unions, I use them separately because they are distinct in their politics and policies, and sometimes data relates specifically to just one group.
- That said, *community banking* refers to the thing that both do—service banking in communities (geographical, employer, digitally, or otherwise).
- Don't forget to download all of the charts in the text and many more from the website. Feel free to use them in your own internal presentations. Just keep all the sourcing and copyrights viewable to others.

Introduction

P rior to the start of the ALCO meeting on this particular Tuesday, the heir-apparent to the chairman glances at his dad's and grand-dad's oil paintings on the wallpapered conference room wall.

If this coffee mug could talk.

First official week as CEO. His confidence is strong as he is well-trained on how to run his family's banking business. And, thankfully, the team that led the bank for the last 35 years has all stayed on to support him.

A deep breath. 7:30 a.m. Time to earn his oil painting!

He kicks off the weekly meeting with a brief, thoughtful soliloquy on legacy and leadership.

The well-rehearsed speech gives assurances that he will embrace the people, processes, and strategy that his father adopted from his father. After some applause and hugs, he leaves to give the same spiel in a few other conference rooms down I-90.

An impressive accomplishment to own and operate a third generation business where only 12 percent[3] of all family-run businesses make it that far, and only 3 percent make it to the following generation. He knows these numbers because he's challenged them his whole life.

Even the bank's examiners remind him of the risk in lending to multigenerational businesses. But it's what you do around here, and, it's worked for 92 years.

And while his goose isn't cooked for running a family-owned and operated business, it will soon be deeply fried for other reasons.

The committees and the meetings, ALCO and otherwise, give a false-sense of control.

In his first day as CEO, this charming, 50-something Wharton MBA and ABA Stonier Graduate School of Banking scholar made a promise to continue sowing the seeds of decay[4] for his 92-year-old community bank.

"No oil painting for you!"

Notes

1. "United States of America before the Securities and Exchange Commission," Securities Act of 1933, release no. 8984, November 24, 2008, https://www.sec .gov/litigation/admin/2008/33-8984.pdf.

2. http://bfi.org/about-fuller.

3. Family Business Institute, https://www.familybusinessinstitute.com/consulting/ succession-planning/.

4. Kirk Dando, *Predictive Leadership: Avoiding the 12 Critical Mistakes That Derail Growth-Hungry Companies* (St. Martin's Press, 2014).

Additional Thanks

To Sean, Gabe, and BenMo. Stan Goudeau and Don Shafer. Marty Sunde and my First Team. My product team, the wingmen, and the rest of my Kasasa family. Paul Blinderman and Shaun Pauling. John Kish, Stephen Rice and The Riverside Company. My buddies in fintech and in community banking. My contributor friends, each of you, for different reasons: I am eternally grateful.

Bankruption

Chapter 1

An Overview of the Bankruption

"Money can't buy life."

—*Bob Marley (final words before death)*

Community Banking Has No Future

Community banks overdosed on arrogance and comfort in the status quo. The vice of Pride plays the long game. She starts harmless enough—young and reckless. Discerning and punctual. But Pride, a generation or three down the line, quite deeply cataracts and sloths. Bankers' kids become loan officers become CEOs become chairmen become barnacle board members of their grandkids' banks.

By and large, community banks are family-begun businesses that have only lasted this long because banking competition was light, with controlled access points. The ultimate problem with family businesses, perhaps, is not pride—it's that blood overrules brains.

Credit unions, you're not off the hook, either.

Quite a bit of legacy thinking going on there, too, with far too many inefficiencies, a model the average consumer doesn't know or care about, and a belief system that outstrips capability. Oh and your boards are typically full of people who have no experience in banking or technology, and zero financial interest in the health or future of the credit union.

If any of that cut a bit too close to home, pay attention, it gets worse.

Because despite the tireless work of many thousands of passionate employees who sought to advance their community institutions from the inside, community banks and credit unions are bloated, outdated, human-powered, ego-driven, know-it-all, do-it-all, whiny, tired, over-regulated, underappreciated customer experience nightmares.

Of course, that's the easy part to fix. Community institutions still have to thrive within the ever-changing banking landscape. And with pole shifts occurring to every foregone conclusion in their business models, top financial institutions today are defining winning strategies that acknowledge and respect these transformative forces.

Although there are a few community banks and credit unions committing to the difficult process of re-examining and changing their business based upon the realities of today, there's not enough to make a difference. Not enough to save the industry from its own damned self.

This is where my brain sat for about a year. My heart crushed; my soul smashed, until I became absolutely obsessed with finding any possible cure to the terminal illness. It only makes sense that incumbents should have one or more advantages. We just need to find them, exploit them, and shore up the weaknesses.

Community Banking Relies Too Heavily on Physical Proximity

Years ago, people in towns across America needed access to capital and a safer place to store their money. Customers lacked the capability to travel too far from home, and bankers didn't want the money they lent to go too far from the safe, so they established a nearby physical location to perform these services. This nearness worked both ways, positioned around the ideal of *convenience*.

Proximity manufactured a false sense of trust between the two parties. Either side trusting the other not to take its money and run—because they have a big, heavy, unmovable structure with columns, or because they live nearby.

And the mutual lie worked pretty well.

This falsehood of belief became further twisted when people learned that the attire they wore to the bank directly impacted how they were treated (e.g., more favorable loan rates). In perhaps an early form of identity fraud, customers would don their Sunday best to get the banker's best.

Somehow, this lie of convenience between the two parties became known as a *relationship*, and mistaken for *intimacy*—a word that connotes personal and honest, shared knowledge—even though the association was, and has remained for decades, anything but intimate.

And over the years, with few exceptions, regulation has reinforced the false benefits of human touch–powered banking by, among other things, raising insurance rates on deposits originated in areas beyond an FI's local branch network. Their assumption: Deposits and accounts sourced digitally (or otherwise outside physical branches) are more inclined to travel to other FIs at a whim.

Today, Data Proximity Yields Intimacy

In 2015, we left behind five exabytes of data exhaust every two minutes: from Periscoped hip-hop concerts to Snapchatted high school home-comings to YouTubed cat videos to less important things like emojiied business emails (see Figure 1.1).

Figure 1.1 Creating Five Exabytes of Data

SOURCE: Berkeley School of Information, 2015
The time, in minutes, it takes humans to create the amount of data from the dawn of time to 2003. Another way to look at it is if you wanted to watch a video of everything that was sent across our global networks in one second of 2015, it would take you about five years of 24×7 screen time.

Not only does each of us leave behind gigabytes-thick data residue daily, but we also have become—consciously and subconsciously—comfortable, and nearly dependent, on our data streams.

These days, well-timed, well-placed, well-modeled informed dig-ital interactions build relationships, trust, and understanding. This all but ensures that any strategy relying solely on physical proximity is a liability.

Data Proximity Has Cast a Very Bright Light on the Cracks of Banking

As Americans begin to taste and feel the ease and fluidity of omni-channel in retail, theme parks, and so on, they learn that innocuous data, like that which sat in ink on paper shopping lists, can greatly enhance their lives. They see how we can talk to devices, and they will do things for us ("Alexa, play some Violent Femmes"). They see how devices can talk to other devices (via Internet of Things) and turn on lamps or adjust the temperature for us (see Figure 1.2). Consumers see all of this happening today, and understand that it is no longer science fiction.

Figure 1.2 Forecast: Internet of Things Devices (in Billions)

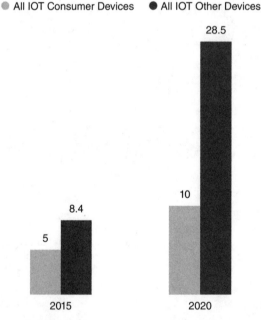

SOURCE: Juniper Research, 2015

The forecasted explosion of networked physical devices, buildings, et al. embedded with sensors and software that collect and exchange data.

Conversely, my friendly community bank teller "helped me" get $450 cash out of an account in a face-to-face transaction, but then wished me a "Bye, Steve" as I began to walk away.

The obvious question then follows, "Why can't the place that houses my most important data, my bank or credit union, use the information I give it all the time (e.g., credit card, bill payments, balance data, timing of future bills, timing of future deposits, etc.) to help me? Why can't banking be easy and protective? Why doesn't my financial provider know me?"

And so today, American consumers bounce between two totally different worlds:

Normal World	Banking World
Digital.	Analog (e.g., paper and wet signatures).
Fast (e.g., sending a letter to another country is now instantaneous).	Slow (e.g., answering an email complaint takes a business day).
Accessible (e.g., I can download a movie on my phone and watch it while sitting on a beach).	Unpredictable accessibility (e.g., I can check my credit card balance on the website, but not in the branch or in an app).
Open communication between people (e.g., Twitter, Facebook Messenger).	Departmental silos (e.g., I have to repeat my concern several times to several different people when I call customer service—even during the same phone call).
Open communication between software (e.g., Slack uses APIs to infinitely extend its capabilities to work with hundreds of other software).	Little to no communication between software (e.g., my bank's investment app cannot share data with my bank's credit card app).
Regular upgrades.	Upgrades?

Community bankers have always stayed behind the curve, in an attempt to moderate risk and lessen unnecessary expense.

But where does risk mitigation end and enterprise risk begin? When does doing the thing you've always done become the riskiest thing you could do? Welcome to the bankruption—the watershed for community banks and credit unions.

Chapter 2

Community Banking Is Broken

What Is Community Banking?

For nearly 200 years, the U.S. economy has been fueled by small, independent institutions lending local money to local people who earned local money that got spent locally.

While the smallest it's been, our financial system is unique across the globe with over 11,000 different competitive financial provider access points (see Figures 2.1 and 2.2).

These small, community-based banking institutions often catered their products and services around their community's specific needs, such as agriculture lending in rural towns, high savings rates for employees, and commercial real estate lending in micropolitan communities.

Figure 2.1 Forecast: Total FIs in the United States by 2020

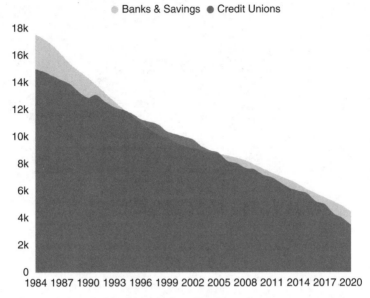

SOURCE: FDIC, NCUA & Peak Performance Consulting Group
The numbers of banks and credit unions have declined steadily since 1984.

Figure 2.2 Percentage of Deposits by Asset Size in the United States

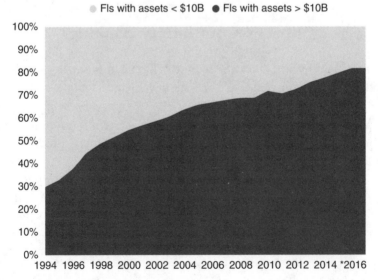

SOURCE: FDIC, NCUA; ★ = Forecast by author
The assets of community banks and credit unions under $10 billion in assets have moved with rigor to large institutions since 1994.

> Until recently, local geography has often defined an institution's "community." While the idea of "locality" was an important distinction for community banks and the majority of credit unions over the past 100 years, some credit unions (such as those related to Special Employer Groups with a nationwide employer base) have successfully demonstrated that communities of people not bound by physical divides exist and still remain loyal to an institution. To compete in today's landscape, banks need their regulators to adjust to a similar nonphysical concept of "community." Credit unions have already begun to do this with the easing of their market area rules to include "website" as a market area.

While the board of governors of the Federal Reserve System define[1] community banks as any bank under $10 billion in assets, the OCC and FDIC both traditionally used the $1 billion threshold.

In 2012, the FDIC, predicting the community banking industry would soon outgrow the $1 billion restriction, set out to add more dials and levers to the definition.[2] Low and behold, the FDIC found there were common attributes among community banks that were not tied exclusively to the size of the bank. (Credit unions, have some patience, please, as the FDIC catches up to you ...)

So, in that study, the FDIC created a whole host of algorithms and fancy math to conclude what most in the industry already knew. According to the FDIC, community banks:

- Follow "tradition" in relationship lending and deposit gathering.
- Have a limited geographic scope.

By focusing the definition of a "community bank" around how and where a bank conducts its business rather than its asset size, the FDIC found the group includes an additional 330 larger banks that would have otherwise been excluded due to the $1 billion asset size cut off point. It also excluded some smaller banks under the new definition, such as industrial loan companies, bankers' banks, trust companies, and credit card specialists.

Let's examine the two characteristics the FDIC uses to define community banks.

1. Relationship Data–Based Lending: Just How Valuable Is That Soft Data?

Community banks are *relationship bankers,* and are important agricultural and small-business lenders (see Figure 2.3), as well as lifelines to mainstream financial services for most nonmetro and rural areas. As the FDIC[3] puts it, community banks have always been "inextricably connected to entrepreneurship."

Figure 2.3   Sources of Credit for Businesses in 2014

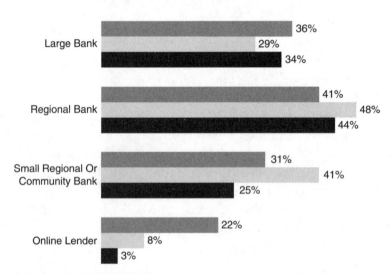

- Startups (<5 yrs in business)
- Growers (profitable & increased revenues)
- Matures (>5 yrs in business, 10+ employees, holds debt)

Large Bank: 36%, 29%, 34%

Regional Bank: 41%, 48%, 44%

Small Regional Or Community Bank: 31%, 41%, 25%

Online Lender: 22%, 8%, 3%

SOURCE: New York Fed; Philadelphia Fed
Regional banks have begun to outpace community banks in lending to "growing" small businesses.

Whereas big banks used strict, standardized lending criteria based on hard data (e.g., FICO), small institutions have traditionally sourced and adjudicated on nonstandardized, soft (or relationship) data learned over the course of a banking relationship.

This local knowledge and flexibility gave community institutions a strong advantage when it came to lending to "informationally opaque borrowers" such as startup businesses or small businesses without audited financials, consumers with irregular income, or those without credit histories.[4]

And it turned out that doing the right thing (catering a product offering to their market in the way the community bankers have done over the past hundred years) was profitable (despite the obvious asset concentration risk associated with the model).

Study after study by the FDIC has shown that prudent relationship lending leads to lower loan losses for community banks than the more traditional "fit in this box" lending of their noncommunity bank counterparts.

However, the tactics of past success will not dictate future success.

Over the past 30 years,[5] the loan yield advantage community banks held over megabanks flattened from 130 basis points (bps) to about 60 bps, median assets per employee increased 80 percent for megabanks (just 30 percent for community banks), and community banks increased expense to asset ratio by 15 bps. All this amounts to a very thin, quickly disappearing (and very "averaged") 15 bps "advantage" for community banks over megabanks.

2. Geographical Focus: Bank Local, and All That, Right?

Remember the popular conversation about too big to fail banks, "big banks are evil" and "bank local" media, fat cat CEOs and their bonuses, big bank fees, and the occupying of various streets? Remember, November 5, 2011, better known as Bank Transfer Day, the day that saw 600,000 consumers "move their money from big banks" to community institutions to stick it to the big guys?

Turned out that all of that dinner table conversation and earned media wasn't very helpful to community institutions. From 2012 to 2014,[6] Chase grew around the combined asset size of all 6,600[7] banks and credit unions under $100M. Wells Fargo did the same. Bank of America purposefully shed about $100B, and Citi remained flat,[8] again, by choice.

What gives? What about all those angry Twitter and Facebook posts and frustrated commenters on blogs? What about the protests and the Move Your Money movement? Didn't any of that do anything to change the sad course for community banking?

Not really.

According to a report,[9] financial assets of credit unions grew from $400 million in 2000 to over $1 trillion in 2015 (see Figure 2.4). That seems decent, but here's the kicker: credit union revenue has been flat, and is expected to remain flat until at least 2020,[10] and, like community banks, smaller credit unions are seeing much higher operating costs for specific levels of production.[11]

Figure 2.4 Assets of US Credit Unions 2013–2015

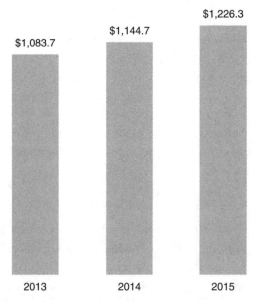

SOURCE: CUNA Mutual Group
The total value of all assets at credit unions in the United States has risen steadily the past few years, yet revenue remains flat.

The majority of American consumers choose their retail banking accounts not to save the local economy or because they care about the credit union movement, but for one of three self-serving reasons: convenience, fees, or features.

In its revised definition of community banks, the FDIC failed to mention that these two defining characteristics (soft data–driven lending and geographical focus) form portions of the group's Achilles' heel.

Over the next few years, advancement in financial technology and data modeling will further undermine the long-trumpeted advantages of relationship lending, bringing to light the costly productivity inefficiencies of human interaction, soft data harvesting and retention, negotiation, and decision making in an increasingly regulated and data-driven industry (see Figure 2.5).

Figure 2.5   Digital Banking Users by Generation in Millions

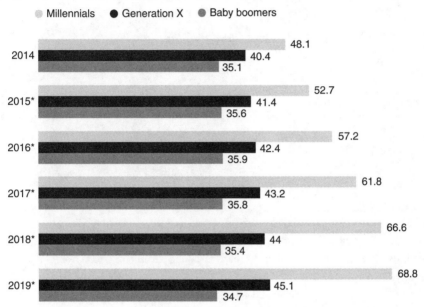

SOURCE: eMarketer (2015) ★ = Forecast. Excludes virtual wallet services like Paypal and Google Wallet. Nearly every millennial in the United States will be using digital banking by 2020.

Where Are All the Institutions Going?

In God we trust; all others must bring data.

—*W. Edwards Deming*

If you've been in this industry longer than a minute, you've heard a speaker or read an article that claimed the declination in bank charters is a direct result of either new fintech competition wreaking havoc on the banking model or greedy bankers causing bank failures (see Figures 2.6 and 2.7).

The truth is, as usual, less exciting. In fact, while the industry has witnessed a serendipitous decline in the number of banks and credit unions,

Figure 2.6   FDIC-Insured Bank Failures by Year

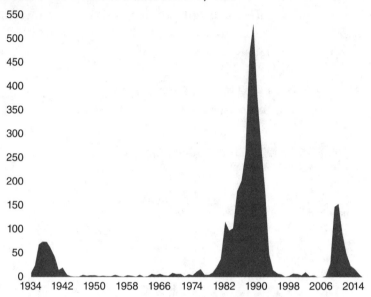

SOURCE: FDIC

Only 14 percent of the total decline in financial institutions since 1980 is due to failure.

Figure 2.7   Number of Bank Charters Issued Compared to Those Currently Operating

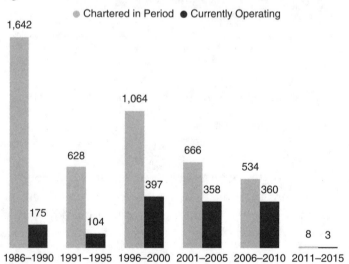

SOURCE: FDIC

Charter consolidation has been a constant in our industry for decades, with only 30 percent of banks chartered since 1986 still operating as independent banks.

the reasons are quite a bit more complex and nuanced than "new fintech competition." To those alarmists who suggest new fintech competition is tearing apart banks, consolidation has been a constant in the US banking industry since 1980.

Back in 1980, banks numbered around 14,000 and credit unions around 21,000. This was just before PCs started entering households, airline travel became more affordable, email forever changed the nine-to-five job, and the world started getting smaller.

Almost 40 years later, it's around 5,500 and 6,500, respectively. Interestingly, only about one seventh of the decline since 1980 is the result of bank or credit union failure; fully six-sevenths of the decline in financial institution numbers since 1980 is due to merger or other, nonfailure, consolidation. Hardly new-age competition—more so evolution.

FDIC's Three Reasons for Bank Charter Consolidation

FDIC teaches us there are three main reasons for charter consolidation, and, as a breath of fresh air, supplements its hypothesis with some really nice data to put it in perspective.[12] While the following is bank/thrift-centric, credit unions and others might find the data useful as well. The three reasons are:

1. Voluntary closures
2. Bank failures
3. Few new charters

Let's look at these in more detail.

Voluntary Closures

When you look at long-term consolidation in bank charters, you must recognize the most critical component: voluntary closures. That's because since 1985, voluntary closures have accounted for around 80 percent of the total bank charter attrition.

Voluntary closures come in three flavors: intracompany consolidation of commonly owned charters, intercompany mergers, and, more rarely, self-liquidation.

Intracompany consolidation of commonly owned charters causes charter consolidation when a bank holding company has more than one charter and decides that it'd be a heck of a lot simpler, cheaper, and so on to collapse two or more of their charters into one. Since the holding company remains in place, this focusing of internal structure does not reduce the number of banking organizations, but it does reduce the overall number of bank charters.

Intercompany mergers are a bit more common than intracompany charter mergers. Intercompany mergers cause charter consolidation when a banking organization acquires a charter or merges with a charter operating under separate ownership. This is typically done to expand the bank's size or geography.

The period from 1993 to 2001 saw the highest voluntary attrition average (5.4 percent), primarily due to effects of the Interstate Banking

Figure 2.8   Voluntary Attrition Rates of U.S. Banks

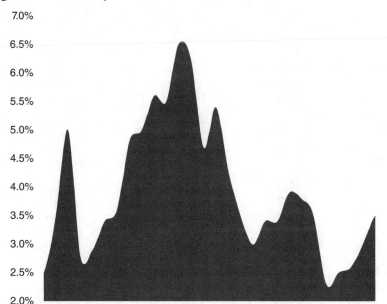

Source: FDIC
Voluntary bank charter consolidation: inter-company mergers, intra-company consolidation and self-liquidation (as a percentage of charters at year-end) in the United States.

and Branching Efficiency Act of 1994 (Riegle-Neal) (see Figure 2.8). With the consolidation of charters within existing organizations and the acquisition of charters operated under different ownership possible, industry consolidation by way of voluntary charter closures ignited the most aggressive period of bank charter consolidation, topping even that of the 2008 recession.

About 65 percent of all closed community banks between 2003 and 2015 were acquired by other community banks (see Figure 2.9), but these days, credit unions are also getting into the community bank acquisition game—especially in the sub-$100M asset community bank market. The 2011 acquisition of Griffith Savings Bank (Griffith, Indiana) by United Federal Credit Union was the first time a federally chartered credit union purchased or merged with a bank.

Since then, 10 similar bank acquisitions by credit unions have been approved by bank shareholders and their regulators, allowing the

Figure 2.9 Community Banks Acquiring Their Own, 2003–2015

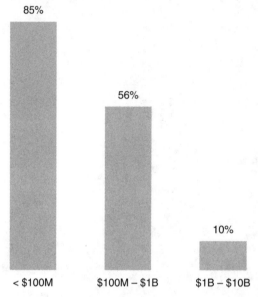

SOURCE: FDIC
Percentage of closed community bank charters acquired by other community banks, by asset size of shuttered bank.

acquired bank to avoid selling to a regional bank while keeping most of its staff and branches intact.

As could be expected, the average size for community banks has grown over time (see Figure 2.10). FDIC completed a study in 2013 that compared the community bank of 1985 to the community bank of 2013, whereby they associate the 3x growth of the 90th percentile, and the 4x growth of the median (and even the 10th percentile) asset-sized community banks, with the enormous acquisition activity that occurred during the 30-year period. Interestingly, the FDIC points out that while community banks saw simultaneous consolidation and growth (on a per bank basis), community banks as a whole remained consistent in offering their local communities necessary banking services.

Bank Failures

According to the FDIC, bank and thrift failures are the second most important factor in post-1985 consolidation, accounting for about

Figure 2.10   Community Bank Assets over Time

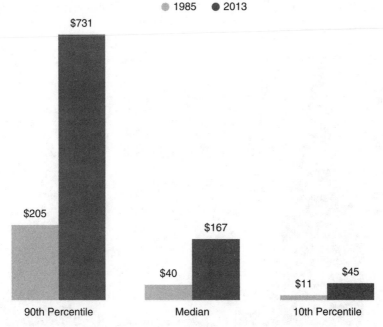

● 1985   ● 2013

Asset distribution of community banks in United States, in million U.S. dollars (1985 vs 2013).

SOURCE: FDIC

17 percent of all charter attrition (or about 2,600 federally insured banks and thrifts).

Post-1980, there are two time periods of sizable failure for banks and thrifts—the first wave driven by the terrible savings and loan crisis and the second by the Great Recession. While the number of the failed institutions is somewhat interesting (see Figure 2.11), the impact of their demise is more easily understood when put in context of the total chartered bank population during the years of failure (see Figure 2.12).

In either chart, you can see two obvious periods of concentrated thrift and bank failure: 1986–1993 and 2008–2013, and a nice, steady quiet period in-between. (Remember, a la FDIC, the year in the chart shows the data at previous year-end: e.g., "1986" is 1985 data, and so on. To avoid confusion, I'll reference the same reporting years as FDIC in the chart.)

Figure 2.11   Bank Failure Rates at Previous Year-End

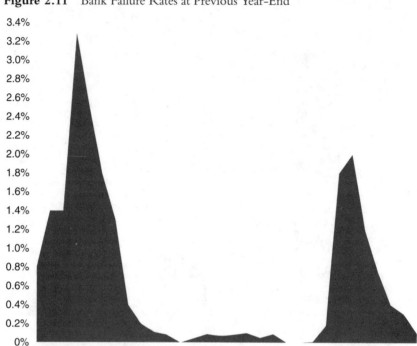

Source: FDIC
This chart shows annual percentage rates of federally insured bank and thrift failure. When put in context of an ever-declining (and nonrenewing) base of chartered banks and thrifts, this chart adequately illuminates the overall impact of the Great Recession failure period (2008–2013) on the community banking industry.

A dark era for Apple, dystopia for hip-hop music, and a period before which most fintech startup geeks were born, 1986 to 1993 saw some complex challenges for federally insured U.S. banks and thrifts. From high credit losses in construction lending and commercial real estate to weathering various (regional) economic slumps, bank (and especially thrift) CEOs had rough waters to navigate during those years. While the average rate of failure over the span comes in around 1.6 percent, the annual rate of failure during this time period ranges between 0.3 percent and 3.2 percent.

The aeon of omnipresent mobile app-based banking and exceedingly heavy-handed banking regulation, 2008 to 2013, not so coincidentally endured the prolonged effects of the entire US residential housing

Figure 2.12   Insolvencies of US Banks

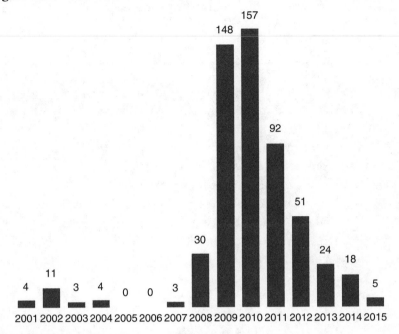

SOURCE: FDIC
While not yet a trend, absolute numbers of bank insolvencies since 2001 show the industry possibly returning to pre-Great Recession insolvency numbers in 2016 and beyond.

market going from terrific to toxic and with it, mortgage-backed securities, jobs, credit scores, bonuses, and bank reputations. The annual rate of failure during this time period ranges between 0.3 percent and 2.0 percent. These two crises account for 97 percent of bank failures in modern banking (1985–2015).

A "noncommunity bank" is not a credit union. The FDIC uses the term "noncommunity bank" to describe the set of approximately 390 banks that do not meet their "community bank" definition. In 1984, a noncommunity bank was, on average, 12 times bigger than a community bank. These days, they are about 75 times larger.

Some fun facts about community bank failure:

- While community banks' rate of total attrition is half that of noncommunity banks, they fail at about the same rate as their bigger brothers.[13]
- Two-thirds of the time that community banks close either voluntarily or through failure, they are acquired by another community bank.[14] This is especially good for the customers of the bank and its community, as it means the acquirer will most likely continue with the same relationship-driven banking practices of the acquired institution.
- In the 10 years between 2003 and 2013, 85 percent of the shuttered community banks under $100 million in assets were acquired by another community bank, and only 9 percent of those acquired were failed banks.[15]
- Only 31 percent of banks chartered since 1986 were in existence in 2016.
- The FDIC believes that bank failure will become far less common (and thus contribute far less to charter consolidation) as a direct result of Dodd-Frank Wall Street Reform and the Consumer Protection Act of 2010 (Dodd-Frank), its spin-off omnipotent Consumer Financial Protection Bureau, and the Basel III capital standards. My bank and credit union friends are begging for what the FDIC is smoking.[16]

Few New Banking Charters

The third point the FDIC offers when considering charter reduction is the very simple fact that new charter creation has historically been quite cyclical.

The last great age of new charter activity (prior to the Great Recession) was 1994 to 2007 (see Figure 2.13). During this time, bank failure was excessively low, and never exceeded 0.1 percent in any one year. Although banking charter creation can offset overall consolidation numbers, the issuing of new charters slows to a crawl during economic downturns such as those in 1990–1991, 2001, and 2008–2009.

Figure 2.13   New Bank Charters Since 1930 (United States)

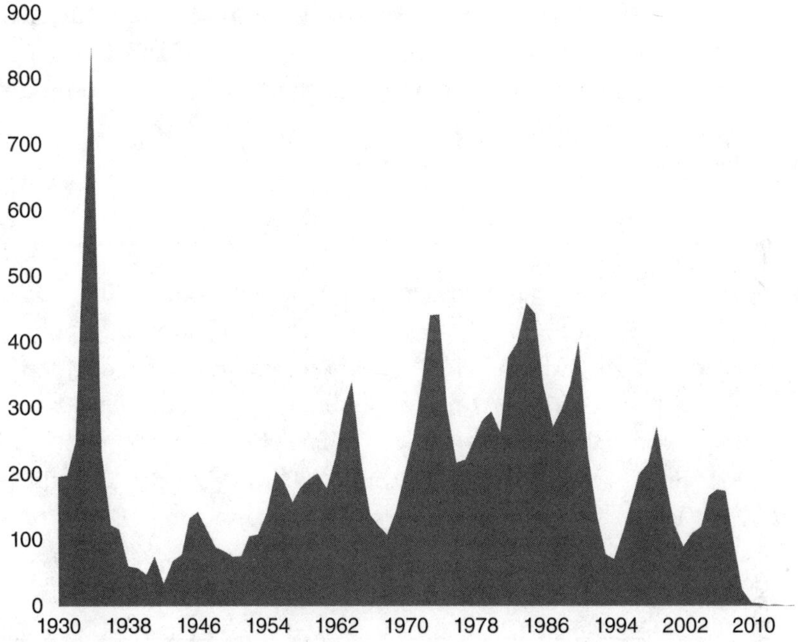

SOURCE: FDIC
Economic downturns have previously slowed charter creation, however, the United States has never seen this long of a prolonged delay in charter creation.

The longer it takes the economy to recover from a particular downturn, the longer the drought of charter approvals. At no point in the past 50 years has this been more evident: economic recovery from the Great Recession was slow, so we saw only 8 bank and 17 credit union charters from 2011 to 2015.[17]

Depopulation and Charter Consolidation Aplenty

During the twentieth century, the agriculture industry endured its own period of consolidation, which left a wake of local unemployment.

This, combined with few nonagricultural local business employment opportunities, forced *brain drain* or migration of otherwise employable talent to micros and metros. All of this out-migration has cast light on the importance of community banking.

A common misconception is that charter consolidation occurred due to the overbanking of rural communities. After all, half of the nearly 1,400 rural counties (containing the headquarters of 1,064 community banks[18]) reported a loss of population between 1980 and 2010,[19] and consistently slowing economic output.

We are using a standard convention[20] whereby 3,238 US counties are subdivided into metropolitan and nonmetropolitan categories. About 1,100 of those counties are deemed metropolitan, and are economically linked to at least one urban core with a 50,000+ population. Metropolitan areas make up about 84 percent of the total U.S. population. One third of the 2,100 nonmetropolitan counties are micropolitan (10,000 to 50,000 people), and two thirds of the counties are considered rural (population under 10,000 people).

But while it is true that rural communities increasingly lose young people (to living in cities) and the elderly (to burials in cemeteries), these are also problems not easily solved by an acquiring bank. As a result, bank consolidation has not occurred in rural markets to the degree of their metropolitan and micropolitan counterparts (with about a 60 percent decline from 1984 to 2015).[21]

In a study of community banks that were operational between 1984 and 2011, the FDIC found that those banks headquartered in rural or micropolitan areas grew half as much as peer banks headquartered in metropolitan areas.[22]

A simple explanation for this lack of growth could simply be the decreased range of lending opportunity for the banks in these markets—fewer and fewer nonagricultural businesses flourished, and fewer and fewer people needed new housing. So these banks saw very little commercial and mortgage lending, and, instead, fought for what little agricultural loan business remained.

You'd think this alone would be enough to demonstrate that the historical model of community banking, focused in physical distribution and bricks and mortar access points, tends to not perform very well when there is a decided absence of potential customers and a shortage of talent (see Figure 2.14).

Figure 2.14 The Number of Community Banks in Depopulating Towns

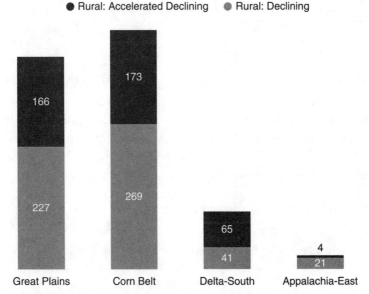

SOURCES: FDIC Call Reports (year-end 2012), 2010 U.S. Census Population, and 2010 OMB Metropolitan and Micropolitan Statistical Area county classifications. Notes: Table reflects only community banks as defined in the FDIC Community Banking Study (2012).
If you're located in a depopulating town and your institution will not alter its directive to solely bank the local geography, you should hope corn starts buying houses.

For what it's worth, today, the median community bank in a depopulating rural market holds about 20 percent of its total assets in agricultural loans (metro-based community banks have about 0.4 percent in agricultural loans).

> Between 1980 and 2010, 41 percent of Corn Belt and 71 per-
> cent of Great Plains counties lost population, making these the
> two largest regions of depopulating rural areas in the United
> States. Together, they account for 835 community banks, 339
> of which have the dubious distinction of residing in accelerated
> declining counties.[23] Imagine the opportunity for these banks if
> they (and their insurer) understood the benefits of transforming
> to a digital community bank!

Another explanation for this lack of growth could be a complete unwillingness to adjust with the times … lack of understanding of
digital acquisition, marketing, and otherwise thoughtless service models.
We'll discuss this more later on.

Conversely, FIs who thrive in sparsely populated areas alter their
weekday hours to cater to the working families for specific needs, rely
on the ubiquitous access of mobile devices (yes, even those in depopulating towns), offer "on-location" service, and otherwise fashion their
institution around their core accountholder base in ways that help it to
manage costs while serving the unique needs of their community.

> 2015 Community Banker of the Year, Jill Castilla, shares her
> roundhouse kick to "brain drain" later in this book.

While positioning your institution in a dwindling community may
limit your appeal to a potential acquirer, and may also limit your future
growth, the incredible shrinking town has proven a bit of an asset in
the realm of financial performance. Over the course of 2000 to 2010,
the pretax return on assets (ROA) performance of 1,091 community
banks based in depopulating rural counties beat the pants off those with
metropolitan headquarters.

Of course, "going rural" isn't necessarily a forward-thinking growth
strategy, either.

Unpacking that successful 10-year performance, one would find that the time period studied included some of the highest prices ever for agriculture, as wheat, soybeans, and corn deliver nearly unbelievable annual net farm income well into the 2010s (Corn Belt and Great Plains rejoice). Couple that with some of the most devastating years ever for metro and micro markets (unemployment, especially construction, by way of the Great Recession), and you'll see how either side experienced anomalies in economies that one might not want to "bank" on.

Community banks[24] are four times more likely to have branches in rural counties than noncommunity institutions. Understandably, town depopulation is a keen concern of community banks and credit unions headquartered in these regions.

To spur growth, 9.3 percent of all community banks in depopulating rural areas expanded into metro markets by 2001, and over 17 percent had done so by 2008. This strategy was a solid win for a few years, delivering twice as much growth as those who did not expand into metro markets, but many of these bankers found themselves lending in areas they had little to no prior experience (CRE, residential, and commercial and industrial).

So, these banks took higher-than-average loan losses (as opposed to their rural peers, who did not expand to metro) during the Great Recession, yet even still, they were much lower losses than metro-based community banks.

Today, many of these institutions have made very successful expansions into metro markets, but they still have a lot of ground to recover. In 1987, community bank's share of total metro deposits was 36 percent, and today, that's around 13 percent.[25] This massive decline in deposit loss is one of the largest indicators of community bank's loss of market share in the United States.

Branch Banking Realities

Not too many discussions on the future of banking pass without a question about the "branch of the future." To me, the branch of the future looks a lot like a mobile device, but I'll set that aside.

For now, let's quickly root ourselves in the recent history of branching, and where we are today in relation to branch closures, and so on (see Figure 2.15).

Figure 2.15   Number of Bank Branches by Year

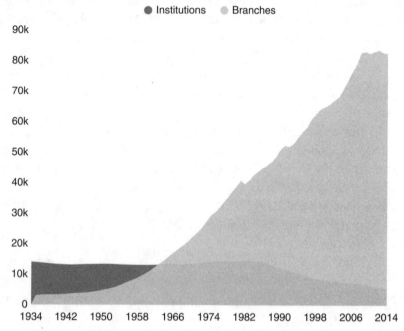

Source: FDIC

The inverse relationship between number of banks and number of branches.

Legislation Propelled Branch Numbers around the Country

In the late 1970s, depository institutions were hamstrung by geographic restrictions, interest rate ceilings, and other corrective measures legislated in response to the Great Depression.

Even by 1979, 12 states were still unit banking states (meaning, FIs could not have a branch at all): Colorado, Illinois, Kansas, Minnesota, Missouri, Montana, Nebraska, North Dakota, Oklahoma, Texas, West Virginia, and Wyoming.[26]

By 1980, nonbank competitive pressures on traditional depository institutions had reached a new high, so legislation was created to ease the branching restrictions across the country.

Not surprisingly, when the branching limitations were removed from these states, financial institutions took advantage. Five of the 10 states that gained the most branches (from 1987 to 2015) were former unit banking states and the other five had other types of geographic restrictions on banking until 1979.

All state restrictions prohibiting branch banking completely disappeared by 1991. Three years later, the United States would see another big legislative change that permitted more banking expansion. The Interstate Banking and Branching Efficiency Act of 1994 (Riegle–Neal) freed up geographic restrictions in two very important ways, which caused the banking industry to witness the highest annual rates of voluntary consolidation yet.

As most things regulation and legislation, Riegle–Neal came much later than the technology improvements that allowed for more efficient branch operation. Remember that by 1994, ATMs had already proven to reduce headcount in an urban branch from 21 to about 13 tellers. Keep this in mind when we discuss the OCC creating a limited purpose federal banking charter for fintech companies and digital giants. These competitors have created efficiency and improve customer experience; the legislation will follow.[27]

First, Riegle–Neal set a standard by which an FI headquartered in one state could branch into (or even acquire banks in) any other state. Prior to this, interstate acquisition was allowed, but varied from state to state. In fact, in 1984 only 16 states permitted unrestricted intrastate branching while just 10 years later, the number of unrestricted states rose to 40.

Second, Riegle-Neal allowed banks who were working around the previous prohibition by operating subsidiary charters in different states, to combine charters from different states into a single "interstate" bank. This led to the highest annual rate of voluntary charter consolidation in the banking industry, which permitted, for the first time in history, expansive geographic branch networks.

To put this in perspective, 10 years prior to Riegle-Neal (1984), 42 states disallowed interstate combinations of branching charters, but by 1994, Hawaii was the only stick in the mud.[28]

These days, Riegle-Neal's crushing blow to community banking is evident. In 1987, banks under $10 billion in assets averaged 4 branches in 1 state, with those above $10 billion in assets averaging 186 branches in 2 states. By 2014, banks under $10 billion were operating, on average, 7 branches in 1 state, while those above $10 billion had 450 branches in, on average, 6 states.

Chief Strategy Officer from CenterState Banks, Chris Nichols, suggests it costs $750,000 to build a branch, and $949,000 to maintain it annually. On average, it will serve 2,500 customers who visit 24 times each year. On the other hand, he can build websites and apps for $650,000 with an annual maintenance cost of $324,000, serving 23,000 customers 122 times per year. We'll cover more on the switch to digital community banking later in the book, but perhaps ego and inertia should not pick a fight with mathematics?[29]

Branch Density Sustains, for Better or Worse

States that had the tightest restrictions on branching in 1979 saw massive boosts to their branch density numbers, while states with some geographic restrictions actually saw a decline in density equal to the national average (see Figure 2.16). The most obvious density decline after 1987 was inside of those states who already permitted statewide branching in 1979 (the non-unit banking states).

Figure 2.16   FDIC-Insured Bank Branch Density

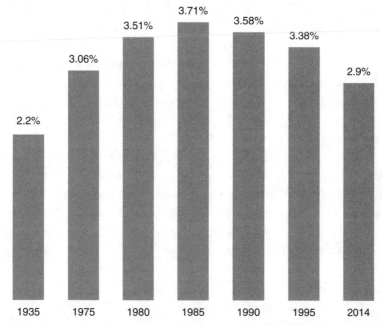

Source: FDIC
The FDIC expresses branch density as the number of branches per 10,000 people.[30]

It bears mentioning that until the 1980s, FIs could not compete on the sexy product benefit of a higher interest rate for deposit accounts. This was due to federal restrictions against paying market interest rates. Instead, FIs needed to differentiate with customer service and number of branch locations.

Unfortunately, most community FI executives grew through the ranks prior to interest rate deregulation, so they force their institutions to suffer with that hangover—trying to win on customer service or branch locations rather than things consumers actually care about.

In addition to the obvious technological advancements between the 1980s and today, an important factor in the overall decline of branch density during this time is the ages-long trend of rural depopulation in the United States. For the 30 years following 1980, 50 percent of the country's rural counties lost population, while overall US population grew by 36 percent.[31]

In spite of this depopulation, branch density remains strong in rural counties. As recently as 2013, branch density was twice as high in rural areas as in their metro counterparts.[32] There are several excuses for this; the most obvious is that depopulation doesn't actually make a physical space any smaller, so branches are still necessary outposts in rural communities.

Excuses are just that, though, and we all have to question how valuable these tired bricks-and-mortar museums will be in the very near future. Or perhaps a better question, how much risk does the expensive branch network impose on a small institution where faster, cheaper, more efficient, and more easily accessed methods of service (mobile banking) are pervasive (see Figure 2.17)?

Figure 2.17   Frequency of Channel Usage (US)

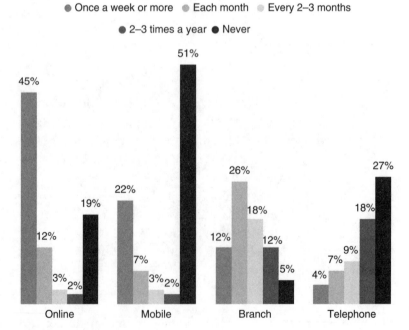

SOURCE: eMarketer; YouGov

By 2014, over 50 percent of the adult Internet users in the United States still had not banked via their primary institution's mobile site or app.

Notwithstanding the very real concern that there may be community blowback of a branch closure or otherwise replacing human workers with interactive teller machines, unless the most rural institutions adapt to the changing technology landscape, taking advantage of ubiquitous (and more efficient) service models, the writing is on the wall for inefficient service models.

But using recent branch closure history data to rationalize your future closure of branches probably isn't the right approach, either. While sensationalists argue that since 18,236 bank branches were closed between 2009 and 2015, traditional branch institutions must be dying a fast death at the hands of direct banking models, the closure of branches is only part of the story. There were branch openings, too. Lots of them (see Figures 2.18 and 2.19).

Figure 2.18   Gross Closings of Bank Branches (US)

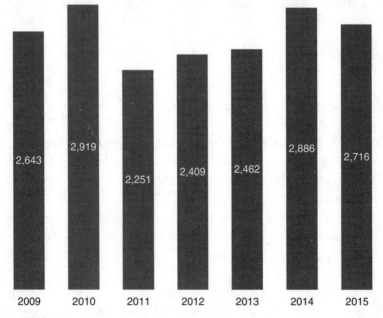

Source: FDIC
Banks have been closing branches at about the same rate since 2009, yet since that time, banks have only shed about 5 percent of their total branch numbers.

Figure 2.19 Gross Openings of Bank Branches (US)

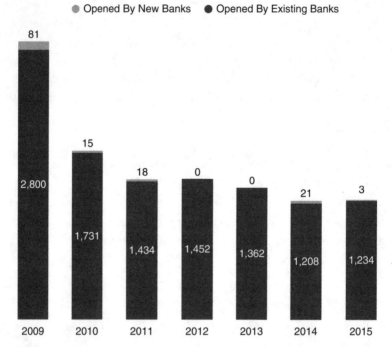

SOURCE: FDIC

Branch openings in 2009 were probably a hangover of planning pre-Great Recession, but new branch openings have slowed over the years.

Of those 18,000 or so branch[33] closings during that time period, only about 2,500 were closed due to failures or mergers. (Remember WaMu and Wachovia?) On the flip side, nearly 11,500 new branches were opened. Not accounting for failures or mergers, that means banks shed less than 5 percent of their entire branch footprint in the several years following the Great Recession.

It's possible that 5 percent would have been even smaller if one of the biggest contributors to new office growth, new bank charters (see Figure 2.20), hadn't fallen to historically low levels (more on this in the next chapter).

It appears that what we're seeing with branch closure numbers speaks more to the larger trend of a change in branch design, sizing, placement, and so on than an overnight shift in retail banking to direct banking (see Figure 2.21).

Figure 2.20   New bank charters issued in the United States by FDIC since 1985.

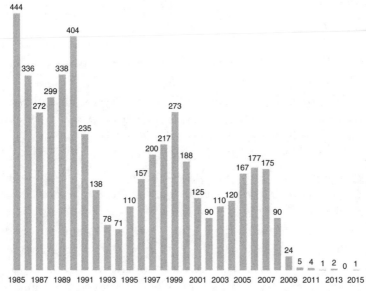

Source: FDIC
A lag in new banks means fewer new branches. To date, zero newly chartered banks have had success in the United States without any physical locations. It will happen, but it hasn't happened yet.

Figure 2.21   The Number of Americans Living in Households with a Direct Bank as Their Primary Bank

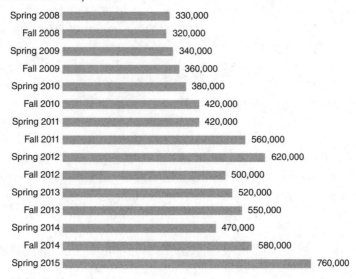

Source: Nielsen Scarborough
It's easy to envision a future with no branches and 100 percent digital distribution, but so far, a very small percentage of U.S. consumers are choosing a 100 percent digital offering as their primary institution.

We shouldn't let history be our guide to the future, but if one were to look in the past, one would find a very similar cycle of branch closures between 1989 and 1995, just prior to a boom in branch growth between 1995 and 2009.[34] A similar branch boom is unlikely to happen again, ever. Anywhere. The world has already changed to more efficient methods of banking delivery and onboarding.

At 2.5 billion in 2016 (and 5 billion by 2020[35]), smartphones have quickly proliferated across the planet, giving everyone (including the billions of unbanked humans around the world) ready access to banking services. As Brett King predicted years ago, nearly every retail transaction except cash deposit (which can be performed by an ATM) can now be serviced on a mobile device—removing all but the emotional excuses to visit a teller.

And so, transactions at branches have fallen hard as consumers and commercial clients quickly shifted to digital technologies and ATMs, which themselves reached location saturation at 425,000 in the United States by 2010[36] (a figure that hasn't budged too much in the years since).

Financial Management Solutions found the average number of teller transactions per branch declined by 45 percent between 1992 and 2013 (from 11,700 transactions per month to 6,400).[37] Federal Reserve saw paper check payments decline from 46 percent of non-cash payments in 2003 to just 15 percent in 2012, while universal credit and debit cards filled the gap at around 58 percent of non-cash payments (up from 38 percent in 2003).

While the number of checks written declined, the volume of non-cash transactions did not. In fact, non-cash transactions grew 50 percent during the same timeframe. Meaning, universal, full-service FIs had to become more efficient while doing more work (a familiar refrain from the 2000s on).

As a direct result of the technology efficiencies, Citi estimates a reduction of 30 percent (or 700,000) retail banking jobs across the U.S. banking industry by 2025.[38]

While the building of new branches has slowed a bit in the past few years, branch networks exploded from 1994 to 2014 for both community and noncommunity banks (see Figure 2.22). This is because the American consumer's traditional need for branches ("I'd like to be able to talk face to face with the person who has my money") has not yet shifted entirely. Unless some cataclysmic event happens to Americans, their evolution to 100 percent digital banking interactions will be incremental and gradual, no matter how much some of us wish it to be instantaneous.

Figure 2.22   Average Size of US Branch Networks 1994–2014

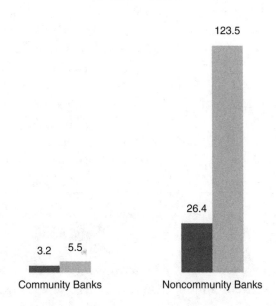

● 1994   ● 2014

Source: FDIC
The average size of branch office networks for US-based community and noncommunity banks. Or, Riegle-Neal in one simple chart.

Branching is terrifically inefficient, and banking executives should be knee-deep in data and analysis to plot the future of their omnichannel approach, but we shouldn't use recent branch closures as a lead indicator for the death of community banking—there are plenty of others.

The De Novo De No-No

The United States is a unique animal when it comes to banking. For nearly 200 years, the US economy roared via local access to capital and financial knowledge from community-based financial institutions.

When geographies around the country experienced economic prosperity, new institutions were formed to fuel that growth. Larger institutions ultimately purchased the smaller guys, and the resulting layoffs increased the pool of experienced bankers who were available to start even more new institutions. A wondrous cycle, indeed.

These entrants, referred to as *de novos,* are wholly new institutions within the banking industry, and examining their numbers and success offers vivid insight into the lifeblood of the industry.

Since new bank charter formation statistics include those who are reorganizing or relabeling their existing institutions, to truly understand how many new FIs are entering the market, it's important to isolate the subset of newly formed banks from simply "charter creation." Unfortunately, for either group, the de novo outlook ain't so rosy.

Referring to Figure 2.23 from the Federal Reserve's National Information Center puts the de novo lull in perspective. Since 1960, there have been two periods of sharp de novo decline: 1993–1994 and 2009–2016 (and beyond?).

Figure 2.23   New Bank De Novos (Since 1961)

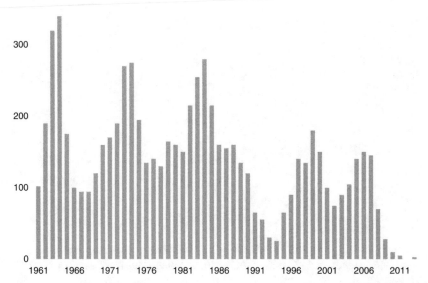

SOURCE: Author's calculations based on data from the Federal Reserve's National Information Center. The number of new commercial banks per year since 1961.

While the years 1993–1994 saw just 28 and 25 de novos, respectively, they were quickly followed with pronounced increases of activity, including the years 2002–2008, which saw over 100 de novos formed annually. However, that surge was followed with the longest sustained de novo drought[39] (2009–2015) in 50 years. In fact, the FDIC saw only four total de novo banks formed and sustained (eight total charters) between 2011 and 2015.

> A 2014 study by the Federal Reserve of Richmond shows that the barren land of de novo banks from 2008 to 2014 accounts for two-thirds of the decline in federally insured, chartered banks.[40]

New credit union charters have been less rare as their bank counterparts, but the numbers are still historically low (see Figure 2.24).

Figure 2.24   New Credit Union Charters (Since 1935)

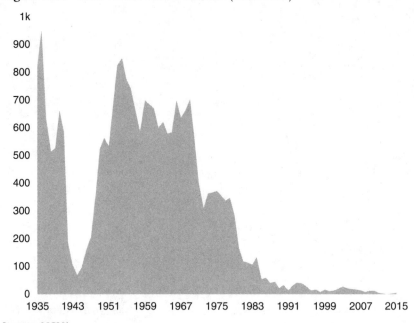

SOURCE: NCUA

The number of new credit unions per year since 1935.

From 2011 to 2015, the NCUA slowed new charter activity to about 17 new credit unions—the lowest number of annual new charter generation in modern US credit union history.

These Days, There Are Plenty of Reasons Not to Start a Bank

Unlike a credit union, banks are for-profit enterprises for shareholders. This means that people start banks like they would start any other business. Bankers are small business people. And every entrepreneur, whether they think of it this way or not, is an investor in their business.

They evaluate the industry they are going to enter. They survey potential customers, determine unsolved problems and find ways to solve those problems that is different/cheaper/faster/more effective than the competition. They perform a SWOT (strengths, weaknesses, opportunities, and threats) analysis of the competition. They craft a business plan and maybe a marketing plan to help guide them along the way. They pitch other investors in an attempt to get more capital for their business.

If you were entrepreneurial and you had expertise in banking, you might consider opening a bank. Let's look at a few of the realities of birthing a bank in today's landscape.

Puny Net Interest Margin. When interest rates are low, it's hard for a bank to make money, and for the seven years between 2009 and 2016, the Fed kept the Federal Funds rate at a historical low which, among other things, helped pushed lending rates into the ditch. As a result, bank profitability, or net interest margin (the spread between deposit rates and lending rates), suffers (see Figure 2.25).

Figure 2.25   Banks' Net Interest Margin

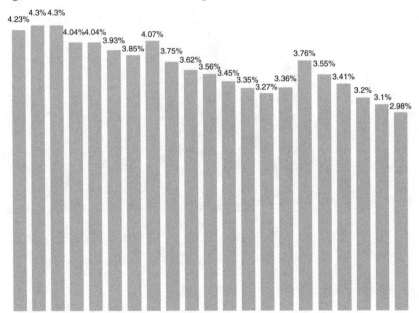

SOURCE: FFIEC
The average net interest margin for banks has tumbled quite a bit since 1995.

While Robert Adams and Jacob Gramlich of the Federal Reserve Board of Governors[41] theorize this lack of profitability as the primary reason for the absence of new banks, a report[42] by Charles Morris and Kristen Regehr of the Kansas City Fed uses historical evidence to disprove this theory. In fact, the (near 40-year) low levels of bank net interest

income (a bank's revenue from interest on loans after expenses) seen during the aforementioned historical low Federal Funds rate is akin to that in
the recovery of two previous recessions (2001 and 1981–1982), but those
recessions witnessed much stronger de novo growth than we currently
see (see Figure 2.26).

Figure 2.26   Effective Federal Funds Rate (Since 1954)

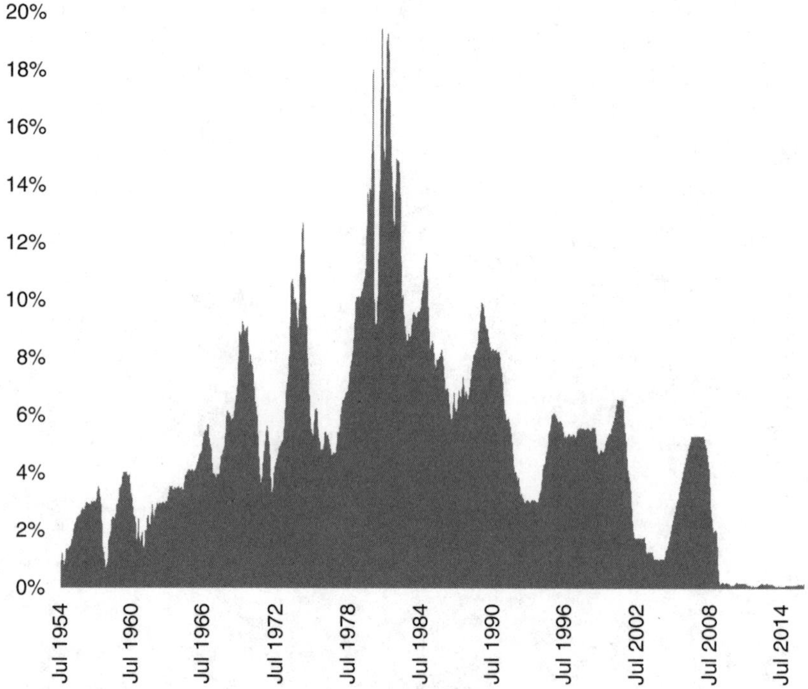

SOURCE: Board of Governors of the US Federal Reserve System
The history of the federal funds rate in the United States.

As the economy strengthens over time, net interest income (and
Federal Funds rates) will naturally improve, creating a more enticing
environment for would-be bank entrepreneurs. So current lack of bank
profitability can't be the entire reason for sparse de novo growth, can
it? After all, anyone who is at all aware of what it takes to become a
de novo understands the years-long application process and would plan
for a stronger economy on the other side of their approved charter. On
second thought, maybe that's why technologists, and not bankers, are
looking at new banking charters.

Expensive, Unduly Burdensome Regulation and Legal Risks.
The original Federal Reserve Act of 1913 totaled 30 pages.[43] Glass-
Steagall (which separated commercial banks from investment banks,
and also created the Federal Deposit Insurance Corporation or FDIC)
was 34 pages. The Sarbanes-Oxley Act (the post-Enron accounting
rule overhaul) was 66 pages. The Dodd-Frank Wall Street Reform
and Consumer Protection Act (Dodd-Frank) is more than 3,500 pages
with more than 3.3 million words (the length of about six copies of
War and Peace), all with the intent to make our thousands of unique,
market-crafted institutions look more like vanilla-flavored financial
utilities. And compliance is still only the second highest concern of
banking executives today (see Figure 2.27).

Figure 2.27 Perceived Challenges for US Financial Institution Executives (2016)

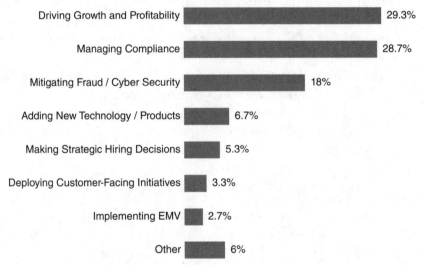

SOURCE: eMarketer; Computer Services
Managing compliance ranks second on the list of top challenges that banking executives believe they
face. Prospective de novo investors might rank it even higher.

> JP Morgan hired an additional 13,000 people in the area of com-
> pliance since 2012.[44]

Much has been written about how the current regulatory environment has led to decreased de novo formation. Heightened scrutiny

during the formation stages, a doubling in the length of time (from three years to seven years) for increased capital requirements and examinations (reverted to three years as of April 2016), and similar regulation requirements as much larger banking institutions (such as Dodd-Frank and its inspired Title XIV mortgage changes issued by the CFPB in October of 2015) add to the myriad reasons one would not be interested in starting a new bank business these days:[45]

- Increased scrutiny and examinations during the formation and early stages—Not too many people, bankers or otherwise, are keen to invite intense oversight and rigorous reporting into their lives.
- Increased capital requirements—From an investor's perspective, committing capital prior to the bank being issued a charter means your capital is locked up for a long while, and it may ultimately not be put to use if the charter is denied. And from the bank's perspective, once you do get issued the charter, you have accumulated a large amount of interest expense from the aforementioned hold on the investment.
- Examined and regulated with the same intensity as a trillion-dollar asset bank—Clearly, megabanks benefit from scale here. As high as the costs of compliance are, the costs of noncompliance are quite extraordinary. Other than limiting compliance risk by limiting the products offered, there really is no way around this.

Proponents of Dodd-Frank believe that community institutions were victims of (and not perpetuators of) the Great Recession. The supporters of Dodd-Frank also believe community FIs should not be held responsible for their big brothers' wrongdoing, going so far as carving out some exceptions for small banks. That said, most bankers believe the law has disastrous consequences for all institutions (not just the mega banks).

The 2014 Mercatus Center's Small Bank Survey[46] showed that existing small banks view the 19,000 pages of regulatory text (with about 60 percent of the rules still undefined[47]) from Dodd-Frank more costly than even the Bank Secrecy Act.

According to the 200+ institutions in the study, Dodd-Frank required more time from noncompliance FTEs on compliance, the hiring of new compliance staff, and increased reliance on outside compliance consultants to fill in gaps between the two. An unreported, yet related, expense is the opportunity cost associated with bank leaders reading volumes of new rules, and attempting to interpret these rules instead of approving loans and performing other actual banking activity.

Dodd-Frank has also forced existing small banks to change their attitudes toward mergers and toward product offerings such as residential mortgages (the second most complained-about banking product; see Figure 2.28).

Figure 2.28   Consumer Complaints to CFPB

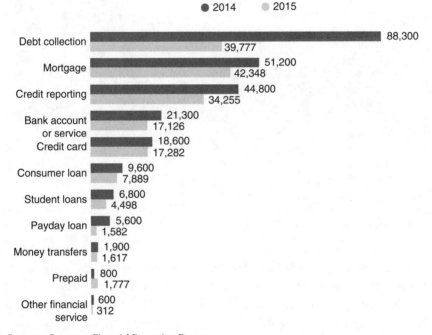

SOURCE: Consumer Financial Protection Bureau
Debt collection and mortgage issues lead the pack for the highest volume of complaints to the CFPB.

On the merger front, over 25 percent of those small FIs surveyed in 2014 were prognosticating merger activity for their institution in the next five years as a result of the known heavy regulatory requirements and the unknown regulatory threat.[48]

At least 15 percent of the small FI respondents to the survey were either discontinuing or anticipating discontinuing residential mortgages (originating and selling off or originating and holding residential

Figure 2.29   US Mortgage Delinquency Rate

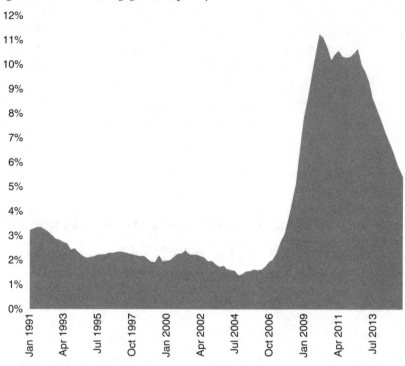

SOURCE: Board of Governors of the Federal Reserve System
Delinquency rates on single-family residential mortgages with banks in the United States. Mortgage delinquency rates are falling, but the volume of new mortgage lending rules will put many would-be community banking lenders out of the game.

mortgages) in the next few years, even though mortgage delinquency rates are falling to pre–Great Recession levels (see Figure 2.29).

Citing the same reasons of burdensome regulation, community FIs have similar attitudes toward discontinuing other lifeblood products such as home equity lines of credit. Altogether, this will have a longstanding, negative impact on the community banking industry.

> For its part, the banking industry has asked for a reduction to verbose, knee-jerk-enacted, and ill-defined regulation such as Dodd-Frank by suggesting the regulatory bodies writing the rules actually understand the financial benefits and the expenses incurred by the proposed regulation prior to adopting it.

> This would avoid situations such as those which the bank-
> ing industry is in today: whereby labor years and untold tens of
> millions of dollars are spent correcting and clarifying the rules
> in following years.
>
> With refreshing honesty, in front of a 2015 Senate Banking
> Committee, federal regulators complained that understanding
> the impacts of rules prior to writing them would make writing
> the rules more difficult.[49]

And if there are added challenges for those community institutions offering mortgages, there are certainly new problems created for consumers looking for mortgages.

While community institutions have had a long history of successfully lending via a personal relationship model, whereby the FI had fairly strong "soft" knowledge of a consumer and his ability to repay, Dodd-Frank changed all of that. Striking at the heart of the decades-strong personal banking relationship model of community FIs, Dodd-Frank requires community financial institutions to reject many of the most in-need of mainstream banking applicants under the guise of "regulatory risk."

In a 2015 ABA study, 80 percent of bankers believe the CFPB's mortgage lending rules will reduce the money available to home-shopping consumers.[50] Another ABA survey showed that in 2015, over 30 percent of banks were forced to deny mortgages to (otherwise approved) consumers in order to comply with the CFPB's new "Ability-to-Pay" rule.[51]

The CFPB estimates[52] that their enacted TRID (TILA-RESPA Integrated Disclosure) changes for mortgage lending will cost the banks $27 more per mortgage, but save consumers $17 per mortgage.

Not that $17 amounts to a hill of beans in the overall context of buying a house of any size, but here's how the CFPB calculates the consumer savings of $17 per mortgage:

- The CFPB assumes the FI pays that banker hourly.
- The CFPB assumes the banker tracks time per project in half-hour increments, and clocks in/out as soon as he starts/finishes each task.
- The CFPB assumes that the banker gets paid $34/hr.
- The CFPB assumes the new rule will save half an hour of a banker's time (there's your $17).

- The CFPB assumes the FI has no added direct or indirect cost for tracking this savings.
- The CFPB assumes the FI passes on 100 percent of all savings from the ludicrously flawed process directly to the consumer.
- Ta-da! $17 can now be returned directly to the consumer by way of a cheaper mortgage.

If you find this idea compelling, you might also be astounded that the Durbin amendment within Dodd-Frank, which gave a reduction in interchange costs to merchants so they could reduce their prices on goods, created near-zero consumer savings.[53] If the government wanted to save consumers some money, I'd start with the three charts in Figures 2.30 to 2.32.

> If you're interested in reducing regulatory costs for your own institution, we have some regtech ideas from a real pro. Read about it in Andy Greenawalt's section toward the end of the book.

Figure 2.30 CFPB—Net Cost of Operations

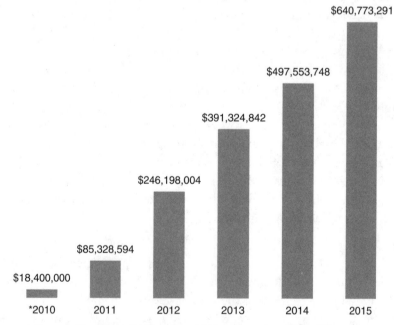

SOURCE: ConsumerFinance.gov *2010 was a partial year of operations for the CFPB.
The net cost of operations for Consumer Financial Protection Bureau in the United States.

Figure 2.31   CFPB—Average Return to Affected Consumers

$$\$588$$

SOURCE: house.gov
The average return to affected consumers helped by the CFPB from its inception in 2010 to July, 2015. Or, $10B US dollars to 17 million people.

Figure 2.32   CFPB Headquarters Renovation Costs

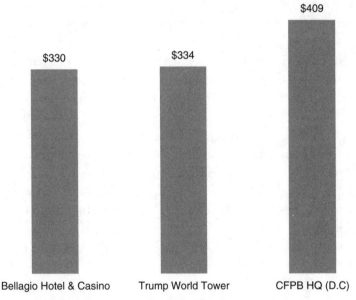

SOURCE: *Washington Business Journal* (December 23, 2015)
The CFPB renovation budget for a building it does not own, as compared to construction costs of other well-known trophy developments (in US dollars per square foot).

When You Have a Limited Supply of New Banks, Community Banking Suffers

Since de novo banks tend to be smaller banks, and smaller banks focus on lending to small business, the decrease in new bank creation will have a damaging effect on the future of community banking. The decrease in de novos will not have a negative impact on the future funding of small business, as many in our industry suggest—there are plenty of very efficient ways for an entrepreneur to get his money today, she doesn't need a community institution as badly as you need her.

The lack of de novos will impact community banking in the following ways:

- Fewer small-asset banks. New banks typically start in the sub-$100 million asset category, so we will see far fewer sub-$100 million FIs.
- Established brands become bigger. In the faceless world of ones and zeroes, name recognition can build trust, and the community FI gets relegated to an unknown and untrusted position.
- Lost advantage in relationship-type lending to small businesses.[54] The small businesses who are ingenious enough will look to the not-so-hidden Internet for alternative solutions to their borrowing needs.
- The simplicity and ease of borrowing from nontraditional sources will open the eyes of small business owners, causing the community banking industry as a whole to suffer the wrath of competition.

At the time it most needs new federally insured entrants and new thinking, perhaps the US banking industry's biggest thorn in its eye is the overreaching regulation intended to help it flourish. Industry impacts aside, the community banker of today has tremendous opportunity to work within the confines of regulation while building her institution for tomorrow.

Before we talk solutions, let's look at some inspiration outside the United States.

The Rise of the Challenger Banks

The United Kingdom Has Nearly 1,000 Financial Institutions, and It Wants Even More Banking Competition

The central bank of the United Kingdom, the Bank of England, maintains monetary and financial stability for its citizens by ensuring low and stable inflation and supervising its 1,700 financial institutions, investment firms, and insurers via the Prudential Regulatory Authority (PRA; see Figure 2.33).

Figure 2.33 Deposit-Taking FIs under PRA in United Kingdom

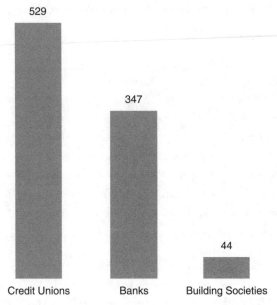

SOURCE: Bank of England
Financial institutions supervised by Prudential Regulatory Authority in United Kingdom (2015).

The financial institution segment in the United Kingdom is similar to that in the United States in that it contains the two poles of banks and credit unions. And, just like in the United States, banks are for-profit entities and credit unions are not-for-profit, member-owned institutions that follow the common operating principles of the World Council of Credit Unions.

> Members of credit unions in the United Kingdom must have a common bond such as an employer group or geography (similar to closed-chartered credit unions in United States). Unlike the United States, however, it is very common for UK-based credit unions to work very closely with small-to-medium sized businesses.

Similar to our old savings and loans (though some themselves are demutualized), is the group that sits between the two poles: *building societies*. In general, building societies are for-profit institutions, owned by their retail account members or shareholders. Building societies specialize in mortgages and savings accounts.

> In 1983, Nottingham Building Society (United Kingdom) launched Homelink, with support from Bank of Scotland. Using a TV set, a rotary phone, and a free terminal, customers could transfer money between accounts, view statements, make bill payments, and even start loans and mortgages—all online. If that wasn't enough, customers could e-mail other Homelink users, and shop with various retailers—something we would, much later, call e-commerce.

Aside from their for-profit status, building societies are most like community chartered credit unions in the United States, in that they do not have select employer group member restrictions.

Throughout the 1990s and 2000s, retail banking strategists in the United Kingdom pushed for retail bank consolidation—ultimately ending up with five large retail banks: Standard Chartered, Barclays, HSBC, Royal Bank of Scotland, and Lloyds. Despite its best efforts, small institutions still persist. And currently, there are just under 1,000 banks, credit unions, and building societies in the United Kingdom, a land mass roughly the size of Nebraska and Kansas.

Just like in the United States, there may be just a few big banks in the United Kingdom, but they make up the overwhelming majority of assets, accounts and deposits. Recently, Bank of England has taken the stance that the United Kingdom needs more competition among their 1,000 financial institutions, so they have eased and modified some of the criteria for chartering.

This Has Given Way to the Creation of "Challenger Banks"

Challenger banks are essentially de novo banks that get approval from the United Kingdom's Prudential Regulation Authority (PRA) and Financial Conduct Authority (FCA) to operate as banks based on a number of factors (not too dissimilar from the de novo application process in the United States).

Also similar to the United States, due to Basel requirements, challenger banks need to hold quite a bit more capital (often, up to 10 times more capital) against their mortgage loans and credit cards than the incumbent institutions. Since no data exist to illustrate the quality and validity of a new bank's lending decisions, challengers must use a standardized model. Experienced, conventional banks, however, can use a much more advanced model that is tied to their exact loan portfolio losses over previous years. (As most things regulation, it's a bit confounding: riskier loans, such as commercial real estate, do not have this requirement.)

That's where the similarities end. On the capital requirements issue, the PRA is working to help ease these anticompetitive rules for challengers. The fact that challengers exist is also a big difference between the United Kingdom and the United States.

Not only has the interest in forming a challenger in the United Kingdom been much stronger than forming a de novo in the United States, challenger applications are actually being approved. The PRA issued 11 new banking licenses in its first two years, with a third of them issued to challenger banks, and the expectation is another 15 challengers will be licensed by the year 2020.

This number is in stark comparison to the PRA's predecessor to bank license approval, the Financial Services Authority (see Figure 2.34).

The New Challengers Will Not Be Universal Banks

Rather than going after business held by the large, established banks, challengers are finding niche markets not well-served by the big players, targeting them (e.g., small business owners in a certain geography), developing a specific product or service to meet their needs, and, typically, relying on digital delivery (no branches, only in-app and telephone for customer support).

This seems to be a sound approach. Study after study of current account (checking accounts without the checkbook antiquity) users in the United Kingdom illustrates fairly happy relationships (see Figures 2.35 to 2.37). Over 80 percent of current accountholders are satisfied with their main financial provider and its digital banking services.

Figure 2.34   FSA–Granted Bank Licenses, by Org

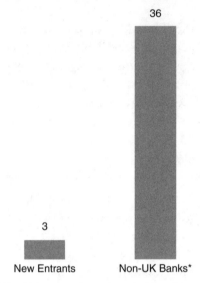

SOURCE: Bank of England *Establishing branches in the United Kingdom, subsidiaries, or UK operating entities.

Financial Services Authority (FSA) approvals of banking licenses from 2006–2012, by type of organization.

Figure 2.35   UK Current Account Satisfaction

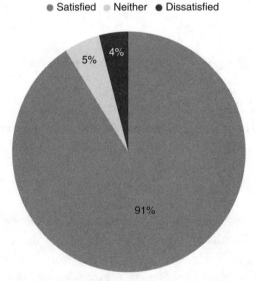

SOURCE: GfK Media and Communications Research; Competition and Markets Authority
Current accountholder satisfaction with their main financial provider in United Kingdom (2015).

Figure 2.36   UK Banking App Satisfaction

● Satisfied   ● Neither / Don't Know   ● Dissatisfied

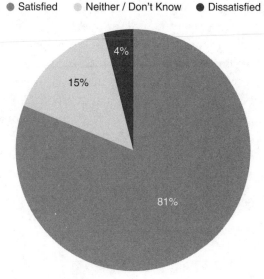

SOURCE: GfK Media and Communications Research; Competition and Markets Authority
Accountholder satisfaction with the banking app from their main current account provider in United
Kingdom (2015).

Figure 2.37   UK Customers on Challenger Banks

● Positive   ● Negative

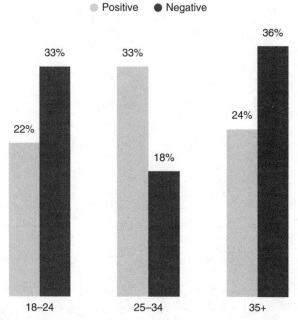

SOURCE: Accenture
Bank customer opinion on usage of the "Pure Digital" bank in United Kingdom, by age group (2014).

From very high overall satisfaction in their banking relationships, to high approval ratings for app-banking, to a near insatiable appetite for physical channels, to current bank customers being fairly disapproving of challenger banks, there's good reason for challenger banks to not focus on the well-served market of the established banks.

This may be why those who have current accounts are not switching in big numbers (only 8 percent of current accountholders switch in a given year), despite having a well-publicized, free, national, fairly automated Current Account Switching Service (CASS) (see Figure 2.38). While not all switchers choose to use CASS, the service, launched in 2013, promises some real benefits for the user, including reducing the time it takes to switch accounts from about 30 working days to 7 working days. (In late 2016, CASS usage will be reevaluated in conjunction with a study on feasibility of bank account number portability.)

Figure 2.38 Switchers of Current Accounts (UK)

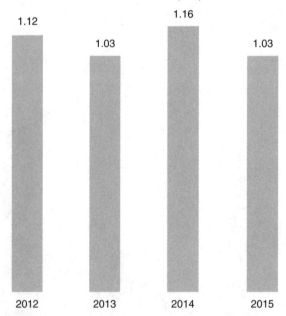

SOURCE: Payments Council

Annual number of customers (in millions) switching their current account provider in United Kingdom.

The switchers using CASS tend to go to banks with branches (see Figure 2.39). The United Kingdom's first challenger bank, Metro Bank,

actually employed a branch-distribution strategy, and has been a big beneficiary CASS. One report showed nearly 30 percent of the switchers
using CASS moving into Metro Bank.[55]

Figure 2.39   Frequency of Channel Usage (UK)

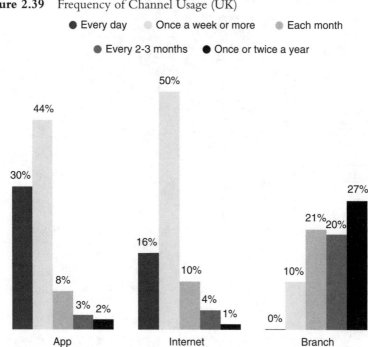

SOURCE: GfK Media and Communication Research; Competition and Markets Authority
Frequency of use by channel for personal current accountholders in United Kingdom (2015).

The multichannel embrace that we see in the United States still exists
in the United Kingdom. In 2015, over 50 percent of current account
customers ages 18 to 44 visited a physical branch at least as often as
every three months, with 10 percent of the population visiting at least
once a week. The study showed no decline in branch usage from those
who used Internet banking or app banking regularly.[56] The consumer
need for branch-based cash and check deposits overwhelmingly drives
branch visits (see Figure 2.40).

As of yet, there is only a small "efficiency" story with a UK
bank pushing its branch customers to digital channels. This is one
case of the United States being far ahead of the United Kingdom in

Figure 2.40   Branch Convenience Importance (UK)

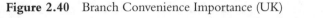

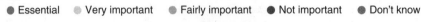

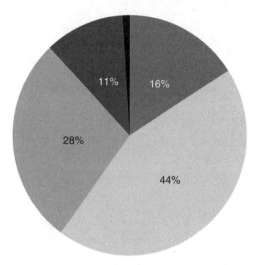

SOURCE: GfK Media and Communications Research; Competition and Markets Authority
Current accountholder opinion on the importance of conveniently located branches of their main banking provider in United Kingdom (2015).

banking laws. The United Kingdom has only recently approved mobile deposit capture.

In 2009, six-employee, $11 million asset WV United Federal Credit Union (now, Element FCU and $28 million in assets) beat USAA to market with iPhone-based remote deposit—winning a Best of the Web award from the Online Banking Report, published at the time by fintech soothsayer Jim Bruene. Begun in 1994, the Online Banking Report awarded "Best of the Web" to companies that pioneered new online and mobile banking features. Read more from Jim Bruene later in this book.

With the United Kingdom's official rollout for mobile deposit capture set for October 2017, there is little doubt that check deposit transaction volume will shift from the bricks-and-mortar channel to smartphone, creating less need for branches over time. No doubt, this is a trend the digital pure-play challengers are banking on.

Or perhaps, as the challengers suggest, they are going after entirely new unbanked consumers—either because they are just turning of age to get a current account or because the target has been otherwise left unserved by the established players. Either way, challenger banks will be very focused on the all-important costs of acquisition and retention, as that, coupled with the fact that most are not planning to offer any other cross-sale services, will be their biggest risks to success.

A Few of the Challengers and What Makes Them Interesting

Although the challenger model is still quite new, with only a few actually live and onboarding customers, the model is proving quite lucrative (by way of return on equity) in comparison to the establishment (see Figures 2.41 and 2.42).

Figure 2.41   ROE for Challenger Banks

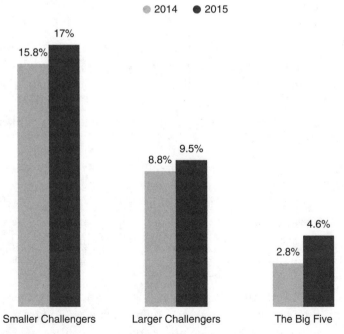

SOURCE: KPMG
The return on equity for challenger banks and the big five banks in United Kingdom.

Figure 2.42   Return on Average Equity (US)

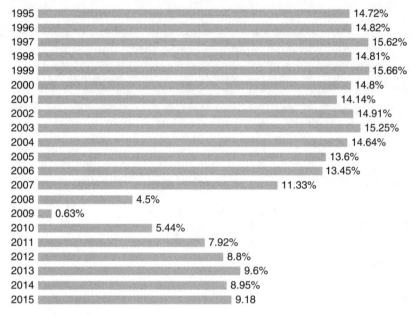

SOURCE: FFIEC
The return on average equity for all banks in the United States.

Aside from the impressive difference in ROE, an overview of some as-yet unlaunched challenger banks in the United Kingdom today (which will assuredly change by the time this text is published, especially in light of the "Brexit") highlights areas of inspiration for bankers in the United States:

- Atom Bank—a brand-focused bank that centers itself on the user: allowing users to rename the bank after themselves (e.g., "John's Bank")—even altering its logo to model itself after the user's chosen bank name. Atom's attempt at bringing the personal side of banking to the digital world continues with allowing users to check their balance by looking into the camera, or transferring funds by using their voice.
- Lintel Bank—will target those in the United Kingdom who have a hard time getting a current account: students and migrant workers.
- Monzo—already has a strong community of developers using and building new things on top of Monzo's APIs, and making its wares

available for free on GitHub. From custom-built online banking to browser extensions to an Apple Watch app, Monzo offers products built by passionate developers excited about a bank that actually gives their customers access to their own data.

- Tandem Bank—gave away a chunk of its bank to early "co-founders"—people who signed up with little more than an email address.
- The term *neo-bank* has come to refer to digital-only banks. In the United States, neo-banks often look like a technology company powering the consumer-facing user experience (brand, user interface, customer support, etc.) partnered with a bank performing the back-end services (KYC, FDIC-insurance, risk, etc.). Although these types of neo-banks exist in other parts of the world (e.g., Number26 in Germany, Nubank in Brazil, or Anytime in France), many banks are taking advantage and applying for the aforementioned Bank of England–issued banking licenses to expand their banking capabilities without the limits imposed by a bank partner.

Of course, the work of the challenger bank is just beginning after attaining its banking license. Just like in the United States, the research and development of accounts and technology that people want (and will move to a new bank for), building trust with the public, and effective marketing techniques are all very real concerns for any new bank.

In China, New Banks Spring from Digital Giants

It all started with a $5,600 loan to a truck driver.

In early 2015, just before Premier Li Keqiang kicked off his "Internet Plus" policy (to increase competition, efficiencies, and drive what he calls "Internet thinking" among companies and government), the premier clicked a button to approve a $5,600 loan to a truck driver.

Accounting for 75 percent of new job creation and over 60 percent of GDP, small business is big in China, but entrepreneurs and small businesses have a very hard time getting the credit they need to build their businesses quickly from the state-controlled banks.

So, Premier Li clicked the big "approve" button, and private, non-government controlled banking was officially alive in China with at least one internet-based bank: WeBank.

Maybe it was irony or maybe it was a symbolic torch-passing: The first bank not run by the government had its very first loan approved by the premier (during WeBank's opening ceremony).

Nevertheless, China has bestowed two very noteworthy bellwethers for community bankers:

1. *The insignificant size of the loan itself: a $5,600 loan to a truck driver.* Prior to WeBank, the truck driver may have had to fill out endless amounts of paperwork and waited for weeks just to be denied or ignored by the state-run banks for his small-dollar loan. Or, he could have gone to a peer-to-peer lending company.

   China's state-owned banks' penchant for lending to state-owned enterprises (over private companies or retail consumers), as well as a housing boom (which has driven home price increases of 50 percent or more within a few years), have given rise to a nearly uncontrollable peer-to-peer lending (or marketplace lending) sector.

   In fact, of the 3,858 Chinese P2P lenders, one third (1,263) ran into real business problems by year end 2015.[57] Of those troubled lenders, 266 have chalked up their troubles to their founder quite literally running away.

   While the "running away" problem is rather humorous, marketplace lending (or other forms of efficient lending as in the case of WeBank) is not.

   Overlooking the little guy for bigger loan opportunities is not just a Chinese problem—it's one that persists across the globe. Marketplace lending or other forms of efficient lending will eat insignificant loans as long as you want to ignore them. Odds are, your financial institution started by making rather "insignificant" loans, too.

2. *Charters!* In addition to WeBank, the China Banking Regulatory Commission approved four other private bank charters—all focused on providing credit and deposit options for small businesses and retail consumers—with another 40 charters pending approval.

   Examine who received, and acted on, the first few charters: WeBank and MyBank.

WeBank's parent company, Tencent, is a massive Internet holding company in China. Tencent's QQ and WeChat (each nearing 1 billion monthly active users) are, in many ways, the Facebook of China.

While WeBank's infrastructure is provided by those fintech providers who have powered traditional banks for decades, WeBank doesn't need the premier to push buttons for loan approvals. Instead, it employs facial recognition, disparate data sources, and machine learning to onboard, adjudicate, and fund within minutes. Most commonly, the app's users pay for necessities like eating out, going to the movies, riding in taxis, and peer-to-peer payments (processing an estimated $556 billion in 2016).

Two letters, but vastly different dynasties, separate WeBank from their nemesis, MYbank.

MYbank is owned by Ant Financial, and is very closely related to Alibaba, or China's (more profitable version of) Amazon. MYbank uses

Figure 2.43   Mobile Banking Transactions in China

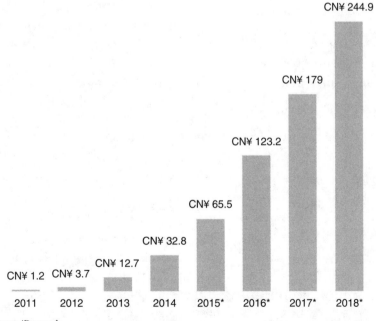

SOURCE: iResearch
Previous and forecast of gross transaction volume of mobile banking in China (in trillion yuan).

Alibaba's extensive history on 400 million users to build extraordinarily intelligent credit models: previous addresses, family-owned properties, previous purchase data, shopping habits and preferred brands, utility bill data, merchants' cash flow, and so on. Today, MYbank is approved to offer loans to consumers or small businesses up to RMB 5 million (about $810,000). Within the first six months of operation, MYbank provided around 500,000 loans to small business customers.

MYbank is pushing the reset button on fintech infrastructure, and will instead rely on its parent's cloud computing company built specifically for financial institutions, Ant Financial Cloud.

Both WeBank and MYbank have massive reach and have the potential to reshape retail and small business banking in China (see Figure 2.43). Of course, if they don't, there are currently thousands of marketplace lending companies in China to pick up the slack.

A Quick Overview of the Fintech Landscape

"I've been hearing about the 'digital onslaught' for 20 years and we're still here. We launched a mobile banking app 6 years late and didn't lose one customer. We have proven we don't need to be on the front end of the spear—or really anywhere near it—to thrive."
—CEO of a $1 billion community bank, August 2015

According to EFMA, today there are over 12,000 fintech companies within 18 segments of the financial industry.[58] (I estimated it closer to 125 million companies and 4,380 segments, but we can go with their number.) This diversity can cause a lot of confusion. I'd like to sort through that confusion, at least for the purposes of this text, as the term *fintech* has come to mean a lot of different things by a lot of different groups these last few years.

"Fintech" Is Nothing New

A very common misconception is that fintech started in 2008 (with the Great Recession and 2009's acquisition of Mint.com by Intuit). This assertion rewrites history, and reeks of ignorance.

The November 1962 Federal Reserve Bulletin uses several pages of data to show the extent of computer-aided automation and related third-party services at commercial banks. At the time, nearly half of those banks reported either planned or existing "electronic computer" book-keeping, which was more advanced than the simple, specific-purpose punch-card systems seen previously.

> "The San Francisco District, in which branch banking is exten-sive, shows the largest proportion of computer-system banks, as well as an unusually large proportion of banks with systems already in operation or being installed."—Federal Reserve Bulletin, November 1962

The Association of Financial Technology (AFT), did not form in 1972 in anticipation of the events of the Great Recession 36 years later. It's had hundreds of member companies come and go throughout its history and has never been more active than today in helping companies with fintech solutions partner, grow, and learn from each other.

Older financial technology might be green-screened with expensive infrastructure and primitive architecture, but it was, and still is, financial technology. And, more often than not, it's been working, rock solid, for decades.

"Fintech" Is Not Necessarily Adversarial to Financial Services Companies

While the Great Recession certainly spurred some entrepreneurs to invent and to capitalize on Americans' disdain for banks (thus, starting fintech companies to compete with certain FI services), the foundation of fintech is in the service of banks and credit unions. Suggesting otherwise is factually inaccurate.

"Fintech" Does Not Mean "Startup Company in Financial Technology or Financial Services"

Some industry commentators will use the term *fintech* and *startups* interchangeably, which is downright confusing. Traditionally, the term *startups* has referred to early-stage, three-people-in-a-garage sort of companies. Let's keep that widely understood definition, and remember that it is completely separate from *fintech.*

Most Financial Services Companies Are Not Fintech Companies (Yet)

While some financial services companies (banks, credit unions, credit card companies, VCs, investment entities, etc.) are starting to refer to themselves as technology companies, a press release and a few simple API calls does not change your spots. This is an admirable start to what is an inevitable conclusion, but the financial services industry today has quite an abyss between it and the underlying financial technology that supports it.

"Fintech" Can Be an Adjective

A company can be a *fintech startup,* meaning its focus is bringing a fintech solution to market. A company can also offer *fintech products,* meaning the company itself is not a fintech company (like Apple), but it does offer a fintech solution (like ApplePay).

"Fintech" Can Be Delivered One of Three Ways

In general, there are three groups of fintech products: White Label, Direct (to consumer or to business), and Gold Label. Let's take a look at those now.

White Label. White Label products are offered to an FI's end users via a white-label strategy, where the technology is developed by a fintech provider, but branded under the FI's name (or not branded at all, like in the case of the core processor).

With White Label, the end user sees the product as a product that is "from the FI," and has no idea there is a fintech vendor behind the scenes. This is the kind of fintech that has been provided to institutions by hundreds of providers for over 40 years.

In a PwC survey, fintech companies believed management and culture were the biggest roadblocks of working with FIs, while IT security led the list of challenges for FIs partnering with fintech companies. These are very important things either side of the equation should keep in mind in a White Label relationship.[59]

Some examples of White Label products and services are Moven's implementations with Westpac and TD Bank in Canada, digital banking from Q2, bill pay from CheckFree, credit card processing from TSYS, etc.

Some credit unions weren't happy with the choices, features, and/or reliability of White Label fintech vendors so they created their own for-profit companies, Credit Union Service Organizations (CUSO), to serve their own needs.

The evolution of fintech CUSOs was logical: technology companies have always had credit unions managing their employees' financial lives, and board members of those credit unions were often selected among notable employees of those respective technology companies.

So for decades, technologists have helped manage and guide technology decisions of credit unions. Many of those starry-eyed builders flocked to the ideals of the credit union movement and the flexible, open working environment.

This cross-pollination between a laid-back financial institution and its technology company host led to a lot of smart people talking big about how they could build a better or cheaper ones and zeroes widget for the CU. Ultimately, someone's bluff was called. Thus, CUSOs were born.

Over time, they too made up the murky entangled noodle soup that is White Label. Some CUSOs do what they do better than a solution offered by White Label, and some do it way worse. Either way, the theory is that the group of sponsoring credit unions benefit from efficiencies of scale.

Direct (to Consumer or to Business). On the other side of the spectrum, you have Direct, which is offered unrelated to an institution. End users of Direct entrust the service directly, and know that an FI is not involved in the service.

Whereas companies sell their White Label solutions to FIs, Direct compete with the FIs, and sell directly to the consumer. Providers of Direct will invest millions of dollars removing user experience barriers that decades of regulation (or perhaps more often, internal compliance officers or external examiners) have placed in front of small businesses who need quick cash or consumers who want an account.

The Direct providers innately understand that community banks and credit unions are hamstrung by their technology partners and contracts, and confounded by contemporary marketing techniques, user adoption, innovative delivery and freemium pricing methodologies. They understand how established institutions operate, so they take advantage of all that waste. All that confusion. All that ignorance.

This is why Direct products often hone in on new business models (e.g., crowdfunding, P2P lending, etc.) that FIs wouldn't traditionally consider due to brand concerns, technology limitations, regulation, geographical restrictions, lack of appropriate risk models, product silos, and so on.

Direct providers can look either brave or stupid, but if they hit it, they hit it out of the park. More commonly than not, the Stanford grads nail the technology, but overlook the difficulties of everything else (e.g., researching to deeply understand the real problem, creating a sales and marketing cycle that attains and retains customers cheaply).

For this reason, it's best a Direct provider not mistake an FI's silence in new markets as a lack of understanding or capability. While Direct fintech may take first steps into markets, the smart FIs are watching, and willing to make profound changes with their massive scale where Directs find opportunity.

Examples of Direct: PayPal, Venmo, Wealthfront, Mint, Square, Stripe, etc.

Direct may soon go after their own charters. While de novo chartering in the United States has been scarce, a glance at Figure 2.44 shows the country still has about 200 FDIC-deemed problem banks. While they may come with a host of their own challenges (poor culture, legacy infrastructure, shattered consumer trust, heavy regulatory scrutiny, etc.), problem banks also have one very big advantage over nonbanks: a very low source of funding and a built-in base of accountholders to cross-sell.

Figure 2.44 Number of Banks on Problem List

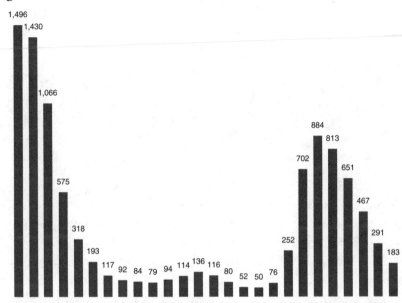

Source: FDIC
The number of banks on the FDIC's secret Problem List at each year's end.

> Picking off a bank on the FDIC's problem list could be one avenue for Direct to nab a charter. It worked for Suresh Ramamurthi from CBW Bank / Yantra. Read Suresh's advice for community banking leaders later in this book.

That base of consumers can be rather limited (by geography), if the acquired institution's charter is not national in nature. The Office of the Comptroller of the Currency is looking into a "limited-purpose" national charter that could push Direct fintech providers directly into the world of real banking servicing.

The limited purpose charter could change the face of the community banking competition overnight, yet would be a saving grace for Direct fintech companies who have had to navigate slow state-by-state licensing and usury laws.

Over the next few years, expect to see many of these problem children (and other too-small-to-compete institutions) get acquired by Direct fintech companies.

Gold Label. In between the two, you have Gold Label products. These are product brands that people recognize and seek out, that are married with the FI's brand of trust and credibility.

> Author and analyst Ron Shevlin first recognized this technique, and named it "Gold Labeling" in a April 3, 2013, article.[60] Ron Shevlin gives his advice for community bankers later in the book.

Like Direct, Gold Label fintech products are unique, brand-first solutions to user problems. But like White Label, Gold Label solutions are designed to help an FI compete and scale and are distributed by FIs to their end users.

In this way, the FI gets to offer the most contemporary, compelling user-centric products without the expense of "building it here," and the fintech firm receives a halo-effect of trust generated by the bank or credit union distributor. This is the best of both worlds for the FI and their fintech partner.

Examples of Gold Label: Kasasa, ApplePay, Simple, Dwolla, and so on.

> Over the years, Direct companies have attempted to cross over to Gold Label. This is fraught with numerous challenges: marketing, pricing, technology, branding, distribution, consumer trust, cultural inertia, etc.
>
> Some examples of Direct to Gold Label attempts:
>
> 2009: Wesabe, one of the early and very popular PFM products, made a last-ditch attempt at Gold Labeling in the year prior to their demise
>
> 2013: Mint attempted to offer their PFM service via FIs with lots of fanfare but no success
>
> 2014: OnDeck partnered with ProfitStars (a company that offers White Label solutions to FIs) with little market impact

As with anything in life, grays abound, but as it stands today, one can fit most fintech into these three buckets. Inside each of these three groups exist start-ups, mid-sized companies, and giants. Not every Direct is neophyte, and not every White Label is primordial. Over the years, financial institutions have invested in Direct and aided in development of White Label via incubators or CUSOs.

The Consumer Is the Change Agent; Fintech Is the Feedback

The noise can obfuscate what's really happening. As interesting, cool, advanced, fun, innovative as financial technology is, it is not the change agent.

Change is forced by the most passionate and evangelical. Depending on which side of the equation one sits, these change agents are fanatics or detractors. They are users, they share stories, and they influence others.

Some of these people care enough about change to build their visions. It's important to see them (whether they actually were or not) as your accountholders.

Consider that something about your institution's products and services is so bad, so lacking, so wretchedly wrong and intolerable, that it forced this person or group of people to work 100-hour weeks to change it.

Let that sink in.

Creating fintech products and building a business is not easy, cheap, quick, clean, relaxing, glorious, or otherwise free of sacrifice. It's quite the opposite. It requires extraordinary passion, talent, and dedication.

Tens of thousands of people around the world are working while you sleep and vacation. They give up birthdays and holidays, delay marriages, and max out their credit cards in order to see to it that something that you do at your institution either stops or begins.

At its most inane, fintech is an enabler of change. Bankers can use fintech companies as vendors, just as they always have, and grow to offer new fintech solutions to their marketplace.

At its best, fintech is constructive feedback. Learn pain points by being engaged with developments in and around fintech, and think of this education as free, constructive feedback for areas of improvement.

Prudent community banking executives will then watch to see how much real-user support these technologies receive. Was this one piece of feedback from one very passionate "accountholder," or are millions of people feeling the same (and willing to put their money behind it)?

Not fintech, nor examiners, nor history, will decide the future of your financial institution, only perspective and existing accountholders. They vote with their dollars and their trust, and those are the only votes that count.

Notes

1. Board of Governors of the Federal Reserve System, *Supervisory Policy and Guidance Topics: Community Banks*, http://www.federalreserve.gov/bankinforeg/topics/community_banking.htm.

2. FDIC Community Banking Study (2012), https://www.fdic.gov/regulations/resources/cbi/study.html.

3. Ibid.

4. Tim Critchfield et al., *The Future of Banking in America: Community Banks: Their Recent Past, Current Performance, and Future Prospects*, FDIC BANKING REV. (2004), at 4, *available at* http://www.fdic.gov/bank/analytical/banking/2005jan/br16n34full.pdf.

5. Stefan Jacewitz and Paul Kupiec, "Community Bank Efficiency and Economies of Scale," *FDIC* (December 2012).

6. http://www.relbanks.com/top-us-banks/assets-2015.

7. CUNA & FDIC, 2015.

8. http://www.relbanks.com/top-us-banks/assets-2015.

9. "Statistical Abstract of the United States 2015," Table 1180, Page 759 (Federal Reserve and US Census Bureau).

10. Statista (2015).

11. David Wheelock and Paul Wilson, "The Evolution of Cost-Productivity and Efficiency Among U.S. Credit Unions," *Journal Of Banking & Finance* (January 2013).

12. John M. Anderlik and Richard D. Cofer Jr., "Long-Term Trends in Rural Depopulation and Their Implications for Community Banks," *FDIC Quarterly* 8, no. 2 (2014).

13. Ibid.

14. Ibid.

15. Ibid.

16. Ibid.

17. NCUA, see Charters by year chart.

18. Anderlik and Cofer.

19. Ibid.

20. FDIC Community Banking Study (2012).

21. Anderlik and Cofer.

22. FDIC Community Banking Study (2012).

23. Anderlik and Cofer.

24. FDIC Community Banking Study (2012).

25. NCUA, see Charters by year chart.

26. Eric C. Breitenstein and John M McGee, "Brick-and-Mortar Banking Remains Prevalent in an Increasingly Virtual World," *FDIC Quarterly* 9, no. 1 (2015).

27. EconTalk podcast (http://www.econtalk.org/archives/2016/05/james_bessen_on.html) on *Learning by Doing* with James Bessen.

28. Anderlik and Cofer.

29. "Are Fintech and Community Banks a Perfect Match?" *American Banker* (April 22, 2016).

30. *FDIC Quarterly* 9, no. 1 (2015).

31. Ibid.

32. Anderlik and Cofer.

33. *FDIC Quarterly* 9, no. 1 (2015).

34. *FDIC Quarterly* 9, no. 1 (2015).

35. World Bank, GSMA, Apple, Google, a16z – slide 8 from Mobile Is Eating The World (2016), http://www.slideshare.net/a16z/mobile-is-eating-the-world-2016.

36. *FDIC Quarterly* 9, no. 1 (2015).

37. Financial Management Solutions Inc., *2013 FMSI Teller Line Study* (N.P., 2013), http://www.fmsi.com/fullpanel/uploads/files/2013-fmsi-teller-line-study-white-paper-00001.pdf.

38. ECB, United States Bureau of Labor Statistics, Citi Research estimates; Citi, "Digital Disruption" (March 2016).

39. Rosin McCord and Edward Simpson Prescott, "The Financial Crisis, The Collapse of Bank Entry, and Changes in the Size Distribution of Banks," Federal Reserve Bank of Richmond, *Economic Quarterly* 100, no. 1 (First Quarter 2014).

40. Ibid.

41. Robert M. Adams and Jacob P. Gramlich, "Where Are All the New Banks? The Role of Regulatory Burden in New Charter Creation," Federal Reserve Board Finance and Economics Discussion Series No. 2014-113 (December 16, 2014).

42. Charles S. Morris and Kristen Regehr, "What Explains Low Net Interest Income at Community Banks?" Federal Reserve Bank of Kansas City, *Economic Review* (Second Quarter 2014), pp. 59–87.

43. http://fraser.stlouisfed.org/publication/?pid=262.

44. David De Cremer, "Why Our Trust in Banks Hasn't Been Restored," *Harvard Business Review* (March 3. 2015).

45. Dodd-Frank Wall Street Reform and Consumer Protection Act of 2010, Pub. L. No. 111-203, 124, Stat. 1376 (July 21, 2010).

46. Hester Peirce, Ian Robinson, and Thomas Stratmann, "How Are Small Banks Faring Under Dodd-Frank?" Mercatus Center George Mason University, *Working Paper* (February 2014).

47. Nicole Gelinas, *Dodd-Frank: Too Convoluted to Succeed*, E21 at the Manhattan Institute (November 20, 2013).

48. Peirce, Robinson, and Stratmann.

49. Hester Peirce, "Scrap Regulations that Thin the Ranks of Small Banks," *American Banker* (February 23, 2015).

50. U.S. Census and Statista (2015).

51. aba.com, "ABA Survey: Regulatory Burden Limiting Bank Products and Services" (July 30, 2015).

52. Financial Register (December 31, 2013).

53. Federal Reserve Bank of Richmond, *Economic Quarterly* 100 no. 3 (2014), pp. 183–208.

54. Allen N. Berger and Gregory F. Udell, "Small Business Credit Availability and Relationship Lending: The Importance of Bank Organisational Structure," *Economic Journal* 112 (February 2002): F32–F53.

55. Personal Current Account Investigation—A report for the Competition and Markets Authority by GfK NOP, April 2015.

56. Ibid.

57. "China's P2P Lending Boom: Taking Flight," *The Economist*, January 23, 2016.

58. "Fintechs: Reinventing Banking," *EFMA Digest* (2016).

59. Personal Current Account Investigation—A report for the Competition and Markets Authority by GfK NOP, April 2015.

60. http://thefinancialbrand.com/47188/future-trend-in-banking-gold-labeling/.

Chapter 3

The Opportunity for Community Financial Institutions

"Everyone has a plan until they get punched in the mouth."

—*Mike Tyson*

"'T hree Six Three' is all we need to know, son," laughed the community bank CEO in a gruff Texan accent. I stare blankly, thinking, "Dammit, I knew I should have gone to banking school."

The smug banker knew something I didn't. Apparently, he didn't need my company to help him compete online. He had something called "Three Six Three."

Not knowing what Three Six Three was, and not wanting my banking-greenhorn to show, I whimpered, "OK, that makes sense." Shaky and defeated, I packed up my battle-scarred Powerbook G4, and scampered to the rental 2005 Chevy HHR.

Disgusted. Outsmarted by my lack of banking knowledge, I now had a six-hour drive back home with yet another "no" to chew on. It was still a year prior to release of iPhone and a decade prior to decent cross-country mobile service, so this drive home—like countless others before it—was lonely. But I was nearing the breaking point of "No, I don't need or want your product" toleration, so this ride's solitude was especially memorable.

I could seemingly sell anything—literally anything—but not a banking strategy to compete and secure business digitally. That's a problem, because as an entrepreneur, success often hinges on your sole sales capability, and I was now coming to the very unfortunate realization that my sales skills had devolved to be the absolute worst on the planet.

For the first half of the return trip, I remember repeatedly thinking: "It was the first objection. How could I simply fold on the first objection? Where is my brain?" In my ad agency days, I would never have let that happen. Back then, I had answers, and if not, I had the common sense to own up to it, and continue the discussion. What happened to my confidence? Damn my nerves and my fear. "This will not happen again. This cannot happen again."

The first three hours of the drive were painful with thoughts of failure, uncertainty, and shame rolling through my head. But by this point, I had wrestled with these concerns for four months. I heard every objection and had carefully crafted data-backed rebuttals for all of them.

Knowing that continuing down this flagellation spiral wouldn't get me anywhere, I spent the next three hours of the drive in absolute paranoia. "How did I miss them? The Internet's a big place, that's how. But really, they must have terrible SEO. Serves them right. Maybe they don't want to be found. So they can pounce on the market. I knew someone would beat me to the punch! The need is too obvious and the market too big. Do they even care about community banking, though? Doesn't matter. All that matters is that someone created a digital marketing business focused on driving business through the digital channels for community institutions, and I am driving home in the dark talking to myself. Tonight I'm finding Three Six Three and I'm going to figure out where the weakness is in their service. How did I miss this? Or maybe Three Six Three is local ad agency trying to expand into digital services. I'm not that lucky. This is a real problem."

By the time I arrived at my Internet oasis, um apartment, I had worked myself up to a frenzy of despair, embarrassment, suspicion, and all around fear. With thorough apprehension, I quickly Googled to find Three Six Three.

I promptly threw up.

Three Six Three wasn't a digital house or an ad agency or a marketing firm. Three Six Three wasn't a technology company. Three Six Three wasn't even a competitor. Three Six Three was, actually, 3-6-3.

Starting in the 1950s, the 3-6-3 rule became quite popular among bankers. Essentially, it was a joke of how easy it was to be a banker, and how little competition the bank has.[1] All a banker has to do is buy deposits at 3 percent, loan them out at 6 percent, and he can be on the golf course by 3 p.m.

That's 3-6-3?!! I wanted to hop in that rental, and drive back the six hours to give that banker a piece of my mind. But instead, frustrated and exhausted, with a bit of vomit still in the corner of my mouth, I passed out on the cold concrete floor of my apartment.

For decades and decades, in certain geographies, if you could get a charter, and you had breathing humans in a town or working at a company, you could make money. And yes, even as late as 2006, the rule that presided over old-school banking was still alive and well in the minds of some banking executives around the United States.

The reason 3-6-3, and similarly, "bankers' hours," reigned over banking is because certain regulation, such as that which prevented inter- and intrastate branching, all but prohibited competition.

A 1984[2] study showed US states with the most inefficient banks were the states that also forbid branch-based competition. And, as one would guess, not only were the less-competitive banks more bloated with costs, they also received above-peer normal profits.

These findings proved true in other findings, even as late as 1990,[3] years prior to the Riegle-Neal Interstate Branching and Branching Efficiency Act of 1994. It should be no surprise, then, that several studies performed during this era cite evidence of other practices found in noncompetitive markets, such as paying far less on deposits or charging higher rates on loans than competitive markets.

You Don't Need to Follow All the Best Practices, but You Should Eliminate the Worst Practices

Yes, some financial institutions thrived when they didn't have to compete. Who wouldn't? But times have changed, thankfully, and tremendous opportunity exists for banking executives willing to see themselves, and their financial institutions, in a new light.

That's the key: Reboots and culture change alike start at the top of the institution. And whether it's the assault of unconstructive noise, a noncompetitive spirit engrained by 3-6-3, curmudgeon board members, decades of customer-service-focused or branch location marketing, depopulating markets, ignorance of innovation, neck-deep regulation, or even simply a longing for status quo driven by the Maslow-commanded need for things physiological and safe, vicious demons plague many of today's community banks and credit unions.

We'll review some of those terrors next, and turn them into a few of the many opportunities that arise when an industry like ours is in the thick of change.

It's silly to cling to a mistake simply because you've spent the last several decades making it. Thankfully, inflection points such as the bankruption require the established players to shed the "what got us this far" thinking, invest in tools that improve efficiency and increase scale, discuss uncomfortable changes to strategy, and, simply, be inspired to test new things.

The remainder of this text holds a slew of executable ideas to help you pull your institution into tomorrow. This chapter contains opportunities to some of the bigger challenges I see in retail community banking today. I hope you find it useful.

Chapter 4 contains pure gold from the greatest minds of our industry. Corralling that range of extraordinary talent was not easy, and getting them to relinquish their best guidance for community banking executives was a near miracle—so please take their suggestions to heart.

The time to act is now. Shall we begin?

Doing Nothing Is Safe, but It's Also Foolish

"It's a lesson." Three days ago she said it, and days of macro and mirco-processing still haven't delivered. Until this afternoon.

Another airport bar. Drippy. Bartender busy. Wait—a slipstream by way of an available bartender. Except he's not a bartender, rather, a careful cashier who thinks he's a friend to all. More a keeper than a tender. The only thing he's got emboldened with alcohol is a Fire Eagle IPA.

Austin's finest. I'll take it. Careful cashier rings me up. Four times over.

Sinking into the airport bar, I'm discovered by a long-lost friend and his companion. He is in clothes that could have only come from the wardrobe of the movie known as the *County of Santa Barbara,* and she in a big round floppy hat as if she just don't care. Freshly spoiled from Austin City Limits.

He throws out a cheers for tomorrow's holiday: Columbus Day. Columbus. The reason we're all here, right?

Another reminder why our industry may soon flatten.

Columbus Day is not a daring or a proud day. It's a lazy day. A day off for those who are weary. Those who have gilded-spoon appetites, and Connecticut broad-leaf cigar-scorched shirts, Bookers' whiskey-stained Dockers, and Rolling Stones' lyrics engrained in their brains. Those whose parents Woolworth escalated over their dreams decades ago. These are the people who rest on holidays. These are the people who stop in a world that doesn't, in a time and a space that drives constant and barrels over the weary.

Mid-cheers, I recall a bar in an old hangar. Across or somewhat near the ol' Blue Plate mayonnaise factory. It's not a terrible place. Aluminum-crested and half-moon shaped. I think it might have fire pits outside, but the warmth was inside the building with the storage-shed design. A band takes the stage and plays for four hours. Those inside the biplane temple had found Mecca. Those outside were just not ready. They missed it forever.

That's what's going on with Columbus Day.

A fiction-filled day off for a few chosen people. The tired, the housed, the bellied…the people Eddie Vedder thanks his Elderly Woman Behind the Counter in a Small Town stars for. The people who were not quite willing to kneel before the flanneled chord of Kurdt. They regret not being ready, but nothing will bring that split-second-decade chance back.

Not the hungry and time-poor fintech startups, but banks and credit unions take a break on this day.

Columbus Day makes one appreciate what he has, which causes one to forget where he was going. It's a fierce and growling and monosyllabic place—a release that takes you to your secret dark. A place you should not visit for long. Some move, and others move in.

There's solace in the familiar, that for once, you are no different. Tradition feels safe and comforting. The comfort will kill. Make yourself uncomfortable.

Expand Your Mind

These days, there is no excuse for banking executives to rely on one single source for enlightenment. No one marketing firm, no one book (well, maybe this one), no one website, no one speaker, no one consultant, no one fintech vendor, no one noise maker should inform your entire outlook on where banking is headed.

Our industry is too diverse, under too much transformation, with too many biases, and too many fortunes at stake to accept one line of thinking as gospel.

Tomorrow's successful community banker will this year attend a few of the many new (Financial Brand Forum, Money 2020, Next Money, Finovate, etc.) and existing association banking conferences to meet other bankers, investigate new technologies, and put to question everything she knows about banking. By getting out of her office, flying to new cities, using Uber when she lands, downloading her Hilton digital key via the mobile app, and simply experiencing the changing world firsthand outside of her cocoon, the banker is forced to think differently, and recognize that today's banking landscape is making the formerly global, quite local.

Whether she wants it or expects it, her mind will soon see the real challenges and challengers her institution faces—well beyond the day-to-day fires. The energy, education, enthusiasm, curiosity, and comradery gleaned from the conference experience will let her recenter herself, as if it were her first week at work, on the future of her institution.

Conferencing can be game changing. And some choice blogs and reports can be the perfect additives (not substitutes) for continued learning outside of the conference. Here are some recommendations to get started:

1. Check out the additional content on Bankruption.com.
2. Follow me, @Waupsh, on Twitter; then follow all those I follow.
3. Subscribe to *Digital Banking Report*.
4. Listen to *Breaking Banks* podcast.
5. Attend your local Next Money events.
6. Read TheFinancialBrand.com regularly.

Correlation Does Not Imply Causation

Often, bankers complain about competition from technology startups that are not overseen by any governing body (yet). Why aren't they regulated? The lack of regulation is why they move so fast / create products that we haven't / attract millennials / whatever! It's just not fair!

Competition isn't fair.

Even still, why should a fintech startup that is not a bank or a credit union be regulated like a bank or a credit union? There are perhaps a hundred reasons why most fintech startups should not be considered and regulated as financial institutions. The CFPB should oversee their interactions with consumers with the same fervor as financial institutions, but they should be regulated based on the exact services they provide, not based on a lazy grouping of "fintech startups."

Presuming that the services provided by the fintech company are moral and fair and all that good stuff, the regulations should keep up with the era, just as they have in other countries around the world. Fintech companies should be allowed to provide aspects of banking services to businesses or consumers without being labeled a *financial institution*.

Uber has demonstrated its separation from taxi services, time and again, in courts all over the globe. The same could be said for aspects of financial services in the United States. We have our European brothers and sisters to thank for the model.

In 2009 (and later expanded in 2015), the European Union adopted the Payment Services Directive, a law that, among other things, increased competition in electronic payments by creating a "payment institution" license. It's all part of creating a single, digital market that will simplify payments for consumers and businesses across Europe.

As a payment institution, a nonbank can supply nearly any type of electronic payment (including direct debit, credit cards, credit transfers, money remittance, mobile payments, etc.) to its customers across the 28 countries in the European Union. Since 2009, many fintech startups in Europe, including Finland-based Holvi (later acquired by BBVA), have gotten their start via a payment institution license.

You don't have to do so now, but in a quiet moment, ask yourself this question: "Why shouldn't the OCC create a similar 'lighter' federal banking charter for fintech startups or nonbanks like Google, Apple, Amazon, or Facebook?" Don't let "because it's not fair" be the response your brain chooses.

> Before you go thinking fintech companies won't want to be pushed into the hornet's nest of regulation, many of them are demanding such changes by the OCC and are even part of a lobbying effort called "Financial Innovation Now" to quickly evolve regulations in the United States. Financial Innovation Now consists of Amazon, Apple, Google, Intuit, and Paypal, etc.

Now, take a look at the number of users on Facebook in Figure 3.1, and imagine how much good Facebook could do by extending banking services to the unbanked around the world. If you don't want to compete against Facebook, sell or merge your FI today.

Uniform regulation went out the window with asset-size carve-outs in Dodd-Frank—you can't have it both ways. Of course, the OCC should study why Dodd-Frank also did away with the Office of Thrift Supervision—specialized "light" charters might simply rehash prior mistakes.

Remember the Riegle-Neal interstate branching discussion earlier? ATM technology pushed branch efficiency forward and enabled the possibility for a bank to operate branches far cheaper than ever. It was only

Figure 3.1   Facebook Monthly Active Users

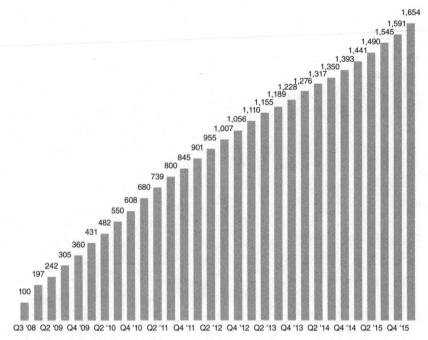

SOURCE: Facebook

The number of monthly active Facebook users worldwide, in millions. Would your institution do anything differently if it knew a "light" charter for Facebook (and others) was on the horizon?

a decade or so before the legislation turned that possibility into reality. Some banks had been using ATMs to automate processes in-branch, were prepared for Riegle-Neal (M&A, compliance, risk, etc.), and took advantage of the new law. Those banks, history has shown, achieved more logarithmic growth than the more exponential growth of those who did not.

Next, ask yourself if your institution is making investments (in human resources, cash, real estate, etc.) today that could be reprioritized to help your FI prepare to turn this limited federal charter threat into an opportunity.

Although some rest easy on their current sub-LIBOR funding source advantage over nonbanks, more prudent community bankers see that as a fairly weak dam that will soon break. The institutions who thrive over the next 10 years will tackle the "competing with nonbanks" question, now, with their executive team and their board.

Because the Real Problem Is Inaction

With shrinking margins, time is not on the side of the banker. Doing nothing is reckless.

Tradition, habit, and the challenges of organizational culture change across a number of humans in a variety of locations can all reinforce slothful dormancy.

There's comfort in inactivity. When one's industry is in transformation, one can easily hedgehog his way into obsolescence. Apathy and indecision can be comfortable and familiar, but, like the sirens' song, things end rather awkwardly.

And if it's not lethargy or inertia, it's fear. Cloaked in a sexy phrase so the entire executive team can feel smarter while cowering, someone at the table mutters, *reputational risk*. Simply uttering the banker safe word quickly sniffs out whatever life, whatever dreams, whatever ember of transformation existed in the institution just six syllables prior.

Goes the refrain: if we do something new and it blows up, what will people think? Is it worth risking all of the consumer trust we've accumulated in our legendary, forty-thousand-year history?

> Certainly "reputational risk" does exist—especially in the financial industry. I'm pushing here for a reason. Perhaps we can have our cake and eat it too?

Call It "Toe in the Water," "MVP," "Whateveryouwant," Just Try Something

In his groundbreaking book *The Lean Startup*, Eric Ries first defined an MVP (Minimally Viable Product) as "that version of a new product that allows a team to collect the maximum amount of validated learning about customers with the least effort".

> Lean Principles can have immediate, profound impacts on any organization—especially community financial institutions. Renown fintech strategist Alex Jiménez offers some key advice on adopting lean at your financial institution in the next chapter.

Delivering the lightest (smallest, least feature-packed, cheapest, fastest, etc.) solution to a problem or set of problems, and, over time, iterating on it in response to feedback makes a lot of logical sense. You eat an elephant one bite at a time, right?

At its core, the adoption of lean principles (like MVP) gives you and your team the freedom and the permission to move. To experiment. To test modifications to processes, products, ideas—while also looking quite industrious and relevant to your accountholders, who have been conditioned to embrace MVP with smartphone app updates.

> It can be difficult to remember this long ago, but the original iPhone didn't come packed with every feature that mobile phone users said they needed. In fact, a very common feature of competitive phones at the time, "cut, copy, and paste," was not found on iPhone until OS release 3.0, almost two years following the launch of iPhone.

When a banking executive frames his team's problems as fintech competition or regulation or reputational risk, all he's doing is absolving his team of their sedentary sins, and perpetuating inclinations of stagnation. The evolved community banker will take a page from the bible of many of his fintech competitors, and embrace transformation—one small step at a time.

Reputational Risk Is Mitigated When You Do It Right

In order to prevent consumer trust erosion when MVP-testing new banking ideas and consumer-facing technologies, best practices dictate you satisfy the following three end-user characteristics:

1. End-users know they are part of an experiment.
2. End-users are clear on the risks involved (e.g., the app may crash and you may not see your balance for a while, etc.).
3. End-users proactively opt-in to your experiment. (When you want to see how a user would behave if they did not know they were part of an experiment, it's best to take this research outside of your MVP.)

From one of the largest banks on the planet to one the newest, Citi and Monzo are two banks charging forward on their innovation agendas while addressing adverse customer reaction before it arises.

Citi FinTech, a related, yet separately run arm of Citibank, was launched in November 2015 to be Citi's conduit to fintech companies, where appropriate, set a startup on an integration path with Citi, and, ultimately, be a catalyst for change across the entire bank.

The fintech-specific investment group for Citi sees Singapore as a favorable country to test in because, among other things, consumers there are enthusiastic guinea pigs. Specifically, its CEO Heather Cox (who has since left Citi for USAA) said, "We see Singapore as a really important hub of innovation … the adoption is so high, the willingness to test and learn by consumers is disproportionately high."[4]

On the other end of the spectrum, you have challenger bank Monzo (United Kingdom). In late 2015, digital-only bank Monzo rolled out its Alpha program in an attempt to get early feedback on real-life situations. The company continuously pushed warnings, "Things will inevitably not work as expected, and you may even temporarily lose access to the money on the card. But we'll work hard to fix those problems as quickly as we can."

By working hard to be transparent with users who want to be on the bleeding edge of their banking experience, community institutions can experiment and evolve, and not be left in the cold.

It's Not a Family; It's a Team

"If you build it, you will fill it."
—Jack Salvetti

C-level banker groupies pack the first five rows like a sober, senior moshpit. Jack is a well-respected strategic consultant for community banking CEOs. With a decades-long track record and a discerning client palette, he has earned the right to wear those trademark glasses.

Rounded vintage, thick dark tortoise frames neatly sculpted around his eye sockets, Jack's eyewear is as defined as his word selection. His anointed banker clients know to listen and to act when Jack speaks. They might not want to hear it, but it's going to be something they need.

This time was no different. In fact, he's said it many times before. Part observation; part threat; zero promise. One sentence, then on to another topic, entirely like a college lecturer or a street corner lunatic.

Certainly the former. My mind hangs back on those eight words like a scratched 45. "If you build it, you will fill it." If you build that multimillion-dollar thing on the corner, you'll need to staff it. Protect it. Vacuum it. Lightbulb it. Pay taxes on it.

But the stymieing board wants a new branch. And on the edge of the county is a fried KFC. Nothing $800,000 and 10 months can't fix.

So you build it, and then you've got to fill it, with a million dollars of overhead, annually (see Figure 3.2).

Figure 3.2   Number of Bank Branches

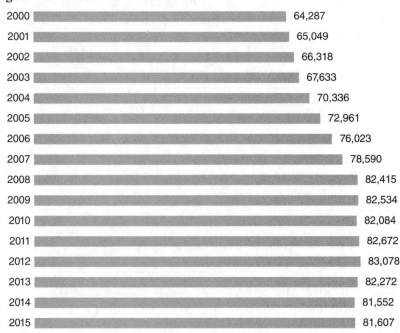

Year	Number
2000	64,287
2001	65,049
2002	66,318
2003	67,633
2004	70,336
2005	72,961
2006	76,023
2007	78,590
2008	82,415
2009	82,534
2010	82,084
2011	82,672
2012	83,078
2013	82,272
2014	81,552
2015	81,607

SOURCE: FDIC
We keep building branches.

The simplicity and rhyme scheme of the eight words makes it fit for an infomercial. But this is not a sales pitch. It's not even an attack or a prognostication of branch death. It's simply a truth.

Unfortunately, so many FIs consider their front line as highly replaceable, cheap labor. Of course, that's what they get in return.

"Cheap labor" is an expensive trap. Rarely is throwing numerous, poorly paid humans at a problem the answer. No savings is more valuable than your accountholders. But that's what you put to risk when you have poorly trained, apathetic, and unapologetic customer service people.

The most effective retail establishments understand that the frontline employee directly positively or negatively impacts their bottom line. Best practices suggest you "open the book" to allow the front line team access and understand the metrics that matter most to your organization, then create a team-based performance plan around those metrics. You need to take it from c-level to sea level with enthusiasm, refined processes, passion, and business acumen.

Gracefully, Salvetti leaves it to the audience to view the truth in context of more macro trends. Nevertheless, we all know that at some point, Jack's phrase may need to change to be a bit more obvious. (I suggest, "If you build it, you will soon kill it.")

Train or Fire the People in Your Organization Who Say, "I Don't Do Numbers"

At a recent banking marketing conference (with about half credit union and half community bank marketers in attendance), a speaker asked the audience to define ROA (return on assets). I think he was going to make the point that the impact marketing can have on an institution. But he never made it, as he soon realized that only three people in the 350-person audience would understand his calculus.

It is impossible to hold marketing leads accountable for creating effective marketing plans if they cannot measure how they help (or hurt) your organization (see Figures 3.3 and 3.4).

Figure 3.3   Number of Bank Employees in United States

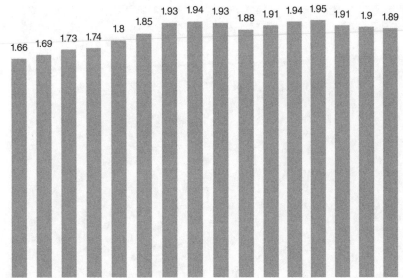

SOURCE: FDIC
The number of FDIC-insured bank employees over time.

Figure 3.4   Salaries and Benefits of Bank Employees (US)

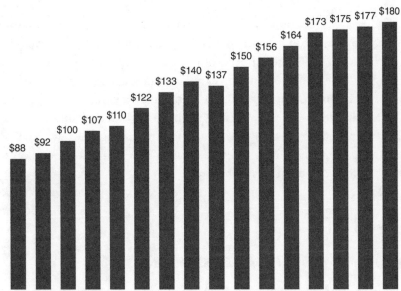

SOURCE: FDIC
Non-interest expense of FDIC banks on employee salaries (in US billion dollars).

Figure 3.5   Shattered Innocence

SOURCE: Author photo
An old bank branch in San Jose, California, now, a gentleman's club

The average community institution in this country has about 40 employees. With a team that small, even one weak link will break the chain. Today's successful community financial institutions demand strong skill sets and coordination across technology, marketing, analytics, et al., who must all be speaking the same language.

Perhaps your entire leadership team should attend banking school? Or, you can build a banking curriculum training program—we have one for Kasasa employees. Failing all that, lots of free education exists on the Internet for your team to self-educate.

There's no excuse for not knowing how your employer makes money. Demand to learn about your business, its measurements, and what makes the institution tick.

Bad People You Must Push; Good People Push You

Train, manage and, where necessary (and it will be necessary), prune your team.

Leadership begins with you. Inform and excite. Don't be the weak manager stereotype of a banking executive. Listen to everyone (including the detractors), prune bad apples, and raise your superstars with clear goals and a career path.

> According to the Center for Generational Kinetics, financial institutions today have four generations of employees serving five generations of end users!

A *Fortune* article suggests that the MVPs of your organization are no longer Peter Drucker's "knowledge workers."[5] Instead, as data and knowledge get further commoditized and mechanized, the most important people on your team are those skilled in the art of human collaboration and team building (aka *relationship workers*).

Studies cited in the article suggest that the most important factor when considering a new employer is its reputation as a great place to work.[6] Thus, the popularity of sites such as Glassdoor.com.

This leads directly to a discussion on culture in the organization, which the typical community bank or credit union translates to "excitement at community events." Excitement is a byproduct, and not a key contributor to an organization's culture.

Instead, *Fortune* suggests a strong culture centers on four main points: mission, colleagues, trust, and caring.

To test this hypothesis, I chose a culture I know very well, that of Kasasa, ranked as one of 2016's top five Best Places to Work in Central Texas (Large Companies).[7] By the CEO Gabe Krajicek's design, Kasasa's culture is centered on four values (named "the Patch"), and by the Chief Culture Officer Nathan Baumeister's lead, Kasasa's culture continues to flourish:

- *Mission*: Its mission is concise, "To help community banks and credit unions win the war against the megabanks and nonbanks." A simple, easy to understand mission ensures clarity and decisive decision making—no matter if it's daily tactical or the multiyear strategic stuff.
- *Colleagues*: To work at Kasasa, a candidate must pass a litany of evaluations, and to remain at Kasasa, an employee must continually deliver

results and live according to the values of the organization. Kasasa has found that by simply nurturing the best talent, it attracts more of the best talent because smart, hard-working people like to work with other smart, hard-working people.

- *Trust*: Kasasa trusts its employees thoroughly; at the most base, Kasasa offers unlimited paid time off. A more powerful demonstration of trust is its value of Five-Star Leadership, whereby every employee is treated as if he or she holds the rank of a five-star general. Irrespective of the role, as a five-star general, it is incumbent upon the employee to provide feedback and ideas for improvement to the other five-star generals, and those five-star generals must make time to listen and respond with either a "yes" or a "no + why" answer. To foster this kind of feedback cycle, trust must exist throughout the organization. And promoting the open environment where a frontline employee could respectfully challenge or offer ideas to his manager or CEO (and receive a direct answer) dramatically improves the organization's trajectory for success.
- *Caring*: One example of caring for employees that exists at Kasasa: their employee-run, employee-funded employee-assistance program called Love Fund. As a Kasasa team member, you can choose to give a small portion of your paycheck to Love Fund, which Kasasa matches. From June 2010 to early 2016, Love Fund assisted nearly 300 employees with everything from alleviation of financial hardships to get-well-soon wishes to a running leg for an amputee employee wanting to (and has since) become a triathlete.

By focusing on its core culture tenants, Kasasa has built an unflappable, focused team that has served it well though the financial crisis as well as the other challenging times of a fintech startup. Any and every community banking institution can and should do the same.

Pressure Wash the Barnacles

Barnacles create such significant drag that the US Naval Academy estimates they increase the Navy's petroleum expenditures by $250 million each year.[8]

Community financial institutions can have their own barnacles, and they typically come in the form of an aged, unimaginative, unresponsive, disinterested board. This is a shame, because a great board can positively transform an organization—as early PayPal CFO turned Sequoia Capital lead Roelof Botha suggests, "Good board members act as shock absorbers, not amplifiers."

At a time when the nimbleness of smaller boats would be an advantage, the would-be community FI trawlers have significant hull drag. For once, small isn't small enough. There's something smaller and faster than you. And they have shock absorbers.

These days, board members are required by regulators to be deeply involved with their institutions. Unfortunately, barnacles hide behind this fact, and use it as an excuse to require undue reporting, which ultimately increases expense and frustration.

A friend of mine is CEO for a $300 million community bank with five branches. In my opinion, the bank's biggest challenge is 12 washed-up centenarian jocks who took an econ class in high school but are respected because they own the businesses their daddies gave them (car dealership, funeral home, plumbing supply business, etc.). They demand a monthly board kit of 200 pages analyzing every aspect of the bank. Every aspect, that is, but the bank's future and its competition.

Board barnacles love to talk banking glory days, opine risk mitigation, and associate blame for transactions long passed. They are not interested in pushing your institution forward, helping you find the talent you need, or learning about contemporary data-marketing techniques. Conversely, check out Figure 3.6, and consider a paradigm change that is statistically more effective.

The coming bankruption introduces even more challenges for those of us in the community banking industry. As community institutions are those who are most at risk for disruption, you will need a team that's stronger than ever to thrive in the new environment. Push accountability of banking knowledge and institutional goals to your teammates, and treat your employees like an evolving team and not like permanent family members. Perhaps most importantly, reduce drag on your hull as soon as you can; you're going to need it.

Figure 3.6   US Returns by Women Directors

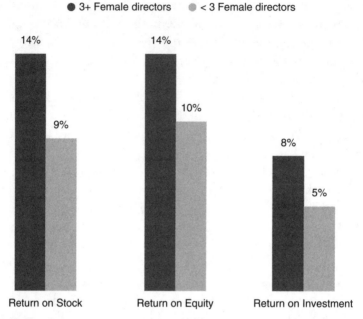

SOURCE: Catalyst, Experts
Returns generated in companies in the United States with female board directors from 2007–2012. If
your board is slowing you down, perhaps this chart will inspire.

Much Ado about Branching

Ginger. I asked the waiter for ginger several minutes ago. Where is it?
After being on the road for a few days, I crave pickled ginger. The pink
kind you find at a sushi restaurant. It's not like I eat jars of pickled ginger
at home, but for whatever reason, pickled ginger is my comfort food.
And I'm uncomfortable right now.

I've been looking forward to the ginger since yesterday, when
Ron Shevlin asked me to join him for dinner. If you've ever spoken
to Ron, you know he likes a good meal at a nice place (and if you've
known Ron for longer than 10 minutes, you also know he expects you
to pay for that meal).

And this place, Nobu, well, let's just say he made a big freaking stink
about Nobu. All I heard from his rant was that we were going to go to
a sushi place, and well, I was set. After all, sushi equals ginger.

Unless, of course, you're at Nobu.

Nobu is one of those affected sushi establishments where the chef chooses the raw fish guts for you and determines how they'll be entwined with vegetables and seaweed and other fish innards and whatnot. Apparently, she also determines whether you get your ginger or not.

Jim Marous is entertaining others with his gruff eloquence—a mannerly gentleman sowing seeds of digital disruption something or other. Ron interrupts him, cordially, for once. Laughter happens. I can't feign a smile. I can't focus. I can't concentrate.

I count the bumps on my tongue as it rubs the ceiling of my blackcurrant-laced and tannin-tanned mouth. No matter how much I drink, my mouth is parched.

Ron blathers some more about the flaws in Net Promoter Score or something else that Ron likes to talk about, but over his shoulder, a siren is carrying pickled ginger as high as the eye can see. I throw it in my mouth as fast as it hits the table.

As the pink stuff whets the arid buds, ears tune in to the table conversation. Brain kicks in just as soon as the topic lands on Brett King. Brett had to duck out on our dinner so he could get home. Jim talks about Brett's podcast that day, and how I missed a great discussion.

Ron and Jim pick up where the day's episode of *Breaking Banks* left off, and I consider lunch a few hours earlier.

Instead of joining the disruption trio on *Breaking Banks*, I chose to sit with Jeffry and Neil at a tall, square-acre table below a gaudy chandelier in a side room connected to a large chef's kitchen off a grandiose living area just behind a grand piano and sky-wide window. The lux pad taunts Las Vegas to play, as only Caesar's Palace can do.

For lunch, we have a private catered meal in a suite that was featured in the movies—*Rain Man, Hangover,* or something else entirely, I can't remember. Either way, it has the allure of a has-been must-be. An odd location, I thought, but soon to be quite familiar. This eloquence would host me several times over the next few days—in various mental and physical states.

The Financial Brand's Jeffry has invited me to join him and Neil for a lunch discussion. Across the table, Jeffry's a slicker, fast-talking fellow with some strong beliefs. Neil, on my right, is a more soft-spoken, yet equal-willed and over-IQ'd overachiever from Facebook. For once, I keep my mouth shut in a feeble attempt to learn something.

> Now would be a good time to go to TheFinancialBrand.com
> and sign up to receive their newsletter. While you're there, get
> a ticket to their annual Forum. Thank me later.

Quiet, that is, until Jeffry and Neil pick on branches. I have a penchant for the underdog, no doubt, but I also see a ton of branch-level data. And, while there is no question that branch banking will undergo radical transformation, and ultimately extinction, there is also no question that branch banking currently cultivates the majority of the primary deposits and accounts in the country.

I have yet to see a profitable US digital banking model that doesn't involve some control over this core relationship—not that it won't happen, just that it hasn't happened, yet.

So, if you need the account, and you eschew the most effective way of opening volumes of accounts, you and your digital banking thing, no matter how transformative, will remain a small player. With all its change, banking remains a volume game.

As I speak up and share my statistics, a confused Jeffry looked at me as he would a visitor from another planet.

How could I not see the writing on the wall?

I do, but timing is everything. In this case, moving slowly with a plan to move quickly might not be so bad.

I understand how to balance the nose and the spite for one's face. Neil, for his part, was open to the idea that branches might still be a maximum-throughput channel for account opening and retail deposit generation (the best funding source for a banking institution), though it's safe to say I could have been from 500 light years away, and the quiet, refined Neil would have been as gracious.

But that's who I am: some dude sitting at the cool kids (lunch) table, but speaking an entirely foreign, somewhat luddite language out of both sides of my mouth. It's not as fun, controversial, or headline-worthy, so I sure don't get invited back!

Look at the Retail Industry as a Corollary

Modern, pure-play ecommerce sites (vs. clicks-and-mortar retailers) are built on a foundation of data-driven insight by agile-thinking, change-embracing talent, and lean business principles. From their inception, these companies have honed their pattern recognition, trend prediction, and propensity modeling skills around the customer experience.

This war against old-school clicks-and-mortar retailers is waged with pixels, clean real-time data, behavioral economics, social media, and psychology.

Clicks-and-mortar retailers, on the other hand, are finding their online and mobile storefronts exploding, and their physical storefronts dwindling in foot-traffic. However, the in-store experience continues to be the most important channel for digital shoppers when making a purchase, and nearly 75 percent of the growth in total retail sales is generated from physical stores.[9]

Quite a familiar conundrum, eh?

With all of their richer, more diverse data, the clicks-and-mortar guys have an opportunity to deliver a more powerful customer experience than the pure-play ecommerce stores ... if they can just get the whole "omnichannel" thing sorted out.

> Read about banking omnichannel strategies from co-publisher of *The Financial Brand* and publisher of *Digital Banking Report*, Jim Marous, later in the book!

Omnichannel strategies utilize both structured and unstructured data to provide more relevant, immersive buying experiences across digital and physical channels. A simple example of this: a store determines that a shopper's shopping list is 20 percent unresolved, on average, when he exits the store.

To solve this problem, the store might incentivize customers to use their mobile app to save shopping lists, offering coupon-matching and in-store routing based on the products on the list. In turn, the store receives more loyal customers who now depend on their app for shopping, more complete shopping list fulfillment, and ultimately, higher average revenue per user.

The investment required for a clicks-and-mortar retailer to deliver omnichannel experiences is not insignificant. Just using the above example, the retailer must manage location-specific mapping of items, display of product availability product at a particular store, in-app or e-commerce purchase (perhaps in-store pickup logistics as well), receipt storage in-app or emailing with high inbox delivery, a unified view of the customer, customer educational signage or videos and other marketing, accompanying business intelligence, and much, much more.

> "A Walmart store-only customer spends on average about $1,400 a year. An online customer only spends a couple of hundred dollars. The customer who shops both online and in the store spends about $2,500 with us on average in a year. So that customer in the middle of the intersection of those two circles is incredibly valuable for us and as they continue to build that behavior, we are going to continue to take advantage of it."—Chief Merchandising Officer for Walmart, Steve Bratspies, at the Raymond James 37th Annual Institutional Investors Conference (2016)

To make that happen, retailers must fight the archaic systems they rely on—system providers who are often unable or unwilling to work together, poor data quality, siloed departments, etc. (The similarities to community banking continue.)

Yet, these retailers are investing the billions of dollars in total transformation because they deeply understand the value of data proximity in delivering a personal experience with consumers. Even more so, they understand the consequences of not providing these intimate experiences.

The Five Words That Will Kill: "How May I Help You?"

Know what I need, and give me proactive service before opening your big mouth to bother me with such a stupid question, that's how.

No matter how Pollyanna this may be, your users have been trained in other parts of their lives to think of you as they think of their smartphone apps—informed and connected to other data points in my life, with regular upgrades.

The discordance between "Normal World" and "Banking World" is unnerving. Like simultaneously listening to Sonic Youth and Justin

Bieber, we are surrounded by warring craft and crap. The genie would fit back in the bottle, if the glass weren't shattered in pieces all over the branch parking lot.

According to a 2015 Gartner study, "89 percent of companies expect to compete mostly on customer experience vs. 36 percent just four years ago." Customer experience is the new customer service, and today's bumpy uninformed service experience aggravates logic and defaces competence.

If your customer experience (i.e., your service) is not continuously informed and upgraded by each particular user's data (task metrics, event knowledge, historical data, and even common sense), you will insult his intelligence and force him into the hands of your competition.

Any banking institution that still requires any human to ask that demeaning question of a customer within the next five years will disappear from existence in the following five.

As Andy Greenawalt Says, "You Are Misusing Your Humans"

Now, Andy was referring to a whole other fossil-powered dinosaur at the financial institution (compliance), but the point remains salient nonetheless: If you are going to pay some humans, don't pay them to do things more poorly than cheaper alternatives (like, say, an automated teller machine).

Omnichannel investments are being made across the landscape of megabanks to advance beyond the worthless small talk, but the "physical proximity equals intimacy" misconception continues to fool even the most hardened community banker (and examiner) today.

These executives are absolutely convinced that they provide a supreme, unnatural, impossibly rich customer service via human-to-human interaction. They fool themselves into an increasingly meaningless, significantly false, and mostly affected legacy claim of smiling, personal service.

> The theory goes, each and every auto loan, mortgage, or commercial checking relationship is so incredibly important to the livelihood of the smaller institution that they take additional customer service steps to ensure repeat business and referrals.

Worse yet, many believe it to be their long-term competitive advantage. To provide contemporary customer service, you have to do a lot more for me than recognize my face and ask me about my cat.

There is no possible way an organization can provide personal customer service via disconnected humans that is anywhere near as remarkable, efficient, timely and friendly as that which can be provided via the aid of contemporary, data-driven, connected devices. The sooner one adopts modern principles, the sooner one can embrace recovery.

The successful community banker of tomorrow knows that data drives understanding and therefore happier accountholders, and adopting an omnichannel strategy is a big step forward for today's siloed and branch-laden financial institutions in the United States.

Community FIs who quickly adapt to the omnichannel world (while overhauling their branch network to optimize efficiencies) will stitch together a more enhanced offering than their pure-play digital counterparts, crossing the intimacy chasm with data and proactive, contextual service.

> As you might guess, for most banking, humans may prefer their human counterpart, but it is better handled by the dumbest, oldest fintech. Perhaps you can reserve these more advanced personal services for certain levels of banking customers, much as the airlines reserve first class service for those who are most brand loyal or are willing to pay the price?

Do Not Let Sacred Geese Live

You know that branch. It's an absolute abomination. Expensive or ugly or both. It's on maintenance mode—you will never invest in it. You and everyone at the institution know why you keep it, but you never, ever say it.

You keep the million-dollar annual overhead sacred goose around for nostalgia. You keep it for proximity to the chairman's home. You keep it because it actually has a room big enough to fit the entire board. You keep it for whatever weak, lame excuse you have told yourself to help you sleep better at night.

A step by step, proven methodology on how to make your branches lean, mean, producing machines is in the next chapter from my friend Hal Coxon. Hal's history of success will speak for itself.

It's time to kill the goose. If it's nostalgia, packrat your archeology exhibit in a nice 10′ × 10′ air-controlled storage unit. If it's because the chairman doesn't like to drive (or can't drive), get him a phone—he probably wasn't doing anything when he came in anyway.

If it's because it had a room big enough to fit the board meetings, tell the board you found a way to save thousands of dollars per year and dramatically increase the speed at which your institution moves— then cut the board by half, and move the meetings to a secure video session.

From robotic tellers to microbranching with interactive tellers to branches on wheels, each of you will have a customized game plan that's right for your institution. The most important thing you can do, how-ever, is evaluate all options, and then quickly execute.

Reevaluating your branch strategy and modifying your physical pres-ence to meet your present and future needs should be one of the easier challenges you have ahead of you. If you can't get past this one with-out too much headache, your institution is just like your sacred goose: cooked.

Market Your Market

Now this is interesting: The sign says that tonight is a songwriter series run by the local Episcopalian church. Waiters see plenty of no-tip one-top four-tops. Bartender greets us with a smile, so we head to the bar.

The singer has a presence. Eyes so dark the whites sparkle. Her too-big-for-her-body feet writhing in red strapped-on heels. A man-dolin case, band-stickered to torn leather first-hand smoke-stained dreams. Grammied by elite; unknown by all.

She stands tall in cuteskulled pants to share her gift. She half-sits, fully present, on a decades-old, Amish barstool. Tapping her feet on the beaten wood floor in time with whatever she's pushing through the solo JBL floor speaker. Guitar pic is MIA.

The lipstick-stained mic is hot. Mids are low. Boyfriend runs the sound, bored.

She plays on, and I ruminate brain drain.

In the mid-2000s, community bankers couldn't not discuss brain drain in their town. Referring to professionals or otherwise educated kids emigrating to the big city, brain drain was the logical excuse I heard for why a certain community FI couldn't attract a younger audience.

A simple demographic study or just a visit to the town would prove the theory time and again. Including this evening, I assumed permanence with brain drain. Twenty-five boomer-to-silent-generation customers in a three-thousand-square-foot pub. Clearly, the singer would need to discuss this tour stop with her agent.

Or, perhaps, she is inspired by the antiquity.

There is a romantic connection between the American heart and the stained-glass-windowed town square tavern—where Main Street is an actual road with coin-operated street parking, and American flags are more common than people. Roadside restaurants with model trains that run the perimeter of the ceiling and all-you-can-eat catfish Fridays.

And, apparently, talented singers writing songs that Episcopalians dissect for truth ...

I glance at the 2″ × 2″ local advertisements plastered all over the paper placemat on the bar. Celtic & Country Collectibles, Minuch's Contractors, Super Siding, Back to Basics Chiropractors, Windgate Heating & Cooling, Tommyhawk's Black Powder & Muzzleloader Supplies, Phoenix Chrysler, Hawktown High's football schedule, and of course, First State Bank.

It's 2016, and the 2″ × 2″s are all local phone numbers and physical addresses. No URLs. No QR codes. Landlines with physical addresses and zip codes. Corn and natural gas may be coming from the ground, but handshakes and sweat power these towns.

> Nearly 1/5 of all US counties would have zero FDIC-insured bank branches if it weren't for community banks. And, community banks hold the vast majority of deposits in micropolitan and rural locations.[10]

My host this evening is the CEO of First State Bank, who tells me that the singer has recently returned after several years in NYC. "She moved back home," he says, "because she missed this place."

Really? Hmm … He suggests the city's skyscrapers were a fine muse for a twenty-something artist, but she had to return to the silo, the tallest thing for a hundred miles.

Owned in large part by her uncle, and otherwise by First State Bank, the large silo just outside of town has been a character in her life since childhood.

The silo casts shade while you play hide and seek, stands tall as a marker for people needing directions at the diner, and proudly shines as a reminder of what hard work can help you achieve.

The man who raised the silo is the same person who raised the singer. He sits with us at the bar—beaming with pride. After her performance, we talk about silos and farming and banking and the price per acre and the changes they've seen in the town.

I ask a lot of questions. I love learning about what makes us all tick, and the group I'm with is willing to share.

The uncle is excited to have his niece back in the place she grew up. In a corner of my mind, I assume it's because singing isn't paying the bills. Why else would you leave the hustle of Time Square for the patience of town square?

"She's a database consultant, and she can live anywhere. So why not a relaxed place where everything's a crapton cheaper?" he says.

Determining if that's a load of bull or reality, I mentally check out for a few minutes—just in time to hear this, "You know, my silo, she renamed him Big Data—'cuz it looks like a picture of data!"

He means "an icon of a database," but I don't correct him. My mind is now racing—completely floored by the direction of this conversation.

He goes on about his niece, the singer. She fled this, her hometown, at 19, but last month, at 33, moved back. Because she could, not because she had to. She's something of a local hero. And, she's hiring. Guess what? That person can live anywhere, too.

I never considered the effect of today's work-from-anywhere liberties on the brain-drained towns. Educated, productive 30-somethings returning to their roots.

Just like in Silicon Valley or NYC, all one needs to work is a laptop and a data connection of some kind. But unlike Silicon Valley or NYC, one can avoid insane housing prices, traffic, and high crime rates.

While they might not have Google Fiber (yet), these small towns have so much to offer someone like our singer/database consultant friend as she begins to settle down. Great schools. Relaxed living. Friendly people. A house. Even a make-shift stage in a local pub.

Brain-drain to brain-gain.

> In 2015, several rural American towns saw positive net in-immigration (meaning families or adults of baby-making age moved into the town), primarily due to oil, natural gas, and shale exploration and extraction.

Purpose Can Drive Change, Too

Recently, I had the opportunity to sit and chat with my friend Jill Castilla, president and CEO at Citizens Bank of Edmond, Oklahoma.

In discussing her story, and the changes she's made with her bank, I discovered another type of brain-gain: the bank recruited Jill back to the town!

Jill is too humble to tell you this directly, but results speak for themselves. Jill turned around an otherwise fledgling bank, directly improved the bank's community and its reputation therein, and, in the process, she was named Community Banker of the Year (2015).

> Yes, Jill is one smart cookie. Make sure you read more from Jill later in this book.

In my opinion, Jill is the premier example of a brilliant mind who returned to her 80,000 person town with a purpose, and has committed to making her bank a strong competitor by focusing on helping the community first.

In her own words, here's why she does what she does:

As a 30-something that moved back home six years ago, the desire to make a difference, not just network, was overwhelming. In earlier years and previous moves, I was focused on developing breadth in my community involvement. Now, it's all about propose and depth of engagement.

It's easier now, in this time and at this age, to be impactful. I try to create opportunities for those that are returning to make my hometown more special to connect and inspire one another. The freshness, optimism, and energy you have after returning home is a renewable resource when you continue to seek out others that are coming back home.

I prodded a bit more, and asked, "What have you done to bring in new banking relationships (retail or commercial) for similar 30-somethings moving back to Edmond (if anything)?"

To develop relationships with this group, we target influencers via social media as a primary source—those that have an affinity for local, own their own small business, or are advocates for community building. I personally reach out to them and, if there seems to be a connection, I meet them in person. We provide a level of accessibility to our executive team, both in the lobby as well as electronically, that's beyond compare.

We've also invested our time, energy, and dollars in community-building activities that this demographic is also connected to. For example, we sponsor the largest food truck gathering in the United States that's located in downtown Oklahoma City.

When we started to hear a call to bring something similar to our suburb, we knew we were building a great reputation when all eyes looked to us to do it. Now, our "Heard on Hurd" local food, music, and shopping festival attracts over 10k to our bank in Downtown Edmond every third Saturday each month.

Social media allows you to connect with others with similar interests, accelerating your ability to be a catalyst for change.

Jill's quite prideful of the path she and her team have taken on the bank since joining. And it's not all social media and fluffy puffery. A glance at Citizen's Bank's Uniform Bank Performance Report shows it is an exceptionally strong bank. I asked her to give any color as to how targeting this audience has positively affected the actual performance of her bank. Here's what she had to say:

We can only sustain our business if we de-commoditize banking. We sold all of our branch real estate, plummeted our deposit rates and slashed our advertising budget.

Banking with us is supporting the social cause to bank local, which deeply resonates with gen Xers and millennials. As a result, we have the lowest cost of funds around and our efficiency ratio continues to drop. We turned around our bank when I came on board and our team has a strong sense of purpose and passion for what we do.

Millennials who moved into their parents' houses to save money, then moved to apartments in the city, will soon be settling down, getting married, buying houses, and having kids.

Repopulation can happen where you make it so. While betting on the discovery of energy below your feet isn't a solid growth strategy, perhaps there is one in making your town marketable to those 30-somethings who left years ago.

Or, you could always embrace the idea of moving from a geographic community to a digital community . . . .

Shift to a Digital Community

Tall with flaking paint, the tall tin ceilings grip copious volumes of mothball-stained air and hover over empty shelves, shells of their former selves. A circular shirt rack strains under the weight of unsold Sesquicentennial tees from 1987. Doublewide aisles straddle an out of place, yet so perfectly placed, era-less $1,000 brown leather Barcalounger.

Ride the checkered tile, extra-long staircase down and you'll discover another world your brain refuses to rationalize. This time, it's not wistful affection, but simply, history. Buried in the uninhabited basement, a sordid reminder of the recent past: the lunch counter.

> For a white Louisiana-born boy of the 1970s, the heretofore solely textbook-experienced lunch counter sits before me as props in a play about civil rights. While not Greensboro, the antiquarian lunch counter and its surrounding cold floor will at once heartbreak, shame, humble, and inspire.

The decades-old grill-tops, soda fountains, clear cake stands, stainless steel napkin dispensers, two-color paper menus, ice cream signage and red Naugahyde booths stand at the ready, as if the establishment were simply closed for the day.

A sparkling-turned-dusty enameled counter snakes three horseshoes along one of the building's two extensive walls. Chrome-backed bar stools spaced evenly, rooted as tree trunks in a black-and-white tiled earth trace the meandering counter.

This five-and-dime is still operating, but would get more visitors as a museum. Other locales in this town square—the bank, the city hall, the overstuffed and disorganized drug store that sells everything the five-and-dime didn't—they are all preserved remnants of an alien, nearly unrecognizable time.

Nowadays, these "depopulated" towns exhibit more aluminum walkers than bicycles, claim more retirement homes than new construction, and tout more Elks Club members than children.

So much America still remains in these single-stoplight towns. But is it all just history waiting to become history? One by one, they fall. They literally die out. Sentimentality loses to economics. Dust to town to dust.

What if your town has absolutely no hope for a population resurgence, and expanding to other geographies is not in the cards?

Price Is Only a Concern in the Absence of Value

In late 2005, I started a company focused on driving business (account and loan leads applications, and openings) digitally for community banks and credit unions. The primary service was named FIRSTBranch after "first chair" in an orchestra, because, I thought, soon community institutions would recognize digital as their most important "branch."

From e-commerce style websites with a sophisticated lead management system to search engine marketing with multivariate tested landing pages, FIRSTBranch incorporated every possible contemporary tactic to target potential accountholders and drive them through a sales funnel to nab the business.

While there were plenty of companies who built websites for banks and credit unions, only FIRSTBranch was focused on targeting prospects and turning them into accountholders.

That was good for press, but bad for business.

I was several months in, and I had visited with hundreds of decision makers across hundreds of community institutions of all sizes and in all market areas. Outside our first two friendly FI sales, I couldn't get any community bank or credit union to bite on the idea of driving business online.

I was absolutely flabbergasted. It seemed the small institutions just didn't get it. Then, I had a conversation with Dale.

Dale was one of the few prospect CEOs who would answer my calls week after week, and month after month. Dale shared with me how he believed his bank needed to compete online, badly. How he understood that his bank's future was ultimately digital. How he thought we were the right people to lead that charge. Every call, though, would end with him explaining that he'd happily take my call next time, but he was just not ready to sign a contract.

I was confounded that I just couldn't close Dale. If I couldn't close the one guy on the planet who deeply understood what we did, what chance did I have of helping the thousands of other community institutions? Then, on one call, Dale asked, "John, if you believe in FIRSTBranch so much, why don't you just have a very low monthly fee and then charge me for each application or lead you bring me?"

Clouds parted.

I finally got it. While Dale, and perhaps other potential clients, understood the high volume of skilled labor-hours involved with FIRSTBranch (search engine optimization, killer design, expert copywriting, paid search marketing, etc.), he did not believe his bank would receive value (new accounts) for the $2,000 monthly fee.

Thank you, Dale Blachford from Liberty Bank in Alton, Illinois, for altering the trajectory of my business. I'll neither forget that conversation, nor how to correctly pronounce "Alton," as long as I live.

In other words, Dale was concerned that he might just be signing up for a service that does a lot of work, but generates no tangible value month after month.

For Dale, reports of success from our first clients weren't enough. He was a CFO prior to being CEO. Dale needed more than allegories to believe, he needed a de-risking of his monetary commitment. He'd happily pay more than a couple thousand dollars per month—if we were truly driving that much value.

It was a sucker bet as far as either side was concerned. The best kind of wager.

By simply modifying the pricing to a paid-on-success model, we de-risked the digital marketing plunge for his institution. He pays very little if the service doesn't produce new account growth, so we are incentivized to use tactics that work to produce as many new accounts as possible.

That was the turning point for our business. We used the new pricing methodology to incentivize hundreds of community banks and credit unions into competing online over the next couple years. (Ultimately, we had to change the FIRSTBranch pricing back to a fixed monthly fee because we drove too many new accounts. But that's a story for a different time.)

In 2016, over 400 community institutions relied on FIRST-Branch to attract and serve over 16 million end-users.

While you still want to meet your product's margin goals, are there services your institution offers that, by flipping your pricing on its head in order to push value as the primary component, might attract more users?

Overcoming the Challenges of the Digital Branch Starts with You

Over the past 10 years or so of helping community institutions achieve digital success with FIRSTBranch, we've learned some very interesting lessons, many counterintuitive. Here's a couple that you can use in your digital journey:

1. *Curb the "method of application" bias.* Recently, a lending officer told me that every loan application submitted through online channels is garbage. I asked him his institution's percentage of garbage applications. He said he got tired of all of the terrible online applications, so he removed the Apply Now buttons from his site's loans pages. He didn't want his people "wasting their time on the dregs of society." After all, he explains, if the applicants had good credit, they wouldn't be so afraid of coming into the branch to apply.

   While I've heard this proto-Neanderthal rationale throughout the years, I'm exceptionally surprised it persists this late in our industry's evolution.

   With all of the data available (much of which is in this book and on the website) on consumer preference, channel adoption, and user experience, the only reason a banker would have to disallow digital applications is that his feeble mind simply cannot distinguish good from bad.

   There is trendy, and there is trend. Digital convenience enjoyed by American consumers is trend.

   And, as a result, you'll receive poor loan applications digitally, just as you do via bricks and mortar. This is a fact of operating a banking institution in this decade.

   The difference between the loan applications you receive is that the digitally generated applications will be far more numerous, and, if proper operating practices are employed, can be adjudicated with less bias, more accuracy, and increased efficiency.

   That's because bankers are humans. And humans, especially in committee, make poor decisions (ahem, Great Recession), come with their own biases that they might not apply in standardized fashion across applicants (e.g., those who apply a certain way are no good—hello, CFPB!), have limited data sets with which to make decisions, and tend to make decisions a bit slower than machines.

In fact, if the data-driven adjudication constructs are left solely to digital applications, it will not be long before the mainstay of the in-branch application is deemed a higher risk for your institution.

Institutions who get left on the wrong side of the bankruption chasm will be those that, among other things, do not curb the method of application bias and wholly embrace best practices in digital targeting, application determination, and onboarding.

2. *There's human in them pixels!* You think your service is awesome? I will prove to you, without even knowing anything about your bank or credit union, that you have terrible service.

Go to your website on your laptop (I won't even set you up to fail with a mobile experience challenge), and apply for a retail checking account. Seriously, do it. I'll wait. (And, don't tell me digital account opening for retail checking accounts can't be done. It absolutely can.)

> Next, apply for a home equity line of credit, a credit card, a retail checking account, and a mortgage. I think you'll soon get my point.

Look, if I walked into your branch and asked a service representative about setting up a retail checking account, would I be told to sit down and that someone would get back to me within one to two business days? Then why do you allow that sort of response time in your digital branch?

I'm not even going to play the "consumers have very little time to get stuff done" card here. I'm playing the "your service sucks, even the easy stuff like digital" card.

Where method of application bias suggests that digital applications are somehow less valuable than paper applications, many community institution cultures seem to forget the even bigger picture that humans sit behind each and every digital interaction.

This means that whether it's an email, a lead, an application, or a tweet, things like response time matter as much as (or even more than) if it were someone in the branch asking the same thing.

You want to get back to me in one business day? I'll move down the Google and find an account I can open instantly, somewhere else. Remember, behind every application is an applicant, and you have plenty of competition.

3. *These dumb biases, and plenty others, start at the top.* You're not the problem. It was the old white man before you. He set you up to fail, and that really stinks. But like a sentimental Eminem track, it happened, and now you need to clean it up.

Just like most things culture-related, modifications to process and reward systems can instrument changes to your team, and how it reacts to these digital predispositions.

For instance, it's very common for digital consumers to find you online, and then come into the branch to apply. To ensure clarity in channel-origination data, Jim Marous reminds bankers to alter any in-branch front-line bonus plans specific to channel origination.

While your team will not alter its thinking overnight, change is possible and requisite to survival. After all, we are heading into the new world of digital community banking.

Welcome to Digital Community Banking

Much has been written about the benefits of a digital banking consumer (if you don't have a subscription to *Digital Banking Report,* do yourself a favor and get one now); suffice it to say that he's starting to look a lot more attractive than the aging, expensive branch-dependent consumer.

And, for all my rants about the value of branches today (e.g., the Las Vegas diatribe with Jeffry and Neil), there are particular circumstances—such as that of the unit bank in a dying town—where certain community institutions should embrace a world with limited physical presence.

Around 2007 to 2008, one of the presentations I gave for community banking association conventions introduced a new definition of *community.*

The thesis (and write-up) for the hour-long presentation started off something like, "Communities are no longer defined by hills, rivers, streams, and railroad tracks," and the point of the presentation was to open the community banking executives' minds to the idea that tomorrow's community banker will consider all aspects of digital communities for market share growth (yes, I even included ideas on how to embrace a "local" digital marketing approach).

The audience feedback from the talks was by far the worst feedback I've ever received, so I probably only gave it 5 or 10 times. I still believe the message was the single most important thing those bankers could have heard, as we were sitting on the precipice of the new economic reality.

I didn't know it at the time, but the next several months would dictate an entirely new playing field in economy, service delivery, communications, marketing (see Figure 3.7), and technology—all but demanding a rethink of what "community" means.

Figure 3.7   Financial Institution Digital Advertising Spending

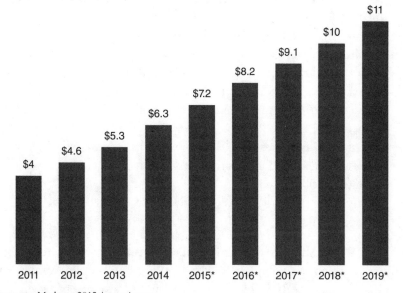

SOURCE: eMarketer 2015 ⋆ = estimate

Financial industry advertising spending in digital media (in billion US dollars). Nearly 40 percent of all digital advertising spending by US financial institutions today is brand-focused, while the remaining is direct response for a particular product or service.[11]

Many types of accounts for the dog lover demographic have been attempted over the years—nearly all shuttered after little success. One of the few that's hung on is the Critter Club savings account at Belco Community Credit Union in Harrisburg, Pennsylvania. Savers earn interest, get a pet shop discount card, and can even be entered into a monthly prize drawing.

The formula for shifting to a digital community is rather simple:

- Research to discover a solution to a problem that a segment of consumers (e.g., dog lovers) or commercial clients (e.g., women–owned businesses) find of value.
- Validate the idea with compliance, risk, etc.
- Run some models to ensure it's a profitable venture for your institution.
- Construct the minimally viable version of it.
- Get market feedback to ensure your initial product will satiate (at least part of) the market need—you can iterate releases later to further develop the product over time.
- Set and share team goals, modify as necessary.
- Finalize compliance with clear language.
- Shore up all the reporting and analysis mechanisms your institution and your examiners might need (for marketing, risk, security, etc.).
- Wrap some marketing around it that cuts through the clutter and attracts your target.
- Test, refine, and retest the user flows to ensure ease of onboarding.
- Obsess over a target acquisition cost, then work to decrease the cost by another 50 percent.
- Accumulate positive reviews and referrals.
- Rinse, and repeat.

It will take a bit of work, but expertise to make this product development happen can be rented or hired, and built on top of White Label or Gold Label fintech providers. And while the investment required to nail each of the steps above can be quite exceptional, all told, it's far less than the cost of setting up a new branch in a new, growing town, and much less than the cost of selling your financial institution at less than book value. The investment looks even more attractive when you factor both sides' total cost of ownership into the equation.

Move over Millennials; Make Way for iGen

As many names as the millennial generation had, their successor generation has more. Now known as iGen, gen Z, or even the centennials, the generation currently under the age of 20 is a group of smartphone addicts and comparison shoppers.

By the time they reach the grand old age of 18, they will have accumulated more hours holding mobile devices than the millennials did by the time they hit the same age. Which is probably why in a 2016 survey, 18 percent of iGen responded that the right age to receive your first smartphone was 13 (which, in case you forgot, is when you're in middle school or junior high).[12]

Aside from the reliance on smartphones, an interesting trend is forming for the eldest of the iGen: they are comparison shoppers, and are always looking for the best deal. Seeing absolutely nothing wrong with comparison shopping on their phones as they're talking to a salesperson in a physical store, iGen rarely pays full price for anything.

It makes a lot of sense when you consider that the eldest of iGen were old enough to be at the dinner table and hear the family discussions or even just watch the news during the Great Recession. They saw the stock market crash, the bank bailout, and the resulting job losses—all impact their parents and older siblings (see Figure 3.8). It is very possible

Figure 3.8   US National Debt

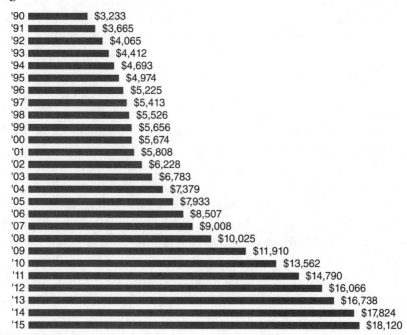

Year	Debt
'90	$3,233
'91	$3,665
'92	$4,065
'93	$4,412
'94	$4,693
'95	$4,974
'96	$5,225
'97	$5,413
'98	$5,526
'99	$5,656
'00	$5,674
'01	$5,808
'02	$6,228
'03	$6,783
'04	$7,379
'05	$7,933
'06	$8,507
'07	$9,008
'08	$10,025
'09	$11,910
'10	$13,562
'11	$14,790
'12	$16,066
'13	$16,738
'14	$17,824
'15	$18,120

SOURCE: US Treasury
The growth of public or national debt for the United States (in billion US dollars). Economic pressures have had profound impacts on shaping iGen.

that these events may have profoundly shaped how iGen will view the economy, money, and banking.

Whether iGen ends up being one of the more fiscally conscious generations in decades remains to be seen, but one thing is for sure: your digital and mobile game needs to be on-point. And since they're already reaching late teens, you don't have much time to act.

Beware the Culture Danger

Neither the expertise, the expense, nor the execution of shifting to a digital community institution should frighten the banking executive in a dying geography. Instead, the risk this hypothetical banker needs to shore up is one of internal culture.

Aging community banking institutions face an incredible chasm in the mind-set of their boards and executives, and all the way down to their front lines. Any and all of them may see a shift to digital as a way to push them out an organization that, in some circumstances, has been their lifelong employer.

The shift to digital community banking will indeed give you and the rest of your executive team the chance to reevaluate your talent base, but you may be surprised that there are simple things you can do to rally the troops. In fact, an April 2016 *Harvard Business Review* found that successful culture shifts can occur based on the revised processes and rewards mechanisms your team establishes. Go leadership.

You may also see that the shift to digital community banking creates new career opportunities for rising stars.

This is a rebirth of your institution, is to be celebrated, and also is not to be taken lightly.

Remember that seemingly obvious things such as method of application bias and associating digital consumers to actual humans like those who used to walk into your branch can be as invasive as a cultural revolution. Help de-risk your move to digital by encouraging team discussions, evaluating individual contributor performance, publicly rewarding changes in behavior, and setting new goals throughout your institution's evolution.

Ensuring strict alignment across the organization is key throughout this transition, and the alignment must start at the executive team and board level. If a team lead is even 5 degrees off from the rest of the executive team, you can expect to have a complete disaster on your hands one year down the road.

Understand Your Technology

> *"If the small businesses that we lend money to knew as little about their own business as we know about ours, we would never lend a cent."*
> —Chief executive of a $1 billion+ asset community bank (2016)

Kamikaze.

A solo fruit fly navigates a fortuitous route, concurrently demonstrating ambition and a lack of restraint. Drown. A violent, expensive death for the plump drone—into a pool of rare, aged red French grape extract resting in the belly of a freakishly clear vessel.

The nectar supplier, a French intellectual eccentric. Or an eccentric intellectual. Either way, a money distributor international a la technology investments.

An Erik Satie in a land of The Monkees, the Frenchman always gets his way. He's quite anxious to do his thing. A fruit fly himself, he is well-trained in Kamikaze assassination.

His target, a vessel of another mother: slow-moving, core processor battleships. He sees them as octogenarian green-screened trolls protecting their gigantic warships from the irreparable harm of fair competition.

And, he's not going to target these guys alone. He's smarter than that. He needs a few banking mercenaries who will join his data liberty battle for a multi-billion dollar valuation.

The Frenchman recruits the few, the proud, the brave, the tech-literate bankers with "We Want You" PowerPoints and, well, quite expensive red wine.

He has constructed what he describes as a powerful new core-processing system using modern architecture and cloud-based infrastructure. And he aims to partner with FIs to replace their aging vascular systems with shiny new pipes that send data back and forth in real time and offer simple integration to any third party (read: fintech startup).

FIs get contemporary technology, extensible architecture, and the freedom to play with third parties. He gets the keys to the data kingdom.

The future … Right?

Your Foundation Could Be a Bit Shaky

Although much of this book is about the flaws in community banking, the flaws are just as well shared with a quagmire of fintech companies serving them (a la White Label). The 11,000 FIs that are out there today rely on a phở of misshapen fintech "integration" via strained partnerships for nearly everything they do.

Hundreds and hundreds of companies selling their single-point-solution, (mostly) distributed software to banks and credit unions. Each point solution centered on serving its institution first, with very little attention paid toward the end-consumer experience. With each of these point solutions, reliability was the forethought, scalability was an after-thought, conversion was the nastiest thought, and integration was a naught-thought.

Over the past several decades, about 20 White Label companies had the right mixture of product, direct sales force, timing, and luck. These guys bought the hundreds of others and kept them running as separate entities under their own armada umbrella.

Those 20 companies became 10. Those 10 became 7. Now, there are about 4.

Today, four-ish separate multibillion-dollar corporations own 80 percent of all White Label point solutions. They don't need to buy the remaining 20 percent. By powering the underlying systems on which the FIs depend, they control the rails, and, as a result, most any other company that wants to work with banks and credit unions.

> According to the World Retail Banking Report 2016, only 13 percent of FIs believe their core processing system can handle a digital banking ecosystem.[13]

And So, the Story Goes, "Free Your Data"

Back to the Frenchman.

Based on what we just reviewed, he has a logical soapbox. "Your core processor vendor should not hold your institution's data hostage. Your data is your data, and you should be able to freely partner with any third party you choose! Join my core, and you will be free." This treasonous rant sounds simultaneously logical and dreamy to many banking executives.

But there are a few issues with his call to action:

- *Risk*: It's a big risk for a banker to play around with a core processor that has fewer than 100 installs under its belt. Newer core processors have not been through the rigor of exams or otherwise demonstrated their value as far superior to the status quo.
- *Conversion*: One of the many dirty "C" words in banking, converting a financial institution's data from the old core to the grass-is-greener core is costly, often negatively impacts consumers as well as employees, invites more examiner attention, and, is also full of risk. Every banking executive has been through one in her career, and every banker who's been through one doesn't ever want to do it again.
- *Competition*: There are many tried and true core processors from around the world who are willing to be quite competitive on price in order to break into the United States. They are willing to open their platforms as necessary to get deals done. Competing against free, battle-tested, and open is quite difficult for even the Frenchman.
- *CEO age*: While the engaging, think-different attitude of the fruit fly might play well to a risk-taking forty-something CEO, the majority of today's community banking CEOs are within a decade of retirement. Fear, uncertainty, and doubt are powerful reasons to enjoy a status quo. There is no need to roll the dice and finish a career with a black eye from a bad core conversion. To borrow from the old IBM line, no one ever got fired for choosing to stick with the existing core processor.

Which takes us to the final nail in the coffin:

- *API initiatives*: We are just now seeing a tectonic shift in how the big four operate. For many years, these legacy fintech vendors have denied the call from their own clients (read Suresh's story later in this book) as well as from fintech companies to open up a set of APIs (application program interfaces) that would allow for the secure extensibility of their core banking and digital platforms. Many industry insiders, myself included, see the lack of API integration into the systems that underpin community institutions as the very reason that CFIs may go the way of the dodo bird. Thankfully, to my knowledge, each of these gigantic core processor companies has now kicked off various API initiatives to answer the call of their clients, and to enable them to more easily work with innovative fintech companies who rely on data access to the core processors. Hopefully, these efforts will bear fruit fast enough for CFIs to adapt.

Ironically, the "your data is your data" line would probably play better with risk-taking consumers than risk-adverse bankers like we see with challenger bank Monzo in the United Kingdom.

Chalk another one up for Direct.

And maybe for the Frenchman, as well. For all my naysaying, he is onto something with his next-gen core processor—there is indeed a market, as community FIs will need some similar solution over the next few years. There will be a few big winners here—four, but maybe five.

A Reliance on Professional Services Means You Get to Focus While Your End Users Get Best-of-Breed Offerings

Years ago, community institutions found solace and success with on-premise servers running core processing and digital banking software in-house. Quickly, the high number and sophistication of breaches, the increased expertise required to successfully manage the systems, and the relative comfort of cloud technologies with regulators and auditors, forced institutions of all sizes to re-associate on premise solutions as high-risk solutions, and move to hosted or service bureau solutions.

By focusing on their actual trade, banking, instead of worrying about the uptime and security of their processing and digital banking software, institutions have been able to decrease risk and operating expense, while increasing end-user satisfaction. As customer experience expectations heighten, just-in-time marketing delivery improves, and security challenges mount, modern community bankers are utilizing a variety of technology vendors (that extend well beyond their traditional systems) to broaden their offerings and capabilities. It's important for community institutions today to re-examine the hosting and management of other non-core services, and consider the advantages of professional service and infrastructure providers.

Service providers can include: marketing automation, customer/ member relationship management, asset liability management, financial reporting, digital lead and application management, account onboarding, digital asset management, document and e-signature, business intelligence or other data visualization software, digital branch management, and more.

For example, the severity and volume of DDoS attacks along with the increased need of sophisticated digital and search marketing skills have forced institutions to look to experienced, industry-focused professional service providers for managing their digital branches. The industry is seeing a similar movement to infrastructure providers like Amazon Web Services, who not only offer attractive pricing but also wrap up security and compliance oversight into tidy packages specifically for the banking vertical.

The sophisticated skills and software offered by third-party providers are quickly becoming must-haves for future success, security, and reliability. Best yet, the offerings are regularly upgraded with new tools and features, increased service-level agreements, and ongoing internal training that can further propel your team forward.

It's Not about Having Access to "Data," It's about Focused Direction

As a banker, getting transactional data from your core isn't really interesting, is it? As with all data, and you'd be sitting on piles of it, you are going to need to make sense of it.

Before you go mouthing off to your core vendor about big data this and data modeling that, the best first step is to sit with your team and make a list of insights that you would like to see, and what problems you would like to solve.

Explore various user journeys, objectives, and long-term goals: What could you do better, easier, faster, cleaner? What does your target want that you have been unable to deliver? Focus and cull down the list, not just in number of items but also in breadth. Group your ideas. The more precise you can get here, the better.

You may find this exercise is best repeated several times with separate teams. Check for consistency in thinking. Explore inconsistent or outsider ideas, as they may lead you to new ideas or opportunities.

If the idea is simply a straggler that needs to be cut or if your team decides it's an important new direction, integrate across team leads and down from managers as quickly as your executive team and board reach consensus.

> Remember, that straggler idea existed because some manager thought it was the direction in which the institution was headed. This probably means that it has made its way into the team below her and perhaps cross-functional teams as well. Double down on daily communication across all levels of all teams to create the habit of ongoing alignment.

Once you've rounded up your distinct set of very concrete ideas, it's time to approach your vendors and request what you need. It's possible they already have what you need (or could build what you need rather quickly) to make significant progress toward your goals. If not, you and they both know you have plenty of options.

Partner, Don't Incubate

"We don't want them to apply online. We love to sit and have a cup of coffee with someone wanting a mortgage. It allows us to get to know them better."
—Chief executive of a $500 million+ asset credit union (2016)

"What's the real reason you shoot a man in Reno?" asks the makeup-caked and sunbaked Bostonian a few stools down in the historic hotel's drafty pub.

Too bothered with other questions and enchanted by the old soul new blues of the nameless guitarist in the corner, I forget to respond for a while. No one cares. But I carry the guilt for at least an ice chewing and final swallow of my spent double Jack and Coke.

Catholic guilt done right—sugar balanced with distilled sugarcane.

It's a dark, stormy, and ginger-beer colored, Naugahyde-painted room.

Ninety years a bar. Lots of history; now, real clean history. These establishments aren't the same since they put the fire out ... Smoke-free, character-free. Even this one, so beautiful and stained, is now a museum. No haze. No clouds. No abyss. Stains don't disappear. Scuffs are obvious and trying too hard. Smells of Clorox and bright lights.

Drinking like a hobo in a tile-floored mini mall, or in some community theatre production, life is staged, shiny, and plastic. Every person in 4K 3-D. Every sound distinguishable from every angle. Music softer. Less fiction, less friction.

People dream in rectangles of various sizes—each with a glass ceiling. No one talks. Not even me. I couldn't even bother to respond to the one person who tried to make a conversation.

Only hackers can eavesdrop. All the information is everywhere. Machine learning scaled amongst the fleet, human learning forgotten by the instance.

Financial institution. The lack of brevity or levity or agility or progression in the descriptor itself suggests things risk adverse, cumbersome, stodgy, slow, ugly, crude, heavy, barnacle-encrusted, targets.

Generous killings are a rare sight, though I expect the frequency to increase quite a bit in the coming years. Not to skip too far ahead; these days we're just approaching the writhing, pleading, grasping-at-straws phase.

And, for all, this phase can last an eternity.

Perhaps most embarrassing for onlookers, this is the stage where both sides, financial institutions and fintech startups, admit their weaknesses and show their cards to, more often than not, much weaker, much noisier opponents.

Alligators apologizing to birds for having teeth.

An opponent by any other name is a partner. Or a vendor. But in the fiery, tormented incubator, which could only be manufactured by the evils of humankind, startups and FIs sniff each other and poke at each other for weeks and months until either side begs for liberation.

More than 30 fintech-focused incubators "mentor" thousands of startups across at least 50 countries—each with allegedly astounding, yet unpublished, "success" rates.

Stumbling past my inquisitive snake-skinned bar mate, hours after her query, I mutter, "Mercy."

Skip the Writhing, Pleading, Grasping at Straws Thing

Over the years, I've had the honor of working as a mentor within several incubators, fintech and otherwise. While some incubators are prodigious bootcamps, most are flailing desperation.

Community FI-sponsored incubators even more so, with very few startups going on to make their way through the gauntlet with the opposing giant, and fewer of those thriving post-acquisition.

Funnily enough, those startups who consider themselves failures in the FI-sponsored incubator process seem to get the most out of the process. Where else can one quickly get an understanding that his product vision is little more than a costly, low ROI feature inside a much larger ecosystem? Or come to the harsh realization that her team isn't as strong, agile, or creative as she thought? Or witness first-hand the due diligence death roll?

Success metrics aside, FI-sponsored incubators exist to thinly guise an FI's (or a group of FIs') fear of failure, fear of missing out, and fear of drowning in a sea of human incompetence. If you are in an organization that is in serious need of showing the market how you can do something (literally, anything, please just help us do something!), the shotgun approach of a well-announced, open fintech incubator could be just what you need to kick the can a bit further down the road.

I can count real successes of community or otherwise non-mega bank-sponsored fintech incubators on one finger, actually: Silicon Valley Bank's "accelerated" Standard Treasury.

A Y Combinator fintech startup intent on equipping all FIs with API-based banking services, Standard Treasury was also a graduate of the MasterCard/Silicon Valley Bank accelerator called Commerce.Innovated.

I first met Standard Treasury's co-founder Dan Kimerling in 2012 when he was COO at Giftly and demoing at Finovate. Even then, Dan struck me as someone who was a bit too smart for his own good. A couple years later, he sold Giftly to GiftCards.com and wanted to chat about his new toy: Standard Treasury.

He knew the enormous challenge of his banking API-driven dream, no matter how logical and obvious it may be to the nonbanking world. From technical limitations to data security implications, Standard

Treasury faced enormous obstacles as an outsider. But as crazy difficult as it would be to make API banking a reality, the payoff for the FIs could be massive.

Instead of trying to patch into the mess work of legacy fintech spaghetti that supports thousands of FIs, my hunch is Dan knew he could be much more effective working inside a single FI. Plus, as long as his patience held out, he could help steer the bank to his vision.

Ultimately, a few years later in August 2015, Silicon Valley Bank (SVB) aquihired the Standard Treasury team, and within just a few months, the $45 billion asset bank began reaping the rewards with its announcement of "API Banking."[14]

To their credit, SVB seems to have been quite purposeful in the acquisition of Standard Treasury. I never asked Dan whether he knew it or not, but as early as March 2014, SVB was getting bad press[15] from the Y Combinator companies they banked for having very little in the way of financial technology under their tech-savvy veneer. In an informal survey of Y Combinator companies who banked with SVB, 33 out of 34 said they were unhappy with SVB's banking tech.

So that's the story of the sole, successful "smallish" FI-led fintech accelerated company that I can recall. The samba no pé of the community FI-led incubator can be a lonely, unsuccessful, and expensive dance best left to the big guys.

Be Interested, Not Desperate

While incubators can garner you earned media and a slap on the back in some circles, prudent community bankers should stay away. Incubators are typically unfocused and yield far less ROI than a community financial institution can withstand, and acquisitions can irrecoverably assault culture on both sides.

If you do find an appealing fintech startup that solves one of your (or your accountholders') pressing problems, it's best (after performing due diligence and risk analysis) to work together lightly at first.

You can work toward a joint venture or another partnership arrangement after certain metrics are met, but remember that even an organization as small as a community institution is far bigger and slower than most startups.

The benefits you want out of the startup, namely: fresh thinking, lean processes, creative talent, and passionate problem solving can all be quickly smothered by the heavy process, no-fail super-committee brainstorming, or other life-sucking practices of a financial institution.

Allowing the startup to live and breathe on its own affords you additional benefits:

- *Expense*: They necessarily will have to find other clients to help them pay their bills.
- *Buffer*: If they don't move in, they won't be breathing down your neck. This buffer will give you and your team the time you need to acclimate to working with a startup.
- *Share the pain*: The startup will make mistakes with, and at the expense of, other institutions. This will make their learning curve less expensive for you.
- *Increased core influence*: An expanded client base for the startup may give them more "pull" when it comes to working with your core processor, as they will have several clients using the same core.

Some Thoughts about Working with Fintech Startups

While we're on the subject, we should probably get this out of the way. While working with startups can be refreshing, educational, and fulfilling, you may also find yourself neck deep in trouble a few months in.

As someone who has made every partnership error in the book and invented several all his own, I'm uniquely suited to give you some things to consider as you head in to any partnership discussions with fintech startups.

Herewith a few nuggets, over and above the typical due-diligence caveats:

- *Startups underestimate the number of fish in their sea.* Every entrepreneur thinks his product is the sole gift from the heavens, and fintech startups suffer from similar delusions. For better or worse, rare is the completely unique idea or firm.

With over 12,000 fintech startups today, it makes logical sense that for every startup, there are 20 similar to that one also trying to succeed. Putting that in perspective, there is more than one fintech firm for every community institution in the United States.

As you attend Next Bank, Finovate, the Financial Brand, Money 2020, and other important conferences, keep in mind that you are surrounded by startups. Collect contact details on LinkedIn, speak with their customers, and do some investigation work on their competitors.

When choosing a partner, use the size of the fintech startup market to your advantage—don't marry the first one you see; date around a bit.

- *Startups underestimate the cost of integration.* Nearly any type of partnership sets in motion a complex set of modifications that goes well beyond the oft-discussed core processor or digital banking integration. Technical integrations may be costly and time consuming for all parties, but like an iceberg, the obvious is rarely the killer.

    Examples of rarely discussed upfront, hidden downstream costs beyond integrations with core processor and digital banking vendor include changes to your: disclosures, internal "training" or learning and development (and any testing tools you may use to verify their knowledge), existing marketing creative and media buys, marketing videos, brochures, compliance documents, notifications of changes to accountholders, tax notifications for users, volume/length of customer service phone calls/emails/chats/etc., product bundling/pricing impacts (cannibalization concerns, expanded offerings, etc.), phone scripts, front-end website/apps, board reporting, internal bonus/incentive structures, business intelligence and profitability reporting and tracking tools, CRM, voice response system, risk, ongoing compliance reviews, vendor and due diligence reviews, additional examinations the partnership may now require, etc.

    Successful partnerships with fintech firms will impact nearly every corner of your business. It's best to uncover this as early as possible, align to success metrics, and plan the timing of functional champions to ease your entire cost of integration and reduce your risk of failure.

- *Startups overestimate the value of the innovators and early adopters.* In his book *Crossing the Chasm,* Geoffrey A. Moore talks about moving from the early market (of innovators and early adopters) to the mainstream market (the market to the right of early adopters). He gives great advice for entrepreneurs to successfully make the adoption curve journey.

  When a market becomes overly frothy, like fintech, it's easy to assume every startup will cross the chasm into regular usage by the populace. Funding fuels press hype, which fuels more funding, and the world's fintech Innovators (myself included) fuel it by trying everything new in fintech ourselves. That combination necessarily means nearly any new fintech startup that gets a TechCrunch mention will receive 10,000 to 30,000 users (depending on the product's scope) very quickly.

  The ramp can be very exciting to the novice entrepreneur (for a brief period), but it can also be extraordinarily misleading to investors and potential partners, as it's filled with fintech enthusiasts, and not real average consumers (see Figure 3.9).

  I can name probably 150 fintech startups over the past five years or so that fall in this category of early "success" only to never make the journey to "normal" user adoption. On top of those 150, there's a factor of 10x that I'm forgetting about.

Figure 3.9   Fintech Adoption and the Bankruption

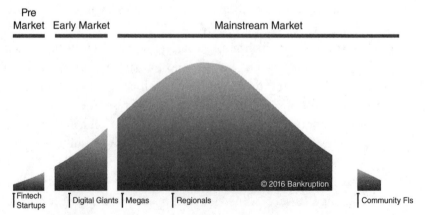

The bankruption chasm illustrated: As newer fintech experiences push further into mainstream consumer consciousness, the consumer awareness and operational effectiveness gap between community FIs and every other banking competitor widens.

You do not want to drag your community institution through this costly journey.

Pay attention to how much of their entire user base actively uses the product over time. Get your team and their kids to use it for an extended period of time. Did you want to use it or did you have to set reminders to do so? Was it a joy or was it work? Remember to see things through your users' eyes: they are not fintech enthusiasts—they are people trying to go on with life without their finances (or lack of them) getting in the way. That's it.

At the end of your testing period, are there more active users on the product (has the initial ramp continued or did it plateau)? The active user plateau may occur for reasons other than the product being a dog, but also you cannot assume that innovator and early adopter hype will translate into success with laggards.

No matter how "awesome" the idea or product or technology, it's best not to assume that your community institution can be the catalyst to successfully move it across the chasm.

- *Startups underestimate the importance of established trust.* In community banking, trust is everything. While consumer trust is rising for fintech firms around the globe, it's in the hands of financial institutions to lose. Odds are, you've spent decades establishing trust with your community; you do not want to erode it overnight (see Figure 3.10).

One way this happens is a potential partner company may quickly cast aside some of your most valued trust-establishing actions and services as outdated tradition or quaint overhead. They may be on to something, or they may be setting your institution up for a very rough trust fall. When in doubt, test it out—with both prospective and current accountholders. Whether you use surveys, demonstrations, usage trials, or other methodologies, take your time and do it right.

Another common mistake is allowing the potential partner to devalue your current base of accountholders or otherwise discount your experience of working with your consumers—either of which might quickly lead you to an irrecoverable world of pain.

A product will have value only if people use it, and you hold the keys to that kingdom: relinquish them judiciously.

Figure 3.10   Influencers of Trust for FIs

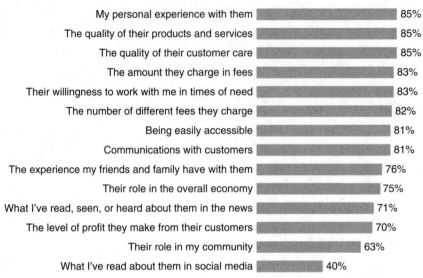

SOURCE: Harris Interactive, Nielson 2014
Factors that impact trust of primary banking institutions in the United States.

- *Startups overestimate human inertia in the world of banking.* Related to the "chasm crossing" point above, when you bank Americans, you deal with inertia. If a startup is convinced it has the best widget around, it might also be certain that everyone will want its widget, as quickly as possible, and be willing to pay anything for it.

  This is another place where your experience in banking might just save you from embarrassment. Even digital banking has high consumer switching costs. Switching to any new service takes time, energy, and desire. Most humans lack any of that when it comes to banking (which is why it's difficult for fintech startups to move to the mainstream market).

  If you want to move the needle for Americans in banking, targeted marketing and timely, relevant incentives are paramount. Shore up your initiatives with the new partner by co-op investing in an iterative incentive-based marketing campaign, which builds over time.

- *Startups underestimate regulation, its added costs to doing business, and its painful sting.* Fintech startups typically do not have experience in the heavily regulated banking environment, and have, on average, less to lose. Your institution can provide a lot of value here, but avoid getting in your own way.

Coach your team to think broadly about what can be done, as opposed to "what we've always done." Engage proactively with your regulators (and even the CFPB) to get their guidance on where you're headed with the potential partnership. You may find the examining bodies a heck of a lot more accommodating on the front-side of a release than ex post facto.

- *Startups overestimate the ease of working cross-generationally.* Many fintech startups consist entirely of millennial or gen Z teams, and your teammates might, well, not be from those generations. And nothing can kill a partnership faster than culture-clash between the two companies.

  You can avoid a veritable catastrophe by catching this one early on, and adjusting your strike team to better gel with the potential partner. It may sound silly, but simply finding someone within your organization who has worked (successfully) with the young folk and appointing them to the team can save you quite a bit of headache.

  You can probably think of a member of your team right now who fits that mold—she does not need to be a millennial (in fact, it's probably better she isn't), and would be excited about working on a new venture. Put her on your project team to help ensure continued, successful communication between your two organizations.

- *Startups overestimate the value of their products.* Many new fintech products are merely features snapped into a pre-existing banking product set or digital ecosystem. For example, the new must-have "product" might be a gaming feature on top of a traditional savings account, or an identity management feature inside of digital banking.

  Without insight that demonstrates the remarkable value (e.g., increased accountholders), all the startup has is "Clippy" (the infamous, obnoxious, and unhelpful Microsoft Office Assistant of the late 1990s, early 2000s), an intrusive add-on that requires a real product with real users to thrive.

  It's important to sift through the hype, rationalize the data, and test within market to determine if you are dealing with a feature or a valuable product.

Get More Efficient and More Proficient with Partners

Without knowing much about your institution, I'll throw this out there: you have too much overhead and not enough expertise across your team to compete long term. I estimate that within five years, you will need half to three-fourths of your currently human-powered retail banking work to either be assumed by technology or outsourced to a whole host of trusted partners.

Make a list of all the tasks you know that your institution should not be doing. What should be vaporized by technology or could be dramatically improved by an expert, reliable vendor? Research specialist companies who have proven success in banking, and next to each task, write potential vendor names for continued due diligence.

While this shopping list will naturally include the obvious technology vendors, it should also consider areas inside your institution that need supplementary help (e.g., compliance, marketing, etc.), as well as rounding out the professional services needed to compete today (e.g., data security, search engine marketing, business intelligence tools, research).

The world has changed, and that's why you are where you are. But as much as it may put you in the defensive position from a service perspective, advancement in technology, ubiquitous, digital access, and the push toward a convenience economy afford you the opportunity to become much more efficient and proficient in how you do what you do.

Some quick examples:

- *Reexamine the technology you use to get things done.* An outdated laptop running Excel can take minutes to save or open a file. Don't cut off your nose to spite you face. From sharing screens with AirPlay to new devices like iPad Pro to project management and communication software like Slack (which works with hundreds of other software to make itself even more useful), hundreds of contemporary technologies have proliferated in the past few years that could propel you and your team forward. Best yet, it's all cheaper, faster, and more integrated than ever before.
- *Hire the best talent, not just local talent.* Use Slack, inexpensive video chat, AWS cloud storage (when implemented with the right

security measures), and inexpensive travel options (Kayak, Airbnb, and Uber) to help you scale your team by finding the absolute best talent—without requiring them to move to your town. Bonus points if you can work with the new talent to arrange part-time or retainer-based services, rather than making them an "employee."

- *Don't get stuck in the rut of one vendor to rule them all.* Users could care less about your desire for "vendor simplicity." No one vendor can be the best at everything. It may be easier for you to manage just a few vendors, but your user does not care or even know about that. Several vendors—working in all areas of your business—can help you and your team scale in ways you never thought possible.

- *Stop doing things that are not core to your business by finding service partners for them.* The new economy has created thousands of services that didn't exist before—allowing you to instantly vaporize work from your physical space, and have the tasks performed by experts at a fraction of the cost of in-house personnel. These services can include website development and digital marketing, automated compliance services via regtech, virtual receptionists, and human resources and benefits outsourcing.

- *Use time-saving services for your organization.* Amazon offers Amazon Business to help you save money on everything from office supplies to breakroom snacks, schedule regular free deliveries for your branches months in advance, or a simple push of the Amazon Dash button can reorder the product instantly so no one needs to spend time ordering the thing.

Partnering with established fintech companies and startups can be an effective way to scale expertise and to ensure your institution evolves with and for your accountholders over time. Reexamine internal roles and responsibilities through the critical lens of someone who knows that nearly every responsibility today is available as a for-hire, professional service with the tap of a finger.

By eschewing the allure of the incubator, selecting partners based on specific achievable goals, and proceeding interdependently, your organization will sponsor a productive, mutually beneficial relationship free of agony and unnecessary expense.

Scale Delivers Results

"This is an expensive business to be in if you don't have the market share and scale."
—Lloyd Blankfein,[16] Chairman, Goldman Sachs

The gin and tonic ran down his shorts and dripped onto the pad of his well-worn flip-flops. Shaking hands wasn't a skill he had perfected over the years, but smiling was. Today was the first day of the rest of his life. He knew it. The floor hit him faster than he anticipated. She laughed; they fell in love.

That was 30 years and three kids ago, and now, for the first time ever, she worries about his stability. She's reading the banking articles too, and they aren't good. Lots of stuff she doesn't quite understand, but she knows Netflix beat Blockbuster.

The small town is smaller, and the graveyard is no longer an empty field. The houses are older than she remembers, and so, too, is the bank's website. He sleeps, though. Still. Completely still. How?

After all these years, is his banking brain just numb to it all? She can't say she feels otherwise. Going through the paces is less interesting than it sounds.

Over the years, he's perfected being still. It's gotten him out of a lot of conversations that meandered way into the too late. He'd play dead and be still. She'd eventually stop talking.

He's always had the answers. Or, at least, an answer. He could figure things out. Always. Sometimes, it would take a few days, but he'd get to an answer. These days, the days are several years longer than they have ever been.

And that doesn't sit well with her. He knows, because he hears her sighs while he lies still. On his stomach, breathing heavy. With a slight, intermittent manufactured snore. His face relaxed; his bladder full; his mind on overdrive.

Wishing for a return. But it won't. It's been a long time since he bought a nice collared shirt, he thinks. That's a dumb thought. Focus. She won't believe he is sleeping. She'll know he just sat there on his semi-fortuitous stomach like a beached, wasted whale.

Lying there; a liar.

Stuck. It's his life's work, sticking, and now he's achieved it at the most inopportune time. Maybe he could never move, he's just assumed that he chose lethargy.

It's not a disease; what he has is a weakness.

What is he supposed to do? Those guys have been writing code since they were in the womb, and his IT guy started tweeting a month ago. The digital giants are engrained with marketing prowess, and his compliance officer scared away his last marketing person four years ago. The startups raised more money than his bank has seen in fifty years, yet will never know the fear of an examination.

His kids think he's lost touch. They want nothing to do with the bank. They laugh at him. They make fun of the board. Of the customers. Of the logo. Of the ATM screens. Of stuff that didn't matter to anyone just 10 years ago.

These days, it's all brands and experiences and rewards and million-dollar marketing budgets. He has none of that. Such a big leap between where he is and where he needs to go. It all seems quite helpless.

For about Fifty Years, the Most Convenient Bank in the United States Was the US Postal Savings System

In an attempt to create more convenient ways to deposit money, and encourage safe savings for those who lost confidence in banks, a June 1910 Act of Congress established the Postal Savings System in the United States.

A consumer would deposit money ($500 maximum, raised to $1,000 in 1916, and then raised to $2,500 in 1918), and earn 2 percent on the savings (local banks were *required* to pay the USPS 2.5 percent on the deposits, with the remaining 0.50 percent used to pay for operation of the Postal Savings System)-see Figure 3.11.

The Postal Savings System hit its peak in the mid-to-late 1940s, with over $3 billion in savings across 4 million depositors and 8,141 "branches" (see Figure 3.12). Talk about attractive banking!

After all, local banks were paying a far lower rate (1.00 percent) on deposits, shaking off a serious hangover brought about by the previous

Figure 3.11   US Postal Savings Offices

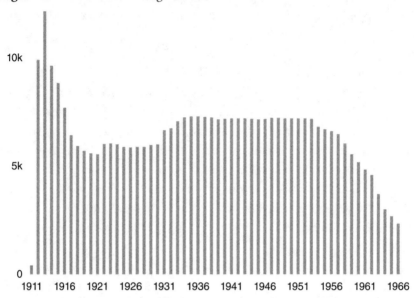

SOURCE: Post Office Department, Annual Report of the Postmaster General, 1957; Statistical Abstract
of the United States 1960–1965
The number of offices participating in the United States Postal Savings program from its start in
1911 to its cessation in 1966. The US Postal Savings System used interstate branching decades before
Riegle-Neal.

recession, reestablishing trust with consumers, and lacking the extended
hours and locations of the thousands of Postal Service depositories.

　　While banks and credit unions these days have more locations than
in the 1940s, they find themselves in a similar situation. It's no surprise,
that yet again, politicians are calling for Post Office banking, which, this
time, would go beyond deposits into lending, as well.

　　This might be quite concerning for community banks and
credit unions who lack the budget, interdepartmental relations with
government or regulatory bodies, staffing, trust, and the branch presence
of the United States Postal Service.

　　Whether the next competitor is the USPS, Google, Facebook,
Ant Financial, or any of the thousands of Direct fintech companies in
existence today, a key threat to the community banking model is its
inherent lack of scale.

Figure 3.12   US Postal Savings Revenue

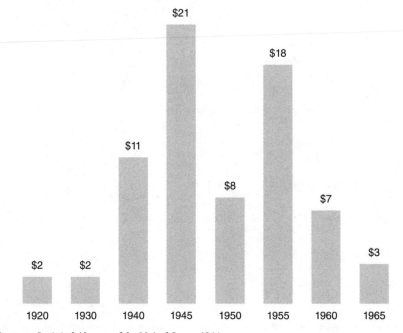

SOURCE: Statistical Abstract of the United States, 1966
Annual revenue for the Postal Savings program in US million dollars (not adjusted). This is income, not profit. Profit for 1965 was about $400,000.

Brand Power

Marketing types love to talk about brand value (how a company's customers and employees feel about the company or product), but I haven't spoken to too many bankers yet who are as infatuated with the idea of brand value, intellectual property, or other intangible assets (see Figures 3.13 and 3.16).

After all, how would the banker measure and prove the quantitative value of such qualitative data? How impactful is the feel-good, intangible stuff to a bank or credit union's bottom line?

According to an Ocean Tomo study of S&P 500 market value, in 1975, 83 percent of the market value was rooted in tangible assets (with only 17 percent in intangible assets).[17] By 2015, you see something incredible happen: a complete flip between the market's perceived importance of tangible (16 percent) and intangible assets (84 percent).

Figure 3.13   Brand Value of Traditional Financial Services (US)

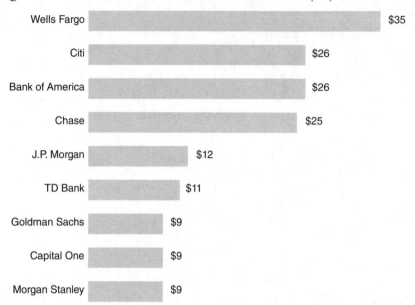

SOURCE: Brand Finance
The most valuable traditional financial services brands in the United States as of February 2015, in billion US dollars.

Don't think we can use the stock market as a benchmark for sanity? OK, fair enough.

Let's look at the impact of this intangible, touchy-feely brandy stuff on the banking industry.

The Average Consumer Cares Very Little about Your Customer Service

While not a research expert, I have spent a good chunk of my existence watching from the other side of one-way glass in banking focus groups, or otherwise pouring over banking research, trying to understand the consumer.

The focus of our research has always had a very particular slant to it: Why does the consumer who banks with the megabank choose the megabank, and what might get them to move to a community bank or credit union?

Research prior to the meltdown of 2008 showed that consumers had no passion for banking. If they considered banking at all, they considered it a private matter. Other than telling their friend which ATM to drive to so they didn't have to pay ATM fees, they didn't talk too much about the features of their banking account(s), the various types of fees charged by their bank, or even admit they ever got hit with overdraft fees from the bank (see Figure 3.14).

Figure 3.14   Average US Overdraft Fee

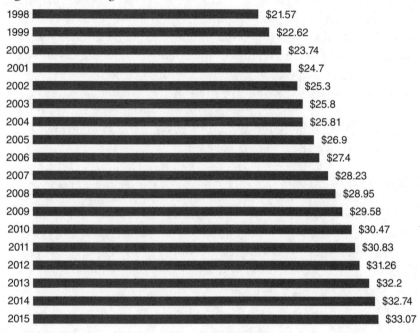

1998	$21.57
1999	$22.62
2000	$23.74
2001	$24.7
2002	$25.3
2003	$25.8
2004	$25.81
2005	$26.9
2006	$27.4
2007	$28.23
2008	$28.95
2009	$29.58
2010	$30.47
2011	$30.83
2012	$31.26
2013	$32.2
2014	$32.74
2015	$33.07

SOURCE: Bankrate
The increase in average overdraft fees, over time, in the United States.

Part of this is because, like in the United Kingdom, consumers didn't really think they had many banking options. Study after study would show consumers describing a sea of sameness with the product offerings, lack of customer service, stagnation with technology, and frustration with fees in the industry.

After all, by 2006, only about 70 percent of American adults were using the Internet![18] Shopping online for a deposit account had not yet hit the mainstream and, according to a Javelin study[19] back then, only 20 million US adults were even attempting to open checking accounts online.

Interviews with the household's primary bank user around this time would yield a primary description of their connection with their big bank: "abusive." If the person was under 50 years old, he probably had no idea what a community bank or credit union was. He might remember his parents having a credit union account, but was 100 percent certain that if they still exist, credit union accounts are reserved for teachers or firefighters.

So, when considering a new place to bank, the unaided consumer thinks about banks that have locations on every corner or banks that advertise aplenty—the national megabanks (Chase, Citi, Wells Fargo, Bank of America) and, to a lesser extent, the 10 or so super-regionals that heavily coat various regions of the country with branches and direct mailers of happy families unpacking boxes in their new homes.

And for years following 2007, focus group after focus group, I'd watch independent moderators describe to consumers what community banks and credit unions are. Without fail, consumers would say, "I bet I get better service at a small place like that."

> If you run a community bank or credit union, and you have advertising that says you offer excellent service, save your money. Every American consumer thinks you offer excellent service (whether you do so or not is another question)—even those who have no idea you exist think that you offer better service. The better message is one that cuts through the clutter and tells them you are not extinct (more on that later).

The moderator then reminds the consumer that they complained for quite a while about the poor service of their megabank, and tells them there is one of these small banks or credit unions down the street. After all, the consumer highlighted bad customer service as their pain point and just admitted that the small institution would solve that problem with good customer service. It sounds like they'll sign up today!

Not so fast, say the megabank accountholders. Actually, it's about more than the service, they say. It's about the products the big bank offers them, they say. They aren't willing to give up the megabank-level products, the megabank-level brand name, and the enormous number of megabank locations for even the greatest customer service in the entire world.

And there's the crux of the problem. For the 80 percent of Americans who bank with a megabank, it all comes back to scale. In the end, scale gives consumers a reason to believe that your product or service is credible. Products and brands trump service, and community banking slips further into obscurity.

Or does it?

Which Takes Us Back to the Scale of Brands

Nearly every community bank or credit union in this country has offered at least one product that consumers recognize by name: Visa or MasterCard.

> A more recent, albeit rather unproven, example is ApplePay. Since its launch in 2014, community banks and credit unions have tripped over themselves to offer a method of payment that they assume their users will (eventually) demand.

A product brand like Visa that's offered at thousands of institutions gives consumers a reason to believe that it's trustworthy, reliable, and, for lack of a more interesting descriptor, "better" than a homegrown product.

By carrying one or both of these popular brands, community institutions know that they'll attract more accountholders than if they built their own open-loop (or closed-loop) payment card network, and branded it something like "FirstSateBankPay."

And Today's Consumers Think Product Experience-First

Throughout my research for this book, I've been forced to page through ancient volumes of text. These dog-eared tomes usually have a directory in the back called an "Index." (Even this book has one!)

Depending on the book, if I were looking for information on "Postal Savings," I might need to look under the Bs for "Banking & Finance," Cs for "Communications," or something else entirely. Looking at the "P" section "Postal Savings Service" was an entirely fruitless affair.

Why?

In order to keep things neat and orderly, humans grouped things by sections. It wasn't until search engines got good at what they do, that they shed the "directory" taxonomy.

Similarly, years ago, if I needed banking services of any type, I would go to your branch (the "directory") and ask for someone to help me.

As time progressed, however, we all became pretty used to searching for exactly what we needed via the old Google, so that now, if we are looking for a product like an iPhone, we don't comb through listings under "mobile telephones," or "mobile providers," or even "AT&T."

Instead, we search by the name of the product, "iPhone X," and then decide which provider we want to supply service to our new phone. Brands, especially for products, deliver results (see Figure 3.15).

Figure 3.15   Share of US Adult Internet Users

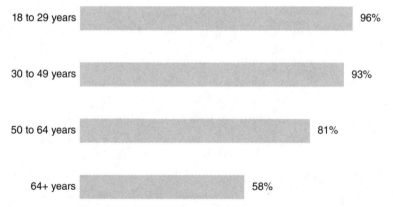

SOURCE: Pew Research Center
The share of adult Internet users in the United States as of May 2015, by age group. The people you want as accountholders use the Internet to find you and your products. How findable are you?

> In other industries, it's very common for small businesses to use product brands to increase scale, decrease costs, boost consumer trust, and provide a sense of focus for its operations. For example, a local athletics store might choose to stock Nikes rather than employing cobblers to cobble its own pair of tennis shoes.

"I spent this last year asking questions, listening to people finding out what leadership meant ... I have some thoughts about what I observed over the last year. Some of them are negative I'll just tell you right off the bat, but I want to be transparent about them because if you don't get them out on the table it's kind of hard to fix them ... We have so many priorities. There's an old quote from somebody that if you have too many priorities you have no priorities.[21] "

—CUNA President/CEO Jim Nussle at the CUNA Community Credit Union and The Federation 2015 Annual Conferences.

The same is true for banking. Instead of searching "First State Bank" first, today, we search by product, e.g., business account, and then, secondarily, we rank them by the provider of the product.

Will your products be found at the top of the search page? Are they competitive to what else is on the page? A Javelin study showed that half of all checking account applications were submitted online and mobile (and, the other half used branches).[20] Do you have a way for people to open and fund the accounts they find online?

People shop for banking products digitally now (turns out that's easier than stopping by every other branch in town picking up brochures), and they shop product-first. Use well-known product brands to scale your institution (see Figure 3.16).

Improve Your Member Associations

"So you're the Cheesecake Factory of banking," I shouted, inhaling the Instagram-flavored, Southern Comforted guitar. "You specialize in hamburgers, salads, fish, chicken, steaks, pizzas, pastas, cheesecakes, fudge cakes, carrot cakes, short cakes, tiramisu, hotdogs, risotto, and anything else I might want to eat. Right? Do you cater as well?"

One cannot age beyond inebriation's joy. So, I refill our glasses of shiraz, killing yet another bottle of McLaren Vale. "You'd be better off as

Figure 3.16 Brand Awareness—Financial Services

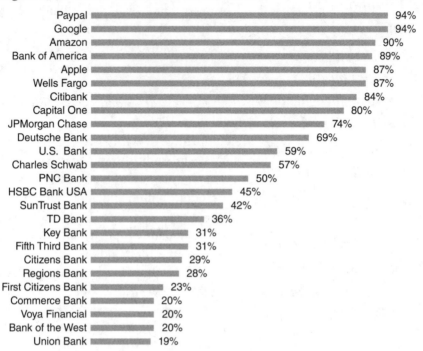

Paypal	94%
Google	94%
Amazon	90%
Bank of America	89%
Apple	87%
Wells Fargo	87%
Citibank	84%
Capital One	80%
JPMorgan Chase	74%
Deutsche Bank	69%
U.S. Bank	59%
Charles Schwab	57%
PNC Bank	50%
HSBC Bank USA	45%
SunTrust Bank	42%
TD Bank	36%
Key Bank	31%
Fifth Third Bank	31%
Citizens Bank	29%
Regions Bank	28%
First Citizens Bank	23%
Commerce Bank	20%
Voya Financial	20%
Bank of the West	20%
Union Bank	19%

SOURCE: Statista; Instantly (2015)

Financial provider awareness by brand in the US. The top three brands in financial services in 2015 were product brands—not financial institution brands.

the J. D. Byrider of mortgages," I suggest to a generations-deep banker counts Hubris amongst his family members.

A sober man would have ducked or dodged or flinched or simply not opened his mouth in the first place, but I continue the ramble gamble, "Universal banking is dead. The days of your bank being the one-stop shop of any-type-of banking to anyone are over."

"Prove it, Nostradamus," he says smugly, as his disinterested girl-friend, a former star of Korean movies (who to her credit, is quite aware he got her on the tail end of her stardom), interrupts the banking talk with a well-timed burp. After a brief laugh, the banker stares, contemplative. "Prove it."

We both knew that time was on my side for that prediction.

Figure 3.17   Most Valuable Brands in 2015

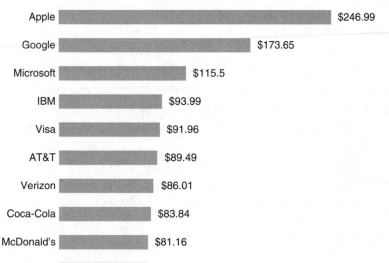

Apple $246.99
Google $173.65
Microsoft $115.5
IBM $93.99
Visa $91.96
AT&T $89.49
Verizon $86.01
Coca-Cola $83.84
McDonald's $81.16
Marlboro $80.35

SOURCE: Millward Brown
The most valuable brands in North America in 2015 (in billion US dollars). Apple's brand was worth $247 billion and Visa's brand was worth about $92 billion. Why wouldn't a community FI want to use some of those brands to their advantage?

"Look, big banks can afford to drop billions of dollars into things that may or may not work. They will be fine. The institutions that are most likely to eat it are the small FIs. The ones with no room for error. History has gotten you this far, but it won't take you into the future. Tomorrow will unfriend the small universal bank, crushing generic institutions under a pile of regulations, busted technologies, crumbled columns, empty coffers, and neglected nostalgia. The days of being everything to everyone are over. We must all choose to be one thing to someone before we are nothing to no one." (Something similar to that came out, if far less coherent.)

One final shriek scratched the top of my aching throat with the hunger of a teenager's tomorrow, and I surrendered my rant. My chords are now blistered raw and beaten and stretched from yelling profane profanities at gentlemen with twice my experience. The quieted and embarrassed vocals spent the earlier part of the week slowly whittling their range to a desperate, awkward, and painful mono-shrill tone.

I motion to my throat as if to signal that it has finished working, and the banker, most certainly relieved, excuses himself to take a call on his phone. Girlfriend hangs out, playing some game on her phone.

What an odd fellow; an untrained pianist with a fake front tooth. A rambling, yet exceedingly allegorical story of how he lost just the one in a decibel-maddening incident five years ago preceded my stump speech on community banking and its impending doom. And, while he hasn't used a Little Giant Ladder System since, he kept his stock in Sears nonetheless.

It wasn't long before the girlfriend spoke up in an accusatory tone, rather frustrated by my simplistic outlook. "What would you do?"

Sympathy set in. And then sadness. If I were a community banker, where would I turn to help me out of this jam? "Perhaps my association could help me," I thought.

A Bit about the Banking and Credit Union Associations

Nearly every state has a few bank and a few credit union associations, with the state associations rolling up to national associations (such as CUNA, ICBA, ABA, etc.). And, there's hundreds more associations—offering camaraderie, political action committees, and industry education.

Political intention varies—from agricultural loan regulation to debit card interchange battles with merchants. As a banker, you have a lot of stuff to worry about, and your associations are there to help you along. They are pretty great.

From an industry analyst perspective, there is an unintended consequence that, if not improved, could toll the bell for the industry in this time of immense flux.

The "Endorsement" Problem

Each association is a not-for-profit organization. Of interest to those more slack-jawed, the associations also have a sister for-profit company that provides "vendor review and endorsement services" for their members. The idea here, is that an endorsement by the organization would help short circuit due diligence processes between a member FI and an endorsed fintech company. Makes sense.

Innocuously, the for-profit company performs due diligence on applying fintech firms. Since FIs (and their examiners) are concerned with operational risk, reputational risk, and the like, the review includes how long the company has been offering the to-be-endorsed product in the market, client satisfaction, financial review, etc.

While this due diligence process may save time for member FIs, it also creates a nice big innovation moat in the industry—only introducing products that have been in market at least three years or longer. By "saving the member FI time and energy of the due diligence process," the association, without intention, casts a rigid template on an industry that needs new, outside thinking the most.

What does the due diligence time requirement (at least three years in-market) and the marketing benefit mean for the member FIs? They necessarily consume years-old industry, product, and technology information. For some products and services, this isn't a bad thing at all—this is precisely what their member institutions want. For new technologies, however, this may be a real challenge.

When the consumer expectation curve was decidedly flat, this wasn't a big deal. It made perfect sense. These days, with the consumer expectation curve off the charts, associations may be doing more harm than good by not including the younger products in some fashion.

Push Your Respective State and National Associations to Adopt More Contemporary Standards for Endorsed Vendor Review

Clearly, the associations should not get reckless with their endorsement process and simply loosen the standards that their member institutions (and affiliated examiners) have grown to trust. Instead, an expansion of the "endorsement" model would help boost awareness of new technologies or marketing approaches for member FIs.

Interestingly, Jim Nussle's quote from CUNA that kicked off this section also marked the inflection point of change inside an association that, in his own words, had many competing priorities. Not only is CUNA now pushing a more focused, pro-innovation agenda across its organization, it is

also knee-deep in the refinement of its endorsement process.
A quick chat with representatives at other banking associations
suggested similar renewed, progressive agendas.

In fact, with small but universal changes, the industry associations can
be a huge help for FIs as they navigate the rough shores of innovation.
Here's some ideas, which I recently submitted to representatives of a few
national bank and credit union associations:

1. *Introduce an additional tier of endorsement, specifically for this cadre of newbie products.* Create an "Endorsement Roadmap" level that is separate
   and apart from your "Officially Endorsed" grouping for companies
   whose products are too young, haven't had enough FI-market experience, or are otherwise unable to meet the standards of the official
   endorsement tier.

   Association leaders might push back on the first step, suggesting they are too busy with political concerns or otherwise lack the
   expertise to evaluate so many vendors. This evaluation could easily
   be funded by the process itself: charge an "evaluation" fee for these
   early products to be reviewed each year, and then use a third-party
   expert consulting firm to perform the rankings.

2. *Create a set of standards for inclusion on the Endorsement Roadmap.* Pub-
   lish a set of requirements and application protocol for the Endorsement Roadmap group. This set of standards will set the stage for
   how a new product or service can be listed *and* evaluated by your
   association for inclusion therein.

   State associations could even take a more localized approach on
   the evaluations. For instance, Midwest associations might find more
   interest in evaluating lending platforms than roboadvisers.

3. *Provide qualitative feedback on Endorsement Roadmap products.* The
   Endorsement Roadmap items should have a healthy, and regularly
   updated, set of common metrics that provide a holistic evaluation
   with gradation—similar to the very informative, but easy to
   understand, filled-circle ratings of *Consumer Reports*.

Ideas on metrics that might matter to an evaluating banker:

- Users (none, some, lots)
- Member FI-beta (none, in-process, complete)
- Funding (none, some, plenty)
- Core partners (none, some, plenty)
- Value to consumers (none, some, plenty)
- SLA (none, some, high)
- Insurance (none, some, high)
- FI clients (none, some, plenty)
- FI pricing (none, low, high)
- FI compliance (none, some, plenty)
- FI risk (none, some, plenty)
- FI profitability (none, some, plenty)
- FI financial literacy (none, some, plenty)
- FI retention (none, some, plenty)

4. *Market the Endorsement Roadmap.* The associations that adopt this direction will be seen as providing real value to their member FIs, but only if they let people know about it. Groups that would find value in the roadmap include the following:

   - *Prospective members*—Show non-member FIs that by simply joining your association they get a clear view of the ever-expanding and ever-evolving world of fintech. People will pay for a good night's sleep.
   - *Existing members*—Every association president I've ever met wants to show additional value to members. This would do just that.
   - *Officially endorsed companies*—More mature companies grow by acquisition and partnerships. That's two activities that would deeply excite those on the roadmap.
   - *Other fintech startups*—More and more fintech companies are attempting to partner with FIs. Give them an on-ramp to making that happen.

After a member FI decides which problems they want to solve for their institution, a simple read of the latest Endorsement Roadmap will inform and inspire them to investigate the service on their own. The Endorsement Roadmap is a spotlight in a dark corner of our industry.

As the world becomes smaller, and global digital brands push into tiny neighborhoods, banking member associations will become more and more important to the continued vitality of credit unions and community banks—in politics, regulation, education, and, of course, trusted vendors.

Associations will need to evolve their practices, policies, and procedures to reflect the new pace of change in the world of compliance, fintech, and consumer expectation. These incremental advances will go a long way to propelling the vestige into relevance.

Work with Entrepreneurs

Embrace the Entrepreneurial Generation with Small Business Guidance

It's a crunchy, salty, wistful evening trapped in the well-rested corner of a red, faux eel-skinned booth. Wretched sports bar courteous enough to keep the TV sound off and the stale popcorn on. Thursday night football is a thing and is happening. Only the locals of some other town who now live in this town care. Can't swing a dead cat without it hitting one or two newly minted natives.

We are all just a few blocks from Central Park, and several too many Guinnesses from detox.

Humanity is riddled with the weak desire of connection. I've been there and done this and look at me do this thing in such a way you've never seen or will ever be able to do, but I'll share it casually as if we were best buds, and you will experience it causally as if you are turning on a network television sitcom.

And we all have conned ourselves to believe it natural and earned and honest and loving. But not one of us does not know or feel guilty that either side is quite self-serving.

And this desire exists everywhere, not simply social media. This sports bar corner is packed with chatty millennials, would-be conversationalists releasing their otherwise retina-screen tethered retinas to several pre-modern shared big screens. A football game.

The crowded beer pong table throws off rowdy discussions of start-ups and apps and delayed financing rounds and unicorns and other buzzwords. Cutting through both beer-powered games with the might of a Snapchat notification, an open laptop displaying a code editor slams and skates across the green, wobbly, soaked table. Something is said, and everyone laughs.

I'm not a sports fan, but I know football when I see it. I'm not a millennial fan, either, but I know the startup elite when I see them, too.

By 2020, the two largest age groups in the United States will be those in this bar: (1) 25 to 29 and (2) 30 to 34—heading toward the late thirties, a time when most Americans who will start a company, start their first.[22]

This Ubiquitous Go-Millennial Write-up Ends with a Rare Pro-Boomer Stance

You've no doubt heard all the statistics on how millennials dread going into a branch, they need technology centered around their needs, they research financial products using the Internet (see Figure 3.18), and all the other obvious data.

We get it: You can't attract the kiddos with your tellers, 9 a.m. to 4 p.m. branch hours, and Rotary Club spaghetti dinners. It turns out that you might, however, nab this entrepreneurial generation with private mentoring sessions and sophisticated online education for starting and running a successful business.

Here are a few points on the generation that may illuminate some common ground between your institution and their life goals:

- Nearly half (41 percent) of millennials want to run their own successful small business.[23]
- Millennials grew up during the technology revolution—so they understand its applications better than you, pops.[24]
- Millennials benefited from exposure to friends and family who are small business owners. In 2013, 3 percent of college freshmen reported that their mothers were entrepreneurs and 9 percent had fathers who ran a business.[25]
- Millennials have had more exposure to entrepreneurship education in colleges and universities than any other generation. In 1975, there were around 100 formal majors, minors, and certificates in

Figure 3.18   Millennial Financial Product Research

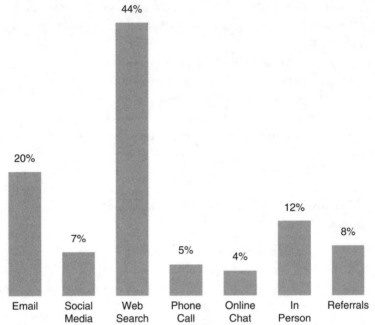

SOURCE: The Principal Financial Group
Preferred methods of research by millennials for financial products and services (in 2015).

entrepreneurship at colleges and universities in the United States.[26] By 1985, there were about 250.[27] By 2008, there were more than 5,000 entrepreneurship courses and more than 400,000 students per year taking them.[28]

• Beyond entrepreneurial classes, millennials have attending higher levels of education, on average, than previous generations. While not a predictor of business success, the added schooling certainly can't hurt.

• Unfortunately, the Great Recession may have temporarily sidelined millennials' capability to become entrepreneurs. The standard source of seed capital for new businesses in America has historically been "housing" wealth. Compared to previous generations, millennials own far fewer homes, graduate with more student loan debt (about $30,000 worth), and delay major life decisions as a result.

- While 24 percent of millennials get at least some of their income from a business they run or own some part of, in 2016, America is still seeing 100,000 to 150,000 fewer startups per year than in each of the 20 years previous to the Great Recession (2009).[29]
- Millennials are the number-one generation in referring their friends to a bank or credit union, according to the Center for Generational Kinetics.

Community bankers who pride themselves on helping small businesses grow may find a very strong future in targeting the entrepreneurial millennial and building an exciting bundle of services around the needs of a budding startup.

To be validated on market research, this could include a special app with instant account opening and instant loan adjudication up to $250,000, mobile deposit capture, a step-by-step incorporation "wizard" integrated with LegalZoom, e-signature capabilities, in-app secure video chat with a personal banker, a button that enables a "drive-to-me" ATM depository (e.g., Idea Bank from Poland), and much more.

And while you're considering entrepreneurial millennials, don't forget the baby boomers.

Boomers, the eldest of whom hit the age of 70 in 2016 (youngest, about 50), have always been seen as the "entrepreneurial generation," have quite a bit more capital to start a business, and may hold the key to entrepreneurship growth in the United States over the next few years.

While their appetite for risk is naturally lower than millennials, boomers are still the wealthiest generation in American history, have tons of work experience, are living longer, and are still chasing that American dream (see Figure 3.19). To that end, in 2015, they were twice as likely to launch a new business as millennials.[30]

Ironically, those at highest risk for failing with tomorrow's entrepreneurs are those existing commercial-focused institutions. Like all things community banking, past performance may not be an indicator of future success.

Figure 3.19   Reasons Retirees Start Businesses

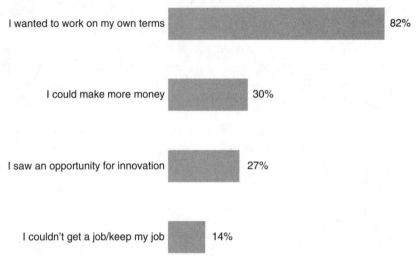

I wanted to work on my own terms — 82%

I could make more money — 30%

I saw an opportunity for innovation — 27%

I couldn't get a job/keep my job — 14%

SOURCE: Merrill Lynch; Age Wave
Retired boomers start businesses for a host of reasons—make sure you're top of mind when they do.

Business newbie millennials, retiree boomers or both can lead you to a new, defensible, and focused position presuming you overhaul your data mining, technology, servicing, and processes accordingly. As a banker with a long career ahead, you're signing up for those changes regardless. Best yet, by aligning your executive team and board on your future service and target now, you have time to research, plan, and iterate deliberately.

Notes

1. "3-6-3 Rule," Wikipedia, 2015: https://en.wikipedia.org/wiki/3-6-3_Rule.
2. Mark J. Flannery, "The Social Costs of Unit Banking Restrictions," *Journal of Monetary Economics* 13 (March 1984): 237–249.
3. Michael C. Keeley, "Deposit Insurance, Risk, and Market Power in Banking," *The American Economic Review* 80 (December 1990): 1183–1200.
4. "Fintechs: Reinventing Banking," *EFMA Digest* (2016).
5. "How to Build the Perfect Workplace," Fortune.com (March 5, 2015).
6. Ibid., McKinsey Global Institute, LinkedIn & Gallop Poll.

7. 2016 Best Places to Work in Central Texas, *Austin Business Journal*, http://www.bizjournals.com/austin/news/2016/06/24/the-best-places-to-work-in-2016-the-winners-how.html.

8. Joshua Saul, "Barnacles Destroy Boats, But Getting Rid of Them Destroys the Sea—Until Now," *Popular Science* (July 21, 2011), http://www.popsci.com/science/article/2011-06/barnacles-destroy-boats-getting-rid-them-destroys-sea%e2%80%94until-now.

9. eMarketer, eMarketer Webinar: Omnichannel Retail—Seven Trends in 2015.

10. 2012 FDIC Community Banking Study, https://www.fdic.gov/regulations/resources/cbi/study.html.

11. eMarketer (May 2015).

12. "iGen—Tech Disruption: 2016 National Study on Technology and the Generation after Millennials," The Center for Generational Kinetics, LLC (2016).

13. "World Retail Banking Report 2016," Capgemini and Efma (2016).

14. Learn about API Banking from SVB here: https://www.svb.com/api/.

15. Jonathan Friedman, "What Startups Think of Silicon Valley," Priceonomics (March 20, 2014), http://priceonomics.com/what-startups-think-about-silicon-valley-bank/.

16. Flannery, 237–249.

17. Andrew Winston, "What VW Didn't Understand about Trust," *Harvard Business Review* (September 23, 2015).

18. Andrew Perrin and Maeve Duggan, "Americans' Internet Access: 2000-2015," Pew Research Center (June 26, 2015).

19. Jean M Garascia, "Online Account Opening Adoption Forecast: The Market Is Ripe for Direct Banking Investments," Javelin Strategy & Research (September 2007).

20. "Digital Account Opening," Digital Banking Report (August 2015).

21. *Credit Union Times Magazine* (October 7, 2015), via a CUNA-provided transcript.

22. Bill McBride, "Census Bureau: Largest 5-Year Population Cohort Is Now the '20 to 24' Age Group," *Calculated Risk* (June 26, 2014).

23. *2014 ICBA American Millennials and Banking Study*.

24. "State of Entrepreneurship 2015 Address," Ewing Marion Kauffman Foundation (February 11, 2015).

25. "The American Freshman: National Norms Fall 2013," University of California, Los Angeles, 2013, http://www.heri.ucla.edu/monographs/theamericanfreshman2013.pdf.

26. Wendy E. F. Torrance et al., "Entrepreneurship Education Comes of Age on Campus: The Challenges and Rewards of Bringing Entrepreneurship to Higher Education," *Ewing Marion Kauffman Research Paper* (August 2013).

27. Ibid.

28. George T. Solomon, "The National Survey of Entrepreneurship Education: An Overview of 2012–2014 Survey Data," George Washington University Center for Entrepreneurial Excellence, December 2, 2014.

29. *2014 ICBA American Millennials and Banking Study.*

30. Kaufmann Foundation, State of Entrepreneurship 2015 Address.

Chapter 4

Advice from Others

I t's one of those singer-songwriter kinds of mornings. Stars are twitching; dawn is bitching.

Another light. This, an Oliva Serie O Double Toro, followed by a crash in the sunbeaten Adirondack. Heavy banana leaves dancing with splintered light palm fans. Dog is barking down the hill. First morning home in three weeks. Sleepy family slumbers. Saber-toothed mosquitos ravage.

Spiritual? Ritual.

Running long on time, and short on fuel. Coldplays. It's not what you wished it was. More spectating than speculating. Comforting.

Always better to be on the outside of a shift. Position yourself there. It's clean and cool. You don't have to explain yourself. You get to ask questions and be an agent of change. Justification is an aside. Counter-cultured is the norm as tattoos and tongue-piercing in 1997, distorting the music all the while.

I think back to the first time I met Brett King. He was working on a new thing called MovenBank.

Brett wanted to learn about how our two ideas might work together (Kasasa and MovenBank). It was clear from that conversation that we had dissimilar goals. He, focused on revolution; we, on renaissance.

In one way, he was right—community financial institutions desperately needed to add digital capabilities to their lineup. They lack the omnichannel capabilities of a full-stack digital bank. And in another way, we were right—community institutions still serve very important needs in their communities, and their branch networks are still assets (at least for the not-to-distant future).

As polite as he is, I doubt he verbalized it in this manner, but Brett seemed to believe that digital banks should be the new community banks and we were foolish for supporting the establishment that can't get out of its own way.

I can't disagree, but it's the incumbents' game to lose.

Brett's team explained that they were intent on starting their own "bank" without going through that whole "de novo" mess. Instead, they were going to let an actual bank handle the hard work of the AML, core processing, regulation, and other messy stuff.

Standing on some sweaty street in Midtown, talking on my year-old iPhone, my first thought glistened, "Genius. Albatross-free."

While this neo-bank model has since been copied over and over again around the world, it was at the time a novel approach, but one that I knew would not work with our FIs' infrastructure.

Moven ultimately selected CBW Bank as its partner institution in the United States, which in hindsight was quite a nice move. Suresh worked hard to make his CBW Bank the behind-the-scenes banking muscle for Moven.

You can read more from both futurist Brett and technologist-turned-community-banker Suresh in this section. These gentlemen have no oil paintings of paternal ancestry hanging in aging yet fortified, fluorescent lit structures, and they are just fine with that.

After all, given a long enough time horizon, futurists are never wrong—just early.

And, We Are in the Future

While Brett and Suresh push bankers and consumers into the future, the eternal question from those laggard bankers is, "Can't we wait a bit longer?"

For the first time in history, Americans have a wide variety of choices in their banking, a multitude of convenient ways to shop for and to open banking accounts, and for once, banking is a table topic. It's mainstream.

All this, when other industries have trained the same consumers to demand more from an experience; that product and design are inseparable.

All this, when money is the cheapest it's been in decades, if not ever.

All this, when there are thousands of financial services startups worldwide in 18 banking segments. One hundred times the number of fintech startups before the 2008 crash—receiving 100 times the amount of investment they need (see Figure 4.1), all working furiously to improve areas of banking most institutions forgot about, while depositing investment dollars that would cripple most community banks' balance sheets.

Figure 4.1   Global Fintech Financing

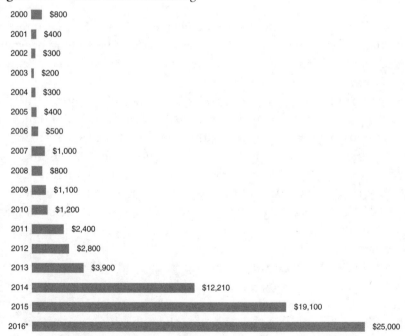

SOURCE: CB Insights *Estimation by author
Estimated investment (in million US dollars) in financial technology companies by year. Total invested includes only data from rounds where round size data is publicly available.

All this, when the world is flat, singularity is near, devices are learning from each other, and realities of virtual and physical are blending.

All this, when new data sources, predictive analytics, artificial intelligence, machine learning, risk models, and user experiences have all begun to make lending and investing vastly more efficient on all sides of the transaction, but are shunned as alternative models by community institutions and their regulators.

All this, when the risk of doing what you've always done has far surpassed the risk of doing nearly anything else.

All this, when "all this" value has fallen exponentially—when banking looks more like a utility (a clunky user interface with a list of gussied-up transactions) than an experience a user would actually pay for.

Advice from Others Much Smarter Than Myself

Over the years, I've friended (and, assuredly, offended) a wide variety of banking experts with a wide degree of opinion. Knowing that I don't have all the answers, I started thinking about getting the best minds in banking today to help think through guidance for the coming bankruption. Wouldn't that increase community banking's likelihood to succeed?

No guts, no glory.

I reached out to the selection of brave, talented souls on the following pages. I asked them to either write what they think might help community banking leaders think through the challenges that they face in crossing the chasm to tomorrow, or to simply answer this question, "If you were a senior-level community bank or credit union leader, what would you do to prepare your institution for the near-term future?"

So here you go, a collection of some of the most advanced thinkers and doers in fintech and community banking today, offering their guidance for you to survive the bankruption.

If you get as much out of their ideas as I did, please support these ladies and gentlemen by engaging with them at conferences; reading their books, websites, and research reports; or connecting on Twitter or LinkedIn. They are actively helping us all by shaping a better future for our industry.

Enjoy!

Oh, and don't forget to read the final chapter, "Finishing Move," where I wrap all this up with one pretty little bow.

Pascal Bouvier, CFA

Kicking off our alphabetically ordered expert panel is Pascal Bouvier, providing a few ideas on spurring an innovation agenda at your institution. If you get a chance to meet Pascal, you'll find a quiet visionary behind actual rose-colored glasses.

> **@PascalBouvier**
> Pascal Bouvier, fintech expert & investor, Venture Partner Santander Innoventures. The following thoughts solely represent his own views.

As the world becomes more networked and as technology allows individuals and corporations to exchange data fluidly amongst themselves and with one another, businesses that rely on opacity, slow processes, and information asymmetry will be existentially challenged. As such, were I the head of a financial institution I would launch a cultural revolution with the end goal of transforming every individual into an Intrapreneur and the organization as a whole into a more nimble and flexible one.

My first steps would be to articulate an Innovation Group around the strategic initiatives of interacting with (a) the outside world (venture investing, platform strategy) and (b) the inside world (cultural education, "new business" builder group, commercial partnerships).

I would make sure this Innovation Group would be independent enough so as to avoid being smothered by the current culture and embedded enough that it would start changing the current culture; and have it report directly to the board of directors.

Finally, I would rejuvenate my organization's board of directors and add individuals who would bring data science, mobile technology, artificial intelligence, platform technology, and innovation skills.

Jim Bruene

The soft-spoken and humble ex-banker, Jim Bruene has been an astute follower of banking and fintech for many years. In fact, from 1994 to 2014, he published Online Banking Report (before passing it along to Jim Marous, who rebranded it Digital Banking Report). During those 20 years, Bruene predicted many trends that shaped banking today. Many of us in the industry would not be where we are today without the thought leadership, curation, and diligence of Jim Bruene.

@Netbanker

Jim Bruene is a financial services industry analyst and early digital banking proponent. He founded fintech innovation platform Finovate in 1995 after leading U.S. Bancorp's pioneering online banking service developed with Microsoft, Wells Fargo, and Chase. More than 10,000 financial execs and 1,500 fintech companies have participated in Finovate events.

Banking Tweens, Teens, and the Under-25s. *In a remote banking world, the most important customers aren't even driving yet.*

In the past, financial institutions didn't get serious about younger consumers until they walked into a branch near their new college campus. But that's a holdover from the branch-banking paradigm that few 18-year-olds today would understand.

Tomorrow's college freshman will arrive fully financially functional with a debit card and mobile account already synced to the parents' bank. Students will stay with the *family's bank* because it's easier that way for mom and dad to maintain an uninterrupted flow of cash for tuition, books, and those never-ending "living expenses."

Banks should be aware of the two trends at play here:

1. Online/mobile banking has eliminated the need to switch banks at major life events.
2. Conversely, mobile/online banking has made it much easier to bank OUTSIDE a customer's geographic community.

It used to make perfect sense to avoid expending resources opening accounts for the under-18 crowd. Their balances were small and lifetime value was negligible. After all, high-school graduates closed their bank accounts when they moved to college. College graduates closed theirs when they moved to their first job. And job holders switched accounts when they landed a better job, and so on.

But that was a different time. In today's remote-banking world, THERE IS NO REASON TO EVER CLOSE YOUR ACCOUNT. You just send in a change of address and keep logging in to the same place.

Look at the opportunity. Today, there are more than 100 million people under age 25 in the United States (see Table 4.1):

- 43 million, ages 15 to 24
- 20 million, ages 10 to 14
- 42 million, under 10 years of age

And 46 percent of U.S. households have children under 18 living at home. If you include households with 18- to 24-year-olds living at home or in college, the total market is more than half the country.

Table 4.1   U.S. Population by Age Range

Age Range	Number	% of Total	Cum %
Under 5 years	21.3 mil	6.9%	7%
5 to 9 years	20.6 mil	6.7%	14%
10 to 14 years	20.0 mil	6.5%	20%
15 to 19 years	21.5 mil	7.0%	27%
20 to 24 years	21.5 mil	7.0%	34%
25 to 29 years	21.7 mil	7.1%	41%
30 to 34 years	19.9 mil	6.5%	48%
35 to 39 years	20.5 mil	6.7%	54%
40 to 44 years	21.0 mil	6.8%	61%
45 to 49 years	22.8 mil	7.4%	69%
50 to 54 years	21.8 mil	7.1%	76%
55 to 59 years	19.0 mil	6.2%	82%
60 to 64 years	15.8 mil	5.2%	87%
65 to 69 years	11.8 mil	3.8%	91%
70 to 74 years	9.0 mil	2.9%	94%
75 to 79 years	7.3 mil	2.4%	96%
80 to 84 years	5.8 mil	1.9%	98%
85 to 89 years	3.7 mil	1.2%	99%
90+	2.0 mil	0.6%	100%
Total	**307 mil**	**100%**	**100%**
Median age	*36.8*		

SOURCE: US Census Bureau Statistics, July 1, 2009

A 12-year-old girl today is expected to live another 70 years (boys, only 65 more, sorry guys). So if those kids won't ever need to close their accounts, it stands to reason that getting them hooked up to their parents' online banking becomes vitally important. And while youth banking won't boost next quarter's bottom line, it doesn't have to be a cost center, either. Reasonable fees, in the $5 to $10 range per month for a basket of services, can make the accounts profitable from the start.

Finally, while it may be many years before you turn a profit on the kid's account, their parents are your bread and butter NOW. And everything you do to deepen relationships with 30- and 40-somethings WILL pay off in next year's P&L.

Therefore, we believe you should not ignore the relatively untapped opportunity for comprehensive *family banking* services that integrate children's accounts (checking, savings, loans, cards, identity protection) with those of their parents. Mobile phone carriers, software providers, and others have proven that there is a lucrative market for parental controls and it's time for banks and credit unions to do the same.

Key Products and Services. Many youth banking programs start by targeting high school students. And while that may be the best chance of retaining them before being tempted by banking offers on campus, it's even better to start earlier, much earlier. In fact, as soon as you catch wind of a birth in your community, you can offer to start a savings account in the child's name. New parents want the best for their newborn, and a savings account where they can sock away a few dollars from grandma and grandpa every year, is the perfect way to start the near-century long relationship.

The following is a list of banking products and services for the older youth and young adult market (18 to 25 years old). Services geared for preteens and younger are much simpler. Tables 4.2 and 4.3 outline banking service by age cohort.

- Debit card/checking
- Spending tools
- Funds transfer (real-time)
- Savings/goals (see Case Study)
- Allowance (with optional ties to chores/goals/achievements)

Table 4.2 Youth Banking Products and Services

Product/Feature	Age Range to Start	Definition/Comments
Allowance/chore manager	5–11	Tool for communicating, tracking and delivering periodic allowance.
ATM fee refunds	18–23	Refund of foreign ATM fees.
Auto loans (with co-sign option)	18–23	Make it easy, and understandable, for parents to co-sign an auto loan; limit the situations where a minor problem (e.g., 30-days late) would be reported on parent's credit score.
Billpay services with bill sharing/splitting function	18–23	Most kids have a small number of bills, but they can be complicated when split with multiple roommates. And due date alerts are very important.
Bonus interest	5–11	With interest rates so low, it's hard to motivate savings based on a dollar or two of interest earned each year. Parents could pay interest bonuses to boost returns.
Business startup loan	18–23	While you may not have a Mark Zuckerberg in your customer base, many young people are interested in starting business. Small loans, under $5,000, could go a long way to kickstart a "dorm room" business (co-signed with parents).
Changing UI (online and mobile)	12–15	The online/mobile interface should evolve as kids grow up. Ideally, shifting every few years, e.g., have a UI for ages 8–11, 12–14, 15–18, 18–22, and so on.
Checking account	18–23	This is still a must-have for most consumers. Paper checks optional.
College savings plans	0–5	It's never too early to start saving for the ever-expanding costs of college.
Communications	5–11	Text, email, chat and in-account messaging.

(continued)

Table 4.2 (*continued*)

Product/Feature	Age Range to Start	Definition/Comments
Credit card (with co-sign option)	18–23	Make it easy, and understandable, for parents to co-sign an unsecured credit card; limit the situations where a minor problem (e.g., 30-days late) would be reported on parent's credit score and/or allow parents to guarantee a portion of the credit limit with a controlled deposit account or high average balance.
Credit scores and monitoring	18–23	Good credit will help young adults secure apartments and jobs and lower the cost of auto and other insurance. It's vitally important to understand and track your credit score.
Credit education, especially cards, student loans, and auto loans	15–18	High schoolers need to understand how credit works so they can make better decisions about college expenses and other big-ticket items.
Customer service via Facebook, Twitter, chat, Skype, email	15–18	Banks need to communicate through the channels their customers are comfortable with.
Debit cards	12–15	The key payment mechanism for the most under-25s.
Deposits by family members (p2p payments)	0–5	Allow family members, e.g., grandparents, to deposit to grandchild's college savings account.
Facebook integration	15–18	Feed alerts and account info directly into the news feed to help young consumers better track their finances.
Financial education	5–11	Make it light and tied to rewards with game mechanics (see "gaming" below).
Forum, financial questions	15–18	A place where kids can go to get questions answered by peers, by the financial institution, and from their parents.

Table 4.2 (*continued*)

Product/Feature	Age Range to Start	Definition/Comments
Friends & family lending	18–23	Interfamily lending, documentation, communications, and automatic payments.
Funds transfer function	12–15	Make it easy for parents to transfer money into their children's spending accounts.
Gaming/rewards elements	12–15	Offer points, badges, leveling up, as positive reinforcement for desirable financial habits (like telling your parents what you spent money on, donating to charity, and so on).
Gift card tracker	15–18	Allow users to track their outstanding cards and balances.
Gift card reselling	18–23	Allow older kids to unload unused cards into the secondary market.
Giving features	12–15	Allows parents to introduce charitable giving at an early age.
Health Savings Accounts	18–23	For those with full-time jobs, allows them to pay healthcare expenses with pretax dollars.
Housing/mortgage assistance (from family)	18–23	Allows family members to kick in one time or on an ongoing basis to help with rental or mortgage expenses (e.g., first/last month's rent, down payment, etc.).
Identity theft protection	18–23	Guards against identity theft, an issue at all ages.
Insurance	18–23	Auto, life, renters, homeowners, business, etc.
Insurance education, especially auto	15–18	Teaches high-schoolers about the benefits and costs of key insurance products.
Integrated with parents' online banking	0–5	Places info about student accounts within the same online/mobile banking interface.
Investment options	15–18	Older teenagers can start learning about, and even participating in, investing their savings.

(*continued*)

Table 4.2 *(continued)*

Product/Feature	Age Range to Start	Definition/Comments
IOU tracking	15–18	Helps kids track money or goods they've loaned out, or borrowed, from friends.
Mobile and email alerts	12–15	Absolutely essential part of any youth banking service.
Mobile app	12–15	A native smartphone app, preferably with at least a youthful look and feel.
Mortgages	18–23	Focus on education, saving for down payments, and enabling family to assist.
Overdraft forgiveness	18–23	Only needed once prepaid users have graduated to full checking services.
P2P payments	15–18	Pay friends using mobile phone number or email address.
Parental controls	12–15	Parental controls begin at the point the child is given a prepaid card for spending.
Parental savings boost	5–11	Allows parents to boost the interest rate by transferring the needed amount from parent acct.
Parental savings match	12–15	Similar to the savings boost, but more of a focus on matching specific savings goals (e.g., you save $100 for the bike, we'll match it with $100).
PFM, full featured	18–23	A good family account will include basic spending/budgeting tools for younger teens, but a full-featured PFM can be introduced during the college years.
Prepaid and debit cards	12–15	
Privacy controls so student can keep transactions private	18–23	At some point, many older kids are not going to want to share their transaction history with their parents. The timing will be different for every family, so this should be optional.

Table 4.2   (*continued*)

Product/Feature	Age Range to Start	Definition/Comments
Rental deposit loans	18–23	It can often be hard to come up with first/last month's rent and damage deposit. This is a perfect way to help kids get started on their own, co-signed with parents in most cases.
Rental/homeowner insurance	18–23	Renter's insurance is often the first insurance policy kids will need all on their own (assuming auto insurance has been added to their parent's policy).
Retirement products (IRA, 401k)	18–23	Retirement savings should start to enter the picture as soon as the child becomes a full-time employee (or entrepreneur).
Savings accounts with online access for the child	5–11	Young children can have online access to their savings as soon as they start going online by themselves (which varies greatly by family).
Savings button	12–15	Make it super easy, and fun, to add money to savings by pressing a button, playing a game, etc.
Savings goals	12–15	Tweens can be introduced to the concept of saving for a goal with easy-to-use tools.
Security assurances, out-of-band authentication	18–23	Young adults should learn how to take additional measures to safeguard their accounts.
Share goals with family members	12–15	Savings goals shared with family members to encourage gifts towards achieving them.
Social media integration	12–15	Delivering information or encouraging discussion through social media platforms such as Facebook
Spending accounts	12–15	At some point, parents will want to enable their kids' accounts for spending; it could be any time in middle or high school.

(*continued*)

Table 4.2   (*continued*)

Product/Feature	Age Range to Start	Definition/Comments
Spending, budgeting, and PFM tools	12–15	These tools should be offered as soon as the account is enabled for spending.
Spending/budget alerts	12–15	Same as above.
Starter credit line to build positive score	18–23	Add a credit element to spending accounts so kids can begin building a positive credit score and thereby understand how to manage credit.
Starter credit cards for those without credit history	18–23	Offer credit cards with small lines of credit.
Startup business services	15–18	For young entrepreneurs, provide basic business startup services.
Student loans	18–23	Offer loan options for college students.
Systematic savings/investing	12–15	Automate the savings process.
Tax prep assistance	15–18	Make it super simple to file federal and state income tax returns.
Temporary prepaid option on credit card	18–23	Allow credit card customers to add funds to their card accounts to temporarily increase their credit limit (effectively making it a partially prepaid account), e.g., add $500 to a card with a $500 credit limit so that up to $1,000 can be charged.
Travel/cash-back rewards	15–18	Rewards are appreciated at any age, but virtual rewards can probably be used before high school.
Unique UI for younger kids	5–11	Create a simple and appealing interface for young kids.
Young adult UI	15–18	Increase the sophistication of the UI as children age.

Table 4.3   Products by Age Range

Birth to 5 (Preschool):

Some parents like to get ahead on savings (especially for college) and set up savings accounts at birth. This also allows family members to put monetary gifts into the child's college savings account at a very early age.

Products to offer:
- College savings plans
- Basic savings and investment accounts

Features:
- Integrated with parents' online banking
- Easy transfer function
- Share goals with family members
- Ability for family members to make direct deposits to the account

5 to 11 (Elementary School):

As kids enter school age, they often begin getting their first lessons on money, often accompanied by an allowance.

Additional products:
- Allowance managers (online and mobile)
- Savings accounts with online access for the child
- Financial education/simple gaming

Additional features:
- Unique UI that appeals to younger kids
- Communications from parent account to kid's account

12 to 15 (Middle School):

Younger teens begin to own mobile phones, use the Internet independently, create Facebook accounts, and spend more money in situations where parents are absent.

Additional products:
- Spending accounts
- Prepaid debit cards
- Giving features
- Contactless stickers
- Savings button
- Savings goals

(continued)

Table 4.3   (*continued*)

Additional features:
- Mobile and email alerts
- Parental controls
- Parental savings match
- Parental savings boost
- More sophisticated UI (online and mobile)
- Gaming/rewards elements
- Mobile app

15 to 18 (High School):

As kids become "young adults," their banking needs become more sophisticated; they may have jobs and pay taxes, yet most are still tied directly to their parents in all matters financial.

Additional products:
- Facebook integration/app
- P2P payments
- Student loans
- Basic spending, budgeting, and PFM tools
- Starter credit account to build positive score
- Tax prep assistance
- IOU tracking
- Gift card tracker
- Starter credit card (with co-signer)

Additional features:
- Young adult UI
- Social media integration
- Credit education, especially about credit cards, student loans, and auto loans
- Insurance education, especially auto

18 to 23+ (College Students):

This is the first age of independence where students may want more financial control and privacy from their parents, while still needing tight integration with their parents for funds transfers. This is also the first time that you can lose the relationship to the local bank or credit union that has set up shop on campus.

Table 4.3 (*continued*)

Additional products:

- Student credit card (with co-sign)
- Auto loans (with co-sign)
- Checking account
- Credit score/monitoring
- Insurance
- Friends and family lending
- Gift card reselling

Additional features:

- Full-featured PFM
- Privacy controls so student can keep transactions private
- Overdraft forgiveness
- Student financial forum
- ATM fee refunds
- Spending/budget alerts

24+ (First Full-Time Job):

This is another life change where traditionally the new graduate will change banks, especially if they are moving to a new location. To retain these customers, you need to decouple their account completely from the parents, while still maintaining easy P2P funds transfers between accounts. You can also pass on price breaks based on the entire "family relationship."

Additional products:

- Investing
- Retirement products, e.g., IRA, 401(k)
- Rental/homeowner insurance
- Mortgages
- Startup business services
- Systematic savings/investing programs
- Health savings accounts (HSAs)
- Housing/mortgage assistance (from family)
- Automated billpay services
- Starter credit cards for those without a credit history

Additional features:

- Travel/cash-back rewards
- Youth-oriented customer service via Facebook, Twitter, live chat, Skype, etc.
- Security assurances, out-of-band authentication
- Temporary prepaid option on credit card

- P2P payments (Venmo, Square cash, or similar)
- Credit card (with optional variable credit line managed by parents)
- Low-value disposable prepaid cards
- Mobile payment (Apple Pay, Android Pay, etc.)
- Student loans (and refis)
- Credit report monitoring/ID protection
- Insurance (rental, auto, bike, cell phone)
- Rent-deposit loans
- Vehicle loans (cosigned)
- Tax prep
- Giving
- Money management tools (PFM)
- Interest rate bonus through parents (see Case Study)
- Business startup loan (cosigned)
- Beginner investing services

Case Study: Youth Savings with Bonus Interest from BECU. Back when my kids were able to save (they are both in college now, so that's not happening), ING Direct and others offered interest rates that actually created an incentive to save. My oldest even enjoyed 5 percent rates for a while. The $5 to $10 in "free money" each month was a tangible reward for giving up the instant gratification from another packet of Pokémon cards and instead socking the cash away.

But today's middle-schoolers and younger teens have come of age in an absurdly low interest-rate environment,[1] with little chance to experience the joy of compound interest. **SmartyPig**[2] and others have created savings bonuses centered around merchant gift cards. That's a clever way to add value, but it can also send a mixed message, "Hey Junior, save $250 and you'll get an extra $5 if you spend the whole thing at Best Buy." For parents who'd like their kids to hold onto that cash (at least until college), there are few options, other than bribing your kids with parent-funded bonuses.

But a few financial institutions have come to the aid of their member parents by dramatically boosting the rates paid on the first few hundred of a balance. For example, in the greater Seattle area, BECU pays 6.17 percent on the first $500 deposited in its Early Saver account (see Figure 4.2). Granted, the rate reverts to pretty much zero (0.1 percent)

Figure 4.2   BECU Youth Savings Landing Page (Jan 11, 2016)

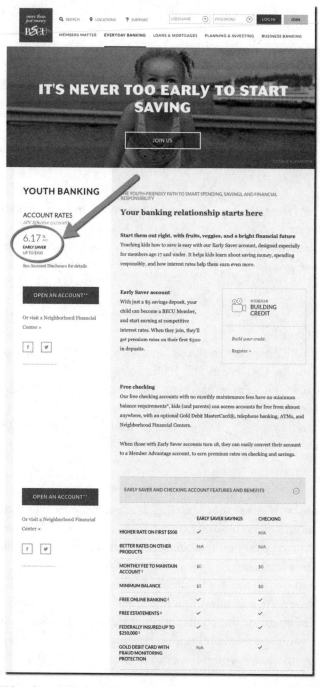

Note: BECU has elevated Youth Banking to one of six choices on its Everyday Banking primary navigation item.

after that, but kids at least get enough interest every month ($2.50/month on $500 balance) to make it feel like it's worth holding the money at the credit union.[3]

Bottom line: Your customers' children are your future. It's worth investing in services to keep them at your FI for the next decade or six. If the $30 annual subsidy is beyond your budget, enable parents to pay for the rate bonus. Let parents "boost" the interest paid on their child's account as much as they want. To provide an extra incentive, you could match parental contributions up to a certain point (e.g., $10/year).

Jill Castilla

While it's a breeze to write about pushing the constructs of community banking, it's not easy to actually do. Jill Castilla has not only done it, she selflessly encourages and inspires other banking executives who want to see similar success in their own organizations. If you get the opportunity, buy this lady lunch and take notes!

@JillCastilla

Jill Castilla is the president and CEO of Citizens Bank of Edmond in Oklahoma. Jill is the recipient of *Bank Innovation*'s 10 Innovative CEOs of 2015, American Banker's Community Banker of the Year 2015, Woman of the Year award from Edmond Chamber of Commerce, American Banker's "Women to Watch," among others.

Community Banks: Let's Bring It. If there ever was a time when bankers should perk up and pay attention, it's now. We're seven years removed from the biggest financial crisis of this generation, Silicon Valley startups are clamoring to get into the financial sector, and in approximately two years, the millennial generation will exceed all others in buying power. As a banker, this gets me to sit up and focus on what's ahead. Despite all of the challenges of regulatory burden and increased competition in the marketplace, community banks are coming up on a pivotal point in time where they can thrive.

Coming from someone who's in charge of a community bank that's been around for more than a century, I can tell you first hand that it's not always easy to usher in change. But coming from experience, it is completely possible to be on the brink of extinction in 2009 and then turn around to becoming an innovative thought leader in the banking space within a span of a few years.

With only $250 million in assets, a shrinking marketing budget (our own decision), and limited resources, we've become the MacGyvers of banking. Give us some duct tape, paper clips, and glue and we'll solve the problem before the time is up. That's the mind-set we have at Citizens Bank of Edmond, and I'm proud to call it a team effort.

Culture change at a bank is not always easy. It's one of those journeys that's like being stranded on a deserted island; you have to dig through thick jungle greens, wade through dirty, waist-deep muddy waters before finally discovering that once hidden treasure you've lost long ago. No, it shouldn't be this hard. But yes, it often can be as treacherous as hunting for lost treasure, but once you find it, it's worth all of the effort.

That's the kind of thing our little bank went through during the financial crisis by getting that regulatory enforcement notice. It's the jolt of action we needed to shape ourselves up, take a deeper look, and wonder who we really are. Through the weathering of years, it's easy to lose yourself in the mix. But sometimes these life-changing scenarios can become the soul-jerking awakening that we all needed. The worst situation can turn into a good one indeed, with the right attitude and strategy.

As an industry, banking was bruised and beaten up from the crisis, and community banks definitely took a toll. But coming out of the other side, there is so much opportunity for growth, change and innovation, it's time to dust ourselves off from the mess and look ahead. Every challenge that's coming our way has given us a new opportunity.

Disruptors are coming into the market, folks say. Bring 'em on! Competition is part of a healthy and growing economy. The concept of banking has been around for thousands of years. Who's to say that new startups can't add to the conversation? In fact, this is one area where many should be perking up and paying attention. What is resonating with consumers? How can I adopt that mind-set/branding/attitude to my bank? What lessons can be learned? These are all things that run through my mind as I discover a new financial disruptor.

It's also encouraging to see that oftentimes, there's a trusted community institution running the back end of many startups. The truth of the matter is, you still need the secure, safe, and sound workings of a bank. Why not go with the local trend and partner with a community bank? We should try not to focus on fighting the disruptors, but think about ways to partner. The financial sector and products for consumers will be even better. Isn't that the goal of banking to begin with? To help people grow their lives? Let's focus on that and bring along as many as we can on that bandwagon.

Also, a word on millennials: They're basically the talk of the town no matter which industry you're in. Maybe the word's becoming taboo; I can sense the eye rolls and preconceived notions coming on. What's really fascinating is that many consulting companies, advertising agencies, and social media gurus are selling the idea that they have the secret to millennials. But what I find increasingly informative is to just go up and talk to the ones you know and pick their brain.

The millennial bunch are a diverse group; there's no study that can sum up the behaviors of all 80 million of them. But many will be more than willing to share about their media consumption habits, why they love a certain brand and what they want from you as a company. Perhaps we could instill millennial advisory boards or brand advocates in the industry. Either way, I can tell you that I gain a ton of insight from interacting with the ones employed at our bank.

What makes a bank stand out amongst the crowd? Social media has been a big differentiator for us and has been a catalyst for many other big things that's shown that we're not your typical bank. In 2012, I had the opportunity to sit in on an industry conference seminar on the importance of social media and how it impacts your search engine optimization results. We had just been released from our regulatory action that same day and I decided to look up what was being said about our bank online. Needless to say, the stories were not all that pleasant. So with a few taps and downloads, I decided to sign up for Twitter that very moment. Community banking for me forever changed.

Social media had a rough childhood. Born in the late 1990s and becoming a full-blown toddler by the turn of the millennium, we all remember the days when you'd be excited to hear that door-open sound on AOL Instant Messenger or get a kudos on your Xanga blog. In its initial stages, social media was wobbling along bumping into tables generally unsure of its identity. Once Facebook came into the picture, it still had to go through an awkward middle school phase. But eventually, we all knew that this small website community created by some Harvard students was here to stay.

As an introverted, risk-averse community banker, social media was not something you think would've been a great idea. But, somehow it just clicked. After that fateful day of joining Twitter, social media became an intricate part of my personal and professional life. Facebook played a big role in my connecting with a new community after our family moved to a new state. Then, Twitter bridged a professional gap and became a place where thought leadership and business connections were to be had.

In a sense, it was a catalyst of our transformation as a bank because of social media's very nature. Transparent, quick to respond, and very sociable, our bank needed all of these qualities to become who it is today. From a time when things were discussed behind closed doors to being completely open, honest and humble about our situation, our employees have stuck through with us and now are some of the bank's biggest advocates. And you need that to make it through.

Everything from our "Gangnam Style" music video to our CBE cash mobs, it's truly amazing to see our team come together after a tough time and just have fun with each other. We're not afraid to share selfies, tag each other in posts, and be silly. Our bank is a family, and we want that reflected in our social media presence.

After doing several successful cash mobs at our local Edmond businesses, we realized there was a need for something bigger to take place. While watching the successes of Bank of Ann Arbor's Sonic Lunch series and seeing Oklahoma City Midtown's revival with H&8th Night Market, it was time to stake our claim and make Edmond a place where people want to hang out. Many cool businesses were popping up in downtown Edmond including Café Evoke and The Patriarch. Each with its own unique flair that adds to the downtown corridor.

When walking into Evoke, our neighborhood coffee shop, you can't help but feel hip. The clean interiors, the chalkboard menu of changing brews and the cool baristas just make it an environment where people just want to hang. The Patriarch is one place where there's no wifi, TVs, or electronics. Rotating food trucks come to share their food with guests, but the Patriarch itself carries only alcohol and carries more than 30 local craft beers on tap at any given moment. We wanted the OKC metro area to check out these cool places in Edmond, but we needed a reason to bring them here.

Enter in Heard on Hurd. With a little more than 50 employees, our little bank has brought in more than 100,000 people to downtown Edmond with a total local economic impact of $2.6 million in just 8 months to what is just a community bank's customer appreciation party. Heard on Hurd is a monthly street festival hosted and run by the bank and takes place from March through October on the third Saturday of the month.

We invite three bands, often with local ties, to come and perform while attendees can nosh on local food and shop at pop-up shops from nearly 60 hand-picked, eclectic vendors. It was just the right mix of activity to get locals out on a Saturday night and to bring OKC metro people to Edmond. Heard on Hurd has struck a chord, and has been rocking out as it progresses.

Because of the event, we've been talking local banking and why we're doing it to many local and national media outlets in print, TV, and radio. Heard on Hurd is essentially the culmination of why local banking is important. You don't expect a national or regional bank to pull off something this big for a very specific downtown area. As a banker and a community member of Edmond, it's part of my responsibility and dream to make Edmond somewhere special. It helps the community, it helps the small businesses here, it makes it that much of a better place to live and, of course, it helps the local banking community thrive.

Heard on Hurd was a win–win all around. Our employees find it a rewarding experience and our community continues to rally behind the event. It also gave us a conversation starter on why local is important whether it's eating, dining, shopping, or banking.

It's the best of times, even though some think it's the worst of times. Banking has a long way to go: We have to become more relevant to consumers, more in tune with the latest technology, more up on the latest ways to communicate, whether that's Facebook or Periscope or holographic videos in the social media future.

As the president and CEO of a small community bank in Edmond, Oklahoma, my focus on the future has never been sharper, our vision has never been bigger and our passion for community and our customers has never been more enhanced. It's time to tackle these challenges head on. Community banks, let's bring it.

Hal Coxon

Years ago, the halls of Kasasa were echoing with rumors of a credit union that successfully built a high-performing centralized sales methodology, and in the process revamped its multi-channel infrastructure to deliver a seamless experience across the digital, phone and in-branch channels.. Hal Coxon was the man leading that charge. I've asked him to capture his best-practices. Here you have it, from a person who actually did it.

> Hal Coxon is an award-winning change agent who worked inside the credit union movement for 16 years. He is currently the president of Northern Illinois Consulting (NIC), a public relations and marketing firm.

The Case for Centralization. In a typical financial institution (FI) retail environment, Members (new and current) open their accounts in one of three ways: Online via the Internet, over the phone via a call center, or by coming into a branch. The concept of centralized sales was born from the desire to improve the overall Member (customer) experience when opening new accounts in-branch.

The primary case for centralization is quite simple: to create consistency, standards, and results for the in-branch experience. On the one hand, those factors are usually built into the new account opening process for Online and over the phone, as these accounts are opened by single workgroups, thus allowing organizations to manage to a set of standards and metrics.

On the other hand, in-branch account opening personnel are by definition spread across different facilities and supervised (if not managed) by different branch managers or supervisors. The results are an uneven experience for the members and inconsistent expectations for the employees.

Two added benefits of converting to a centralized model are operating efficiency and scale. Realizing improved operating efficiency is a long-term play, something that will be achieved over time, and more easily for FIs on a strong growth path. Once implemented, it is also much easier to scale the business using the centralized model; that, of course, is when the real cost savings can be expected.

Approach. There are several steps required in order to assure a smooth transition to a centralized sales model. First, it requires buy-in from the C-suite, as the impact of this change touches operations, Member relations, lending, credit office, human resources, technology and whichever additional department handles retail delivery. Clearly, there are many different stakeholders involved, each of whom may have a distinctly different agenda for why they support or oppose a centralized model.

Once buy-in is achieved, the next step in the process is to create the expectations for the Member experience. Challenges include how to construct the centralized remote "virtual session:" voice only, voice and data, or voice, video, and data. The selection made at this step will also impact how documents are exchanged, as well as compliance considerations.

Support from the Technology Department is an absolute must, of course, as a successful conversion to a centralized model requires absolute buy-in from the ultimate stakeholders: the FI's Members/customers. To a large degree, their buy-in will be determined by the functionality and ease of use … and that means technology working fluently, correctly, and intuitively.

The third step is to map the new account opening workflow, which will most likely result in creating new processes. This is where the convergence of compliance, document exchange, cash handling, and the member experience will require creative thinking, along with a willingness to accept change: This will not be "business as usual." This step also requires contemplating how to handle exceptions to the centralized model; for example, exceptions may arise from members resistant to change and technology, or the limitations of the types of accounts the FI can open digitally. Identifying these potential exceptions—and how to handle them—is perhaps the most important step required to assure a successful conversion to a centralized model.

Next up, it's time to identify, recruit, and train the centralized team, starting with managers and supervisors, then the new accounts representatives. It's important to note that different skills will be required for employees working in a centralized environment; therefore, it is a given that not everyone currently working in account opening positions (and/or supervisors of these employees) will meet the requirements of the new positions.

Compensation will also be a key element in recruiting the right people to join the centralized team. While the strength of the existing sales culture at the FI will influence how the compensation model is created, a variable-based compensation model that motivates productivity and relationship development is strongly recommended.

Another important consideration will be where to physically locate the centralized team. The good news is, the FI will no longer be bound by the limitations of any specific branch location. This advantage is offset by the fact that world-class connectivity will be a "must"—and access to that connectivity is crucial to creating a seamless experience for the member/customer.

Implementation. Once all of the above steps have been put into place, it's important to choose the implementation plan. While there are endless choices for the best model, the three most logical are the following:

- Convert one branch initially, then evaluate, course correct, and identify the timeline for converting the remaining branches.
- Create a conversion timeline that folds one branch at a time, with the timeline for branch #2 determined after all the "bugs" are worked out of the initial conversion, then subsequent branch conversions folded in as practical on a go-forward basis. This is essentially the same model as the first option, with one huge caveat: FIs with a large number of locations will logically take a much longer timeframe to complete the conversion across the enterprise.
- Create the plan, test it until you are satisfied that all the "bugs" are out, then convert all of the branch locations at one time.

Although a strong case can be made for (and against) each of these three models, some considerations in making the decision include the number of different branch locations; FI's comfort with technology;

the FI's existing sales culture; and, the organizational comfort with change—just to name a few.

Human Resources Considerations. There are several human resources considerations that go beyond recruiting and training the new centralized sales team. For example, it is highly unlikely that every employee currently in a front-line position will be appropriate for a position in the centralized environment.

There are many reasons why these employees will not fit into the parallel roles in the new model. They may not be comfortable communicating via video and electronic document exchange; they may lack the necessary sales skills that are necessary for success in the centralized world; and, they may simply be unwilling to adapt to change, and so on.

The FI needs a forward-thinking transition plan for these employees as part of the conversion process, as employee buy-in as a key ingredient to the formula for success. While *transition* could be interpreted as "termination," that approach has serious negative connotations, is risky at best, and would be the least desirable approach. Here are some other options for consideration:

- Recruit impacted employees to other areas of the FI that match their skills and experience.
- Consider these employees for new roles that may result from the transition.

The first option can also be a bit tricky. First, it's important from a morale standpoint for any reassigned employees to be in a position of relatively equal (or perhaps even greater) value to the FI; otherwise, you risk the appearance of a "demotion." Second, it is important to avoid creating artificial "positions" just for the sake of saving an employee. In short, any reassignment should represent value to both the employee and the FI.

In contrast, the second option listed above looks at new roles; hence, it should create a positive impact on morale because the new model might create new opportunities for existing employees. Although these new roles would differ from one FI to another based on how the model is created, a few logical examples would be sales processor; sales assistant; new accounts specialist; and, concierge.

The sales processor and sales assistant positions are self-explanatory; here are working definitions for the new accounts specialist and concierge. The concierge would be a "greeter on steroids," someone whose primary role would be to help a member (customer) coming into a branch get comfortable with how the new model works—clearly a vital cog in the success of the model and the acceptance by customers. The sales specialist might be available in the branch to handle any accounts that may not be supported for remote account opening based on limitations, if any, of the core processor, as well as being available to handle that rare person who "refuses" to open an account in the new environment.

Another significant HR consideration would be the impact on the roles of employees remaining in the branch. For example, if a branch manager currently oversees new accounts representatives, that duty will no longer be applicable in the centralized environment. If the FI adopts the new accounts specialist and concierge positions, how will these positions be "graded" relative to other positions? No matter what, roles in the branches will be different!

The bottom line: There will be many human resources considerations that will arise as a result of a transition from a branch-centric to a centralized model. The good news is, there is an equal number of possible ways to resolve these considerations in a positive fashion. The culture of the FI will ultimately decide which solutions are adopted.

Success Metrics and Operating Efficiency. At the end of the day, it will be important for the FI to have a plan for measuring the success of the transition to the centralized model. How success is measured will depend largely on what is most important to each bank or credit union. Here are some areas to consider:

- Improved consistency of the member/customer experience
- Creating more consistent expectations for staff performance
- Faster and more consistent lending decisions
- Increased product and service penetration for new members/customers
- Member/customer satisfaction scores
- Impact on total headcount
- Whatever else is most important to the FI

It is also important for FIs making this transition to understand that this is a long-term play. As with any change, there are likely to be higher costs during the transition phase, resulting primarily from a need to avoid disrupting the existing member/customer experience during that period. There may also be compensation changes for employees with redefined roles in the branch, especially if there is a significant reduction in responsibilities.

Additionally, if the FI adopts a variable-based compensation plan for salespeople in the centralized environment, it will be important to have metrics established to assure the new compensation is equitable for everyone involved. After all, highly successful sales personnel in a variable-based compensation model may—and *should*—begin to earn more than many managers. The FI needs to be prepared for this eventuality, or it faces two potential problems: jealousy of the comp opportunities of sales people; and the risk of creating an environment that discourages (or even punishes) the income opportunities for its best producers.

Penny Crosman

Over the past several years, if you've read an article about financial technology and banking (and it wasn't in The Financial Brand), odds are, Penny had a hand in developing or writing it—making her first suggestion for community financial institution leaders all the more poignant.

@PennyCrosman
Penny Crosman is editor at large at *American Banker*. Prior to taking this role in January 2016, she was editor in chief of *Bank Technology News* and Technology Editor of *American Banker*. She has had senior editorial roles at *Bank Systems & Technology, Wall Street & Technology, Intelligent Enterprise,* and *Network Magazine,* among other titles

---

1. *Be wary of advice, especially coming from journalists.* There are hundreds, if not thousands, of writers, pundits, consultants, and others who gleefully and repeatedly say banking is doomed, the branch is dead, fintechs are the future, run for your life. They get applauded on Twitter and LinkedIn. They should all be viewed with deep suspicion.

2. *Stick to your core mission.* One day several years ago, I was riding in a car down a long country road with the CEO of a small Wisconsin bank. All around us was a bleak, barren winter landscape, nothing but snow-covered dirt for miles. The kindly banker looked around at the place he loved and said, "This is as close to heaven as you're going to get." I secretly thought to myself, "I hope not," but I admired his deep appreciation for his part of the country. Then we visited some of his customers—a local cheese maker, a veneer company, a farmer. He was obviously friends with these people and wanted their businesses to succeed. It came out that he had cut them a break here and there when they fell on hard times.

   This is why community institutions are important and need to survive. That understanding of the people with whom you do business, their character, their needs, their troubles, gives you the ability to make sound lending decisions and provide off-the-books help. Venmo, Apple, and the large banks can't compete on this front.

3. *Let your mobile apps shine.* One of the neat things about mobile banking apps is that you get tons of direct feedback from users on the Apple App Store and Google Play. It always amazes me that FIs will allow hundreds of bad reviews and complaints to sit out there in the open, and appear to not address them with fixes and updates. When apps don't work properly or lack basic features everyone else has, customers are not going to stick around. They don't have the patience. This is probably blindingly obvious, but it seemed worth mentioning.

4. *Upgrade your mortgage technology.* Some of the oldest and most outdated technology in banking is on the mortgage side. Yet for many people, the loan they use to buy their home is the most important financial transaction they will make in their life. These customers are going to want a quick answer and an intuitive experience, like the ones Quicken Loans (which recently came out with an "eight-minute" online loan) and Google are building.

5. *Partner with interesting fintech and alternative lending companies.* Everybody is saying this these days, but it's true. Some of the most innovative community institutions are those that have hooked up with startups. Radius Bank in Boston works with LevelUp, a mobile payments provider, SmarterBucks, which has a debit card

rewards program for paying down college debt, and Aspiration, an online investing startup. Lincoln Savings Bank in Waterloo, Iowa, works with savings startup Qapital. CBW Bank in Kansas is allied with Simple, Moven, and Ripple Labs (for cross-border payments). Partnerships mean you don't have to do all the work and shoulder all the expense yourself.

6. *Be yourselves and continue to be good.* Community bankers are known for being friends to their customers, giving them sound advice even if it's counter to the institution's goals, being patient through hard times and generously contributing to and helping their communities. All of this will come back to you in some way. Even if it doesn't, it's still a good way to be.

Matt Davis

If you work at a credit union, odds are you know, and have probably hugged, Matt Davis. If you run a community bank, it would serve you well to go hear Matt speak or ping him on Twitter. Not everything he says will resonate with you, but it will resonate with the audience you want.

@CUWarrior
Matt is a leading thinker, writer, and doer in the credit union movement. Beyond founding gameFI, 6thStory, CUWater Cooler.com, and CoopWaterCooler.com, he is widely known for inspiring credit union leaders to leverage innovation, cooperation, and technology to further the impact of member-owned financial cooperatives.

Relevance is in the eye of its beholder. What is relevant to a steelworker in Bethlehem, Pennsylvania, starkly contrasts with what is relevant to a schoolteacher in El Paso, Texas, or a high-powered real estate executive in New York City. These examples diverge in their economic status, schedules, expertise, and often in their personal aspirations. Likewise, their needs are different. They define convenience differently. What keeps the real estate executive up at night may not matter at all to a schoolteacher, and vice versa. As such, they have very different reasons why they need a financial institution in the first place.

Many financial services firms have rendered themselves irrelevant because they have forgotten a key fact: financial institutions are in a human-centered problem-solving business. At the core of problem-solving is the relentless pursuit of understanding—of who it is the financial institution is trying to serve, and the problems (big and small) that those humans face every day. Empathy for the schoolteacher in El Paso cannot be gained from a spreadsheet. It is earned through intimate observation, discussion, and experience.

In the early days of credit unions and community banks this was not such a problem. A credit union may have had its only "branch" in its single sponsor's breakroom. The branch manager was often a volunteer or an employee of the sponsor. The board consisted entirely of the sponsor's employees or retirees. Empathy didn't take much effort, because there was no difference between those being served, and those providing the service. Community institutions didn't have to guess what their community needed, because they lived there, too. Decisions were made locally by those who knew their customers the best.

Before we get nostalgic for that approach, let it be said that modern technology has allowed financial institutions to provide truly amazing products and services at prices absolutely unimaginable in the old model. Scale has allowed financial institutions to be more efficient than ever and roll out technological and service innovations that have undoubtedly improved consumers' ability to borrow, spend, and understand their money. Few would give back ATMs, mobile banking, debit cards, or mobile deposit capture to relive the days of George Bailey and Bedford Falls.

But as financial institutions have grown, so too has the distance (geographic and otherwise) between their decisions and the people that they serve. That scale has replaced small, but precise target audiences with much larger population archetypes. While this is a natural progression, it forces executives to make decisions that serve the middle of the bell curve. The edges get ignored as outliers—simply too small to make a difference.

The problem is that financial institutions have all done the same thing. They are fighting in the bloodiest of waters for the exact same fish. Their products are the same. Their branches look the same. Their websites, brochures, and employees look the same. To Joe Consumer, they are the same.

This is at the heart of financial institutions' relevancy problem. Banks and credit unions have sacrificed problem-solving precision for problem-solving directionality. If you are relevant to everyone, you are likely relevant to no one.

Financial institutions for way too long have assumed that relevance can be gained by keeping up with the Jones—that somehow offering the same products and services as market leaders will somehow put them on equal footing. Executives take a wait-and-see approach to product and service innovation/adoption, assuming that they are mitigating risk in doing so. In many ways this approach simply exacerbates the relevance problem. While Will Ferrell's character in *Talledega Nights* is only mostly right when he says, "If you ain't first, you're last," his point is well made. Financial institutions have been tragically slow to adopt new technology, products, services, and business models.

So what can financial institutions do to become relevant again? There are four primary things that can be done:

1. *Win the insights battle.* Big data has been a buzzword for way too long. Still, financial institutions haven't optimized its potential. Even worse, they have misused it. Fancy graphs, charts, or predictive analytics that guess a customer's "next best product" only scratch the surface of what financial institutions can do with the petabytes of data in their collective possessions. Behavioral data should be as aggressively pursued as financial data. Portfolio performance matters, no doubt, but it only tells part of the story. He with the most insights wins. The financial institutions that can find patterns in quantitative and qualitative data that can predict when financial struggles will occur and intervene in a respectful, yet timely, manner are the ones that will regain relevance. The complexity of modern life does not exempt consumers from personal financial responsibility, but it does heighten financial institutions' ability to shepherd them through their financial lives. Timely intervention and empathy are as important to relevance as pricing, location, and product assortment.
2. *Become hyper-local.* "Buy local" is not just a phase. Consumers are increasingly preferring to do business locally with people who are empowered to make local decisions. For the small credit union or community bank, this is good news. But for the large regional,

national, or mega bank, all is not lost. The Desjardins Group model in Quebec could serve as a possible model that can offer the scale necessary to efficiently provide high quality financial services, while providing customers with local decision making. Desjardins is a federation of nearly 400 credit unions and $230 billion, serving nearly 6 million members. Most closely described as franchises, each credit union has its own board, prepares its own financial statements, and operates as an autonomous legal entity.

While this may be a difficult or impossible model for many institutions to implement, the general concept is not. A homemaker in Winston-Salem, North Carolina, wants to know he can look his decision maker in the eye, not wait for the New York office to approve his loan. Financial institutions that can provide local community involvement, governance, and understanding will be the ones that fend off irrelevancy.

3. *Breed instead of buy.* The regulatory environment doesn't necessarily encourage innovation, but financial institutions' general wait-and-see approach to innovation and new product/service adoption is costing precious time and money. Venture capital has fueled a fintech revolution—one that financial institutions themselves should have been leading. Nearly $3 billion was raised by fintech startups in 2014 alone, just one of many signs that innovators all over the globe see fundamental disruption of financial services as an inevitability. It is also a sign that financial services firms have rested on their laurels. Instead of keeping pace with consumers' evolving needs with experimentation and innovation, the banking industry hoped its legacy infrastructure and high barrier to entry can sufficiently stave off external competition. It hasn't worked.

The startup world has aggressively nibbled at the edges of relationships and revenue streams that financial institutions have taken for granted. Seemingly every meaningful payments, process, service, and product innovation related to financial services in the past decade has occurred outside FIs' collective walls. Instead of controlling their own destinies, financial institutions have sat back and waited for disruption to happen. The hope, it seems, is to let the good ideas die risk-free and gobble up the great ideas once they have garnered sufficient traction. In doing so, the banking industry simply overpays for innovation that should have been created internally and virtually guarantees fundamental disruption.

4. *Work together.* The open sharing of ideas is far from a hallmark of the banking industry. As financial institutions have grown, they have no doubt experienced even greater pressure to keep strategies, tactics, and ideas as secretive as possible. The assumption is that banking is a zero sum game—a win for any bank is a loss to every other financial institution. If the market is truly winner take all, this approach may make sense. However, the current regulatory environment and the onslaught of nonbank competition in the industry suggests that perhaps financial institutions are better together. Google, Apple, Wal-Mart, Bitcoin, CFPB, and Lending Club are much bigger threats to banks' livelihood than traditional financial institutions. Finding ways to collaborate on product development, back office efficiency, regulatory influence, technological investment, and risk mitigation may be the difference between survival and a slow death march.

Relevance is far too subjective for a one-size-fits-all approach. By seeking empathy, becoming hyperlocal, taking innovation seriously, and collaborating, financial institutions at least have a chance.

Julie Esser

Another credit union leader and great hugger (come on, bankers, step up your hugging game!), Julie Esser is a quiet and calculating thinker who's not afraid to ask the tough questions of fintech providers.

@JulieJEsser

Julie Esser is vice president of alliance development for CUNA Strategic Services, an affiliate of the Credit Union National Association (CUNA). As a member of CUNA Strategic Services' senior management team, Julie is responsible for directing the entire development process from conception to implementation of new strategic alliance relationships.

I've been very blessed to serve in the credit union industry for more than 30 years. I've seen a lot of change—both positive and negative—over the course of my career. If I were a C-level credit union executive today, I'm sure a number of things would keep me up at night in regard to planning for the future. However, I would focus my strategic planning around three particularly impactful areas: consolidation, branding, and technology.

Consolidation. When I first started working in the credit union industry, there were more than 10,000 credit unions in the United States. Now there are just over 6,000. According to a recent Filene Research Institute study, credit unions will continue to decline by 150 to 250 institutions per year through 2025. You'll notice remarkably similar contraction patterns among banks. Conversely, the credit union movement on the whole is experiencing significant growth in memberships and total assets. Generally, economies of scale drive the need for consolidation; think about all the redundancy in human and financial resources associated with building and maintaining a credit union's back-office operations.

Branding. The importance of branding, especially in payments, and the need to attract younger members should cause concern for credit unions. On the payments side, we're seeing the financial institution's brand taking a back seat to consumer-facing product brands. As a C-level credit union executive, I would worry about maintaining relevancy. Furthermore, credit unions should be thinking hard about who their members are today—and who they will be in the future, since the average age of a credit union member is 47.

Technology. The credit union industry relies heavily on outsourcing and is well-positioned to adapt to new technologies and improve members' financial lives. However, as consumers' appetites for convenient services continue to grow, credit unions of all sizes will be challenged to make the necessary investments to satisfy their younger members.

I've truly learned what it means to be part of a cooperative and to understand that principles such as "people helping people" and "not for

profit, not for charity, but for service" mean more than simply offering better rates and lower/fewer fees. I'm very thankful to be part of a
remarkable industry.

John Fishback

*John Fishback is a battle-scarred community banker, as well as a student of the
industry. If you get a chance to corner John about banking—do it. Even you
credit union folk could stand to learn a thing or two from this fellow.*

> **@JTF_CEB**
> John Fishback works in CEB's Financial Services Practice,
> where he is part of the Commercial Banking and Retail
> Banking Leadership Council research teams. John sits on the
> boards of Fishback Financial Corporation, a community bank
> holding company, and of First Bank & Trust of Brookings,
> South Dakota.

I have never underwritten a loan. Though I started my career as a
teller, and now both work as a management consultant to FIs and sit
on the board of a community bank, I do not have first-hand knowledge
of how it feels to apply the disciplines of underwriting to a client or
customer. But I have been thinking about underwriting a lot, because
I think there are at least three things having to do with underwriting that
might prove helpful to bankers navigating a period of significant change.

Reconsider "Sales Culture." The reason we need an underwriting
process at all is that you need the money back. What institutions do is
unique—lending, because it includes an urgent need to understand the
client deeply, is not selling.

There's been a notion out there for at least a decade that what FIs
need to do is to build a sales culture. And certainly, there are changes
afoot that mean that any institution that is just opening its branch doors
in the morning and waiting for customers to come in and buy their products will find itself short on revenue. But adopting a pure sales approach
isn't likely to work for FIs.

Even leaving aside the risks of selling loans rather than lending money, my colleagues at CEB have shown that what drives retail banking customers' loyalty is help from their FI in staying on track toward their goals. Commercial banking customers are more likely to do business with bankers that help them solve business problems, rather than just advocate for their deals within the institution (indeed, some of my colleagues have shown in *The Challenger Sale* that teaching clients something, rather than matching products to their needs, is the most effective approach to sales in all industries).[4]

And we shouldn't lose sight of the fact that the Fintech startups increasingly taking share from FIs position themselves as helping to solve customer problems, not as product sales machines.

Appreciate the Value You Create. Because underwriting is the mechanism for building that client understanding, it is not only valuable to institutions, it is valuable to customers as well. One of the bankers I work with recently said to me, "Our job is really just to understand the world" and then to try to understand what is likely to happen given a variety of scenarios.

In 2012, *American Banker*'s summer reading list included a great old book, *Practical Bank Credit*, and reading it provided a wonderful reminder that the customer's financials are only part of the story.[5] Underwriting effectively requires understanding the customer's life or the client's business—what is their strategy? What are their assumptions? What is true about the industry? How effective is management?

For businesses, a rigorous testing of management and strategy can be incredibly valuable—and that is precisely what underwriting is. For individuals, a clear-eyed assessment of their financial position can be a wakeup call, or a confirmation of the right path. What bankers do is valuable.

We should be clear, though, that the activity of understanding the business and presenting the FI's assessment, not the mechanism or person that completes that work, that makes underwriting valuable to customers. Underwriting needn't be done by a committee or a person to be valuable. Their full assessment of a business needn't be delivered face to face to provide valuable insight, but there can be no question that underwriting deepens a client's understanding of themselves.

Banker, Underwrite Thyself. So underwriting is what sets what bankers do apart from selling, and that same deep understanding of customers creates value not just for the FI, but for the customers the bankers work hard to understand. But too many bankers fail to apply the same discipline to their own institutions. Reporting and reviews focus on financial metrics and performance. Far too much strategic planning bears greater resemblance to budgeting (take last year's revenue and add a percentage) than to true strategy. But bankers—exactly because they are bankers—have the tools needed to evaluate:

- *Our purpose*—Whom was our institution formed to serve? Is that still whom we primarily serve? Is serving that set of clients how we make our money? Do the goals that we started with still drive our investments?
- *Our performance*—Do we understand our own performance within the framework for success we have set up? Do we set goals that have both a "what" (10 percent loan growth) and a "how" (by increasing penetration of the local buggy whip sector)? Do we have a view on what kinds of things our team members should be doing individually to produce the right outcomes as a group, and have we put in place a system that provides accountability and support on those activities while allowing maximum autonomy for employees?
- *Our customers*—Do we understand our customers' current needs and preferences and how those are changing? Are we familiar with broad trends in product and channel usage outside of our footprint, and have we considered what our response to those trends should be?
- *Our people*—Do we understand our local labor markets and pool of talent, and do we have a set of routines and plans in place to provide challenging and rewarding work and development experiences for all levels of employee and job seeker?
- *Our industry*—Do we understand the broad industry context in which we are operating? How are national and even international banks changing regulator and customer expectations? Are the businesses that are currently profitable for our institution subject to margin pressure from either other FIs or from nonbanks? Do we understand and have a plan for the industrywide changes driven by technology and regulation?

Credit unions and community banks—like all banks—are operating in a moment of significant change. But this moment is unique in that the challenges it offers do not necessarily get easier with scale. Community institutions able to develop an understanding of their competitive position and relative strengths should be able to use those strengths to their advantage. Doing so will require a deep look inward to understand their current position and future prospects. The good news is, that is what bankers are uniquely qualified to do.

Andy Greenawalt

Most discussions with Andy Greenawalt end with one feeling like a child learning how to ride a bike. To give you an idea of the scale of Andy's foresight, he created security in the cloud a decade before anyone stored anything there, and he created regtech nearly a decade before it had a name. As a community banker, odds are that if Andy's doing it, you'll want to do it, too.

@AndyGreenawalt

A Connecticut native, Andy is a Fintech serial entrepreneur, sometimes writer and philosopher. Currently the Chairman of Continuity, accomplishments include the invention of Security-in-the-Cloud with Perimeter eSecurity, Inc., 500 growth with two companies, and he currently serves on the board of the Yale Entrepreneurial Institute.

Regtech, It's Time to Update the Last Pre-Modern Area in Banking. On a typical week, the first regulatory change, with about 50 pages of dense legal information, will arrive by mid-morning on Monday. This item will need to be read and analyzed to understand if it applies to your organization and what changes are really in there.

By the time you've digested the information and made all applicable changes to various policies and procedures and got your staff up to speed, you will have invested a somewhere between 2 to 200 hours to get that update in place. With the typical issuance taking 40 hours, you'll go into the coming week with a backlog of four since a typical week will see five issuances. This adds up to over 250 changes per year going back decades.

This current reality is what led some in the regulatory community to lay out the choices of, "grow, merge or die." If you're a community banker it's obvious that you'd like a few other options.

In looking at the choices between "grow, merge or die," it turns out that there is a fourth choice that holds material promise—evolve. The reasoning behind the dire alternative is the belief that innovation is over, and the only means of progress is the size of your financial institution. So while these alternatives would hold IF innovation wasn't possible, it is.

The compliance industry, and profession that supports financial institutions in these regards, exists in a premodern state. In the world of compliance, it's as if the information age never got here. The delivery of "help" is still focused on consulting hours, documents, or other deliverables from the premodern period. While nobody set out to do this on purpose, a series of anti-innovation reflexes took root and have held the industry back from the massive gains technology affords. It is this intersection of need from surging regulations with antiquated solutions that is giving birth to a new category within fintech coined as regtech, or regulatory technology.

Regtech looks at the intersection between the operations of businesses in the financial services industry, and the wide array of regulatory requirements on them. Regtech looks to bring technology solutions to areas that still operate in a premodern state. In the premodern world, the regulatory domain was left ill-defined.

Without the information infrastructure of data dictionaries to lock in the various data elements and labels, and taxonomies to associate them in logical relationships with one another, human effort has to fill all of the many cracks. For regtech to really become something, it needs to bring standards to this murky refuge of nineteenth-century thinking. So the question is how to make sense of it.

For the community financial industry to make sense of how this would help, we need to understand where various solutions might land. As a way of framing the issue, it is helpful to understand that there are only six key objectives of a compliance management system to satisfy the expectations of examiners. In meeting these six objectives in a well-articulated manner, an organization demonstrates that it understands the issue, has installed the infrastructure, and routinely meets its regulatory obligations.

Although these objectives aren't specifically framed by regtech, they serve to define the broader objectives that can narrow the domain into more manageable areas for technology solutions. Each of the objectives has data needs, organizational dynamics, constituents, and more, that serve to paint a picture of what types of regtech solutions could assist with them.

The six objectives of a compliance management system are:

1. *Know*—The first objective is to know which regulations apply to you. While easy to say, with monthly changes in products, and daily changes in regulations, keeping current with an organization's state of understanding is, as we say in engineering, nontrivial.
   - *Regtech opportunity*: Regulatory taxonomy

2. *Adapt*—Given the rate of 200 to 300 regulatory changes per year, just at the federal level, there is a very pressing objective for banking organizations to be able to economically adapt to the new or modified requirements.
   - *Regtech opportunity*: Regulatory change management

3. *Delegate*—With the vast array of requirements, determining where they should be met operationally is another material challenge and for that reason meeting the objective of the delegation of the work and/or responsibilities is critical to meeting requirements.
   - *Regtech opportunity*: Mapping of organizational roles to regulatory requirements

4. *Do*—This objective is where the rubber meets the road with the execution of regulatory requirements throughout a banking operation. Thought of broadly they are either operational or transactional in nature.
   - *Regtech opportunity*: Regulatory awareness workflow technology and transaction assistance.

5. *Verify*—With both operational, technical, and transactional activities, in a regulated environment we must trust, but verify. Verification falls into the three areas of quality check around transaction preparation, ongoing process monitoring, and in-depth system audit.
   - *Regtech opportunity*: Data analytics, benchmarking, real time thresholding

6. *Improve*—As any defects are observed in the large and complex infrastructure that financial institutions operate, they must marshal resources to improve that area in a timely and transparent way. Defects can be transactional, a client-related issue, or structural with a particular functional area within the organization.

• *Regtech opportunity*: Regulatory awareness issue tracking system

The six objectives taken together represent the full range of objectives an organization needs to meet for an examiner to be comfortable that everything is well in hand. Now given the traditional nature of community banking, these ideas around regtech likely seem a bit foreign and look like something from science fiction, however, it's in technology that a bright future lies. Given the dynamics in the broader fintech market, the time to move toward that future is now.

The fintech market, with Internet only banks, payments, lending and advisory innovators, exists to disintermediate traditional banking models. In 2014, it saw a tripling of investment in the United States with almost $10 billion invested across 500 firms.

While as a consumer with smartphone in hand, it is a thrilling time as we see innovation offering us options that were unthinkable just a few short years ago, however, it is very unsettling for our industry. Fintech competitors are forcing a rethink of the operating models of banking by investing billions in innovation, and redefining consumers' expectations upward every day.

These dynamics both illuminate new paths of innovation as well as force our industry to adopt the best innovations if we are to remain competitive and be capable of generating margin.

In the emerging regtech sector, we are seeing the best of technology and innovation brought to this age-old problem to dramatically change the economics of compliance. In doing this, it is attacking the ballast that is weighing the traditional model down—the operational costs.

Simply put, the operating model for most organizations is too costly to remain competitive into the future as is seen clearly in the efficiency ratio trends over the last 20 years.

With regtech, there appears to be the sector breakthrough that allows for a bulk shrinking of the cost and complexity of managing regulatory requirements, and therefore the complexity of running a financial institution. This could very well be the sustainable innovation emerging now that will change our industry for decades to come.

Matt Harris

Matt Harris is one of the foremost experts on fintech, startups, and the sobering reality of investing. As an outspoken thinker, it's not unusual to find Matt poking and prodding entire genres of fintech—cutting through the hype to find the return.

> **@MattCHarris**
> Matt Harris is a venture investor at Bain Capital, where he focuses on financial services and fintech companies.

Fintech as Force Multiplier. Fintech is entering a new phase, one that creates the opportunity for community financial institutions to compete and win.

Fintech, of course, is shorthand for technology-driven innovation in financial services; it historically referred to startups and other entrepreneurial firms, rather than to incumbent financial institutions.

The first generation of fintech startups very much set themselves up in opposition to the existing FIs, and appealed to customers based on the argument that "banks suck." What choice did the institutions have but to react? Thus began fintech 2.0, which has been characterized by a sense of confidence amongst the FIs that they can compete with these startups, and successfully fend them off or co-opt them. FIs like Capital One started buying fintech firms, and many other banks and broker-dealers started venture capital arms, innovation labs, and other "intrapreneurial" efforts.

Increasingly, we are entering yet a new phase. On one side, the entrepreneurial fintech firms are realizing that reinventing financial services from scratch is harder than it looks, and that partnering with FIs may not only be pragmatic, but necessary.

On the other side, institutions are realizing that, regardless of their whopping technology budgets, building delightful products is not their best thing. As such, and in a delightfully Hegelian way, we are approaching the synthesis of these two phases, one where the best-of-breed fintech firms partner with FIs of all stripes to reach, cross-sell, upsell, and retain their customers.

The single largest beneficiary of this new phenomena will be community financial institutions. These smaller banks and credit unions have had it rough for a while now.

As banking moved from being a local business to a national business, these smaller players faced competition from the behemoths, who could offer better products and use their economics of scale to undercut on price. Community FIs still have strong local brands and relationships, but those advantages can't overcome significant pricing disparities and product deficiencies.

But that can all change now. A community bank or credit union, through partnerships with fintech firms, can now not only match Chase, Citi, BofA, and Wells on price and product, but significantly outmatch them. Fintech effectively neutralizes the scale advantages of the large players and allows smaller financial institutions to offer a full, modern product line that compares favorably to the larger players.

The key is not to wait.

We know that the large banks are inherently sclerotic, due to hyper-regulation and the challenges of their unwieldy size. Community FIs are theoretically nimble, due to their small size—they now have to be actually nimble, as well as decisive. Only the first movers have a chance to win. First, small institutions ignored fintech. Then, they were scared of it. Now, they need to leverage it as a force multiplier.

Pradeep Ittycheria

Few technologists are truly conversant in Direct, White, and Gold Label fintech. Even fewer have the real-world experience of managing those various architectures across millions of consumer accounts, including the security, business intelligence, and various data-driven marketing activities that come along with it. Pradeep is a unique talent indeed, and a guy you want on your side.

@Pradeepi
Pradeep is a technologist and entrepreneur with cross industry experience in software engineering management, product development, strategy, and corporate development. He has been a member of management teams that have turned around companies and created value for investors through successful exits.

Pablo Picasso once said, "Good artists copy, great artists steal." There is no shame in copying something that customers love about the big banks: convenience.

The definition of "good service" has changed. Financial management is no longer about an individualized experience. The shift to digital banking and investment services has meant that the proximity between provider and customer is no longer significant. The need for high-touch, human-powered service is becoming less important for younger customers. Why would the average 25-year-old go into a community institution branch when Samuel Jackson pops up on Pandora telling him how easy it is to bank digitally with Capital One?

The trick is not just merging your local credibility with all the cool technology one can get with the big banks—like a complete digital banking experience with a strong mobile presence. Your institution needs to also market like the big banks. That doesn't mean it needs a multi-million-dollar advertising budget, rather, it needs to market smartly. Use data-driven, digital, one-to-one marketing instead of billboards that look like they are from the local car dealer.

Traditionally, community institutions have not had to innovate because they leveraged their localized footprints and had captive customer bases for their services.

The first community institutions that faced the brunt of the large bank innovations were the banks in big city suburbs. Larger banks are now coming to small town America either as Direct, Internet-only banks or hybrid banks with some branch presence.

At this point, community institutions still have a strategic advantage with lending to local businesses. The traditional high-touch, personalized business models currently work well in business banking and perceived value of service (see Figure 4.3). There is a lot of speculation about branch banking dying, but branches will have a longer runway with commercial banking.

Since community institutions do not have the resources to compete with the large banks, they need to start looking at third-party technology and marketing solutions that reach far beyond the expertise of their core vendors. These are fintech companies that specialize in unique digital banking enhancements, consumer-friendly payment mechanisms, rewards processors, analytics and business intelligence tools, and financial services marketing solution providers.

Figure 4.3 Small Business: Lender Satisfaction Score, 2015

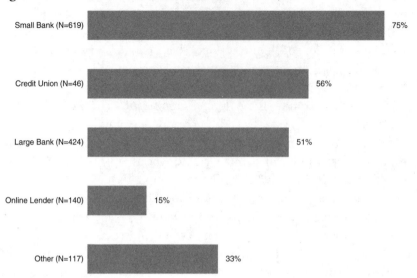

Small Bank (N=619) 75%

Credit Union (N=46) 56%

Large Bank (N=424) 51%

Online Lender (N=140) 15%

Other (N=117) 33%

SOURCE: Federal Reserve Bank
US small business satisfaction of lender, by lender type. Applicants were approved and received financing.

Fintech startups and other nonbank competitors have exploited friction in regulated banking that make it more difficult for customers to obtain what they want. While the big banks can buy some of these upstarts (like in the case of BBVA acquiring Simple), community institutions need to leverage partnerships with companies like Circle or lending platforms like Kabbage and OnDeck. CFOs may be worried about letting some of these systems manage funding operations, but compromises will have to be made between balance sheet management, account acquisition, and retention.

Community institutions have been pretty poor at leveraging their own consumer data such as knowing where their accountholder is getting his/her car loan or that only one person in the household has an account with the institution (see Figure 4.4). Use analytics solutions or have third parties mine your data to gain better insight into consumers. Marketing, now and in the future, will always be data-driven.

Community bankers can remain in a state of denial, waiting to merge or be acquired, or they can take the fight to the big banks by using technology more effectively. NIH (not invented here) is a mantra that works

Figure 4.4 Small Business: Lender Dissatisfaction

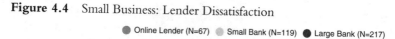

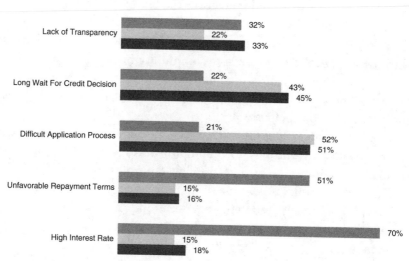

SOURCE: Federal Reserve Bank
The percentage of US small business firms who received financing in 2015 and were dissatisfied with the lender, by type and reason.

well in this case. Partner with technology providers, market like the best consumer product companies, and give yourself a fighting chance.

Alex Jiménez

Regularly named one of fintech's global influencers, Alex has managed digital banking strategies for banks of all sizes and led the Digital Channel Committee for the Consumer Bankers Association. Alex deeply understands the challenges that institutions face in regards to the pace of change and is passionate about helping organizations cross the chasm effectively.

@RAlexJimenez

Alex Jimenez is a digital banking and payments strategist, focused on innovation and fintech. He has over 20 years of experience in financial services, including banking, wealth management, and insurance.

The pace of change seems to have exponentially increased in the digital age. US banks and credit unions have managed change in the past 100 years, but the increased speed over the last few years has shown the cracks in a system based on risk aversion and conservative thinking.

In the next ten years, change will continue to accelerate. To keep up with the pace of change, CEOs at community banks and credit unions will have to approach their organizations differently than they have in the past. They will need to build organizations that thrive on change and are focused on the customer.

For many organizations, such a change requires a major shift in company culture. One way to accomplish this change is to apply *lean principles* throughout the organization in a controlled process. An FI that applies lean principles, sometimes called *kaizen* (as it is known in Japan), becomes a continually improving organization.

Management of such an organization requires managing by facts and speaking with data, particularly data related to the customer and productivity. A focus on good processes that bring about good results becomes paramount. Defining root causes for any problems that arise results in corrections to processes. Teamwork emerges as the preferred way to function when continuous improvement is "everybody's business."

Changing culture demands a combination of both "top-down" and "bottom-up" activities. The top-down involves the CEO and the whole executive suite, as leadership must set out the vision and be supportive for the change to occur. The bottom-up involves informal leaders throughout the organization that can make sure to implement the change.

The top-down approach begins with the CEO. CEOs should honestly examine the organization and determine the level of effort that such a culture change will require. If there are existing efforts to affect a culture of continuous improvement, perhaps those efforts can be leveraged or refocused. Next, the executive leadership should be engaged in the examination. The CEO should be very explicit about the goal, clearly stating why it is required. Hire professionals to train the executive leaders on lean principles and tools. Before training anyone else, the CEO should get buy-in from each of the leaders. They should be tasked with completing small-scale projects using lean with the support of the experts. If any of the executives aren't supportive of the process, the CEO should determine whether those executives belong in the future organization.

At this point, the executive leadership should clearly identify the vision, mission, and organizational metrics for the transformation initiative. Metrics must include employee engagement, overall customer engagement or satisfaction, as well as financial and operational metrics. They should put together a cross-functional planning team that includes the CEO and formal and informal leaders in the organization from various areas and ranks. The planning team should report directly to the CEO, and its main goal will be to oversee the direction of the initiative.

Transition to the "bottom-up" part of the roll out begins with the planning team. The planning team should be trained on lean principles and tools, followed by a discussion on the goals and process for the transformation initiative. Items for discussion and definition include goals and their relationship to customer engagement and satisfaction, barriers to the initiative, and opportunities to leverage existing culture, processes, and systems.

The planning team should also plan a kickoff meeting for a pilot team. The pilot team will consist of a group of informal leaders within the organization that are tasked to apply lean to everyday processes within the organization. The planning team should define the goals of the meeting, the people involved, and how the meeting will unfold.

The pilot team kickoff meeting should be a large-scale event focusing on lean training (first part of the day), and defining a plan to roll it out throughout the organization (second part of the day). The event will begin the "bottom-up" approach. The outside experts will train the participants and coach them after the kickoff. The pilot team participants will leave the kickoff meeting ready to apply lean to their everyday processes.

As results and lessons come in from the pilot team's efforts, they should be shared throughout the organization. Dissemination of these results should be facilitated through a concerted effort that reflects the "bottom-up" approach driving the change. Slowly training more working team leaders should follow, expanding the pilot to eventually include the whole of the organization.

The planning team should plan regular meetings to monitor the change, make adjustments to the process, and celebrate successes. At the executive level, leadership should also track organizational metrics and determine what is working and what is not and help the planning team to make changes.

The CEO should avoid giving special titles to staff trained in lean. Many of the organizations that have had problems with truly transforming a culture that is focused on change, failed by giving people specific roles (change managers, champions, green belts, black belts, scrum masters, kaizen leaders). These roles became the only change agents within the organization. The majority of the organization should become change agents.

CEOs should ensure that customer focused initiatives, such as CRM, business intelligence, voice of the customer, customer complaint tracking, and segmentation are specifically included in the early rollout. As noted previously, lean principles include management with data; projects that have customer data as their central focus become key in the transformation.

Building an organization that thrives in change and is focused on the customer is a difficult proposition. A deliberate approach to engage the executive suite and all the leaders of the organization, formal or informal, must be taken. Training and coaching managers or a given few change agents within an organization is not enough to bring transformational change.

Community banks with less than $10 billion in assets have lost over half of their market share in the past 20 years. If community banks and credit unions want to compete with the larger FIs that have grown their market share, they need to implement different approaches. FIs that continue to focus on what has worked in the past will face increased competition from larger FIs, as well as new fintech entrants, and face extinction.

Further consideration should be given to the rapid speed of change in products and services. As technology continues to affect the pace of change, FI CEOs should also consider borrowing a page from fintech startups. As an add-on to rolling out lean, FIs should consider implementing agile for project teams in areas of technology, product, and service development.

Although lean focuses on the repetitive workings of a service organization, much of the work done by project teams have a complexity and speed that is better served by agile. The agile approach for software development relies on iteration instead of scheduled releases. An iterative approach blends well with activities like FI projects in technology and product development, where changes can be applied regularly.

Applying agile methodology to the overall management of projects will allow FIs to adjust at the speed of new competitors who are building their cultures on top of technology developments based on agile. A similar but much more focused implementation approach to agile could be taken as described above, except limiting these kind of teams.

An organization that strives to continuously learn to improve will thrive in the changing environment. Use of customer data will grow and will drive the direction of the organization. Processes will adjust continually, and not just when problems arise. Product teams will continually redesign products and services. New employees hired will change their roles regularly, and nimbleness will be a desired competency.

Brett King

Just read his bio below. It's safe to say that few people in our industry crank out more work product than Brett King. He's a powerhouse of curiosity, a futurist with a killer accent, and an all-around loveable guy with an eyebrow muscle that is probably insured by Lloyd's of London. Spending time with Brett will inspire you to create the future.

@BrettKing

Brett King is an Amazon best-selling author, a well-known industry commentator, a speaker, the host of the *Breaking Banks* radio show on Voice America (an Internet talk-radio network with over nine million monthly listeners), and the founder of the revolutionary mobile-based banking service Moven. King was voted as *American Banker*'s Innovator of the Year in 2012, and was nominated by *Bank Innovation* as one of the Top 10 "coolest brands in banking."

The future of many financial institutions remains uncertain. In the next 10 years, more changes will take place in respect to the way we bank, the products and services banks provide, along with numerous new entrants who appear extremely bank-like in their positioning, but don't have a charter. The biggest change or impact will simply be in access to basic financial services, and what that will mean for redefining the nature of the bank account.

Within the next 10 years, more than 2 billion unbanked individuals will get access to basic banking for the first time, but this won't be through a bank branch. The increased compliance and KYC workload that banks and their customers have had to endure as a result of 9/11 and increased AML and identity scrutiny have actually worsened the lot of lower- to middle-income individuals in many developed countries.

In the United States, despite one of the highest branch density ratios in the world, financial exclusion has accelerated, and this has forced customers to frequently use alternative financial service providers like prepaid debit cards, check-cashing services, and payday lending. The problem here is not lack of financial education or financial literacy, but simply that entry into the formal banking system has become more difficult. Regulation has not only hampered banks but has simply excluded more and more customers because of the friction and complexity it has brought with it.

This is why the fastest-growing savings product in the United States today remains prepaid debit cards. Why mobile payment initiatives like Venmo, Stripe, and Braintree are outstripping all of the traditional modalities like cards and checks in terms of growth. In fact, checks are disappearing faster than ever, and yet most banks still insist on selling checking accounts to new customers who may never write a check in their life. Developed economies like the United States, however, are not where the real action will be.

The 2 billion people who will get access to their first banking experience in the next 10 years will almost all come through mobile banking, wallet, or mobile money technology. In Bangladesh with bKash, Kenya's M-Pesa, and other initiatives in the Philippines, China, and elsewhere, the growth in simple value stores tied to a phone is like nothing we've ever seen.

The growth in mobile money services is showing the fastest-ever financial inclusion shift in the entire history of banking, and it is happening in such compressed time frames it is simply unbelievable. Historical projections of financial inclusion improvements globally prior to the factoring in of mobile were less then 10 percent of the actual improvements we're seeing due to the use of mobile in money transmission and basic banking.

All of this means that by 2025, more people will be doing their banking on a mobile phone, and more people will have got their first banking experience on a mobile phone, than those who have walked into a bank branch and signed an application form. This has to change the way we think about the nature of a bank account itself.

For traditional bank players, mostly they'll watch this from afar wondering what all the fuss is about, until suddenly they realize that many of their branches haven't opened a new account in months. By the time most smaller banks realize this shift in behavior has taken place, it will already be too late.

While many bankers optimistically trust in their physical presence in the community to support modest growth in their customer base, what they don't realize is that friction is the biggest legacy that banks carry today.

Every fintech company in the world right now, and there are by some estimates more than 40,000 of them, are all working on simplifying the day-to-day banking, payments, and credit experience. This simplification is mostly about just removing friction from long-held processes that have got more and more complex as time goes on.

Technology and experience design are absolutely critical to removing that friction, but it also has some interesting side effects.

Today vendors like Mitek can provide banks with algorithms that use smartphone cameras in a mobile banking app to verify an identity document like a driver's license or passport. Combined with technologies like facial recognition, and data mining and profiling of customers, we now have the incredible situation where a mobile application combined with some fairly simple IDV software is more than 10x better at identifying a fraudulent ID than a human in a branch. Not only that, but the cost of acquisition through a mobile app sign-up is often 1/50 of the cost of a traditional checking account acquisition in-branch.

This all leads to one very inevitable conclusion.

If, in five years, you cannot process most of your retail banking product applications in real-time via a phone, not only will you be absorbing massive risk and fraud, but you'll be seeing radically declining revenue numbers.

The single biggest risk a bank has today is simply the insistence on signing a physical piece of paper to open an account.

Viewed through this lens, the only course of action for bankers today is to immediately and significantly invest in both the technology to acquire customers completely digitally, but also in partnerships with the likes of Apple, Facebook, Google, Uber, AirBnB, PayPal, and the myriad of fintech players now recrafting the user experiences around payments, lending, savings, and investment.

Dan Latimore

Attend most any conference in and around banking or fintech, and you'll find Dan Latimore, furiously taking notes and looking pensive. Even though he has led research groups for and worked in more big names than you can count, Dan remains a student of the industry, especially where focused on the consumer and technology-enabled strategy.

@DanLatimore
Dan Latimore leads the Banking group at Celent, whose analysts study the business implications of new technology. In addition to managing the team's overall topic portfolio and a keen interest in behavioral economics, Dan focuses on the banking ecosystem, digital, and innovation.

Some frameworks verge on being trite because they work so well. The SWOT analysis—focused on strengths, weaknesses, opportunities, and threats—is one of them. I'll show how smaller financial institutions fare in the framework, particularly in the context of the changing digital and technology landscape.

Strengths

1. Great customer relationships
2. Deep local knowledge
3. Long-term view (for mutual firms)

Weaknesses

1. Small scale (budget, technical expertise)
2. Lack of digital data
3. Bifurcated customer base

Opportunities

1. Build on existing customer relationships.
2. Partner to implement digital technologies.
3. Emphasize local knowledge, leverage digital to more fully embrace the ecosystem (e.g., local merchants and charitable causes).

Threats

1. Aging customer base
2. Competitors using technology to offer more compelling products based on digital insights
3. Fintech competitors

The diversity of smaller financial institutions is staggering, so there's no one-size-fits-all approach. Some fundamental advice applies to everyone, however.

- Focus on your customers, both existing and new. Tailor experiences that will serve them well.
- Differentiate yourself from competitors.
- Take advantage of your heritage; build on strengths and add new ones.
- Recognize the very real threats and seek to augment your weaknesses.

Most importantly, realize you can't do it yourself, and partner appropriately.

Jim Marous

This section is full of @FintechMafia members, and Jim Marous is perhaps its Godfather. It's nearly impossible to tame Jim's enthusiasm for things fintech and digital banking, and his article below highlights that passion. You already read The Financial Brand; now go see this guy speak, and subscribe to Digital Banking Report. It will be the best investment you make this year.

@JimMarous
Named as one of the most influential people in banking and a Top 5 Fintech Influencer to Follow, Jim Marous is an internationally recognized financial industry strategist, co-publisher of *The Financial Brand*, and the owner and publisher of the *Digital Banking Report*.

How to Be the Primary Financial Institution in the Future. Now more than ever, banks and credit unions need to step out of our collective comfort zone, digitizing and diversifying in response to the changing consumer. While branches aren't vanishing as quickly as some predicted, the financial services industry can no longer follow branch-centric models. Instead, the "Bank of the Future" represents an omnichannel, client-centric, self-directed digital model that many financial executives admit may be beyond their scope.

Digitization of the entire organization is viewed as the primary enabler of most bank and credit union business objectives. Regardless of whether the focus is increasing revenues or profitability, decreasing costs or meeting regulatory guidelines, digitization is seen as a central investment priority.

Overall, 94 percent of banking executives interviewed say that having a digitized omnichannel customer engagement strategy is important to their future success, with 37 percent admitting that future success of their business is "entirely dependent" on digital customer engagements. Despite the recognition that digital technology initiatives are urgently needed, 88 percent say they see significant challenges in moving toward digitization (see Figure 4.5).

Figure 4.5   Current Banking Priorities

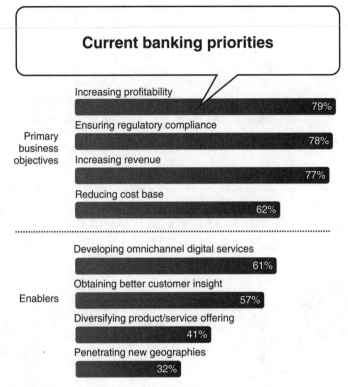

SOURCE: Oracle © November 2015 *The Financial Brand*
Lots of "priorities" for today's banking executive, but only 34% of them feel the future success of their business is entirely dependent upon digital consumer engagement.

The Fintech Challenge. Every publication talks about the transformation of banking and that today's retail banking competitive landscape is far removed from what existed a decade ago. Much of this change has been highlighted by the rising influence of new digital competitors that are impacting all levels of banking.

No longer do retail banks simply vie for customers against other retail banks. Instead, we are witnessing an influx of new, tech-savvy, digital competitors—fintech startups—all eager for a piece of this lucrative financial pie.

The foundation of these changes is caused by changing consumer demographics and expectations. "The world's largest demographic, born after 1980, are now millennials. These customers have grown up in the era of Facebook and Amazon; an era of instant communication, one-click purchases and 24-hour delivery. If a supplier can't provide a service, they don't wait—they find someone else who can," says the report.

More than half believe that both private-label banks, alternative payment providers, and even credit-card providers will be major competitive threats—a greater percentage than are worried about other currently operating banking organizations (see Figure 4.6).

Figure 4.6   Banking Industry's Perceived Threats

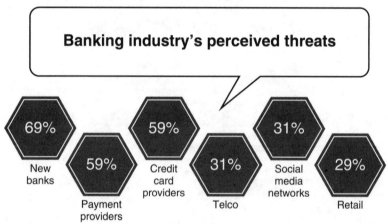

SOURCE: Oracle © November 2015 *The Financial Brand*
Banking executives perceive some obvious threats, but it's quite possible the biggest competitive threat over the next few years is yet unnamed.

The Digital Delivery Gap. The banking industry is not standing still as these changes in expectation and competitors occur. Most organizations recognize that digital customer engagement is the way to respond to the changes in the industry. Key services that are among the most important to adopt include mobile payments and real-time data synchronization, spend analytics, and even digital advisory services.

Despite all being recognized as important by over 80 percent of banks, there appears to be a failure to commit to delivery of these services, with only 24 percent providing real-time synchronization,

19 percent providing location-driven services, and only 30 percent currently providing real-time analytics. In other words, the gap between importance and ability to deliver is more than 60 percent for three of these capabilities. And while the importance of providing mobile payments is viewed as the most important component of digital engagement, the gap in capabilities is still 50 percent.

One of the reasons for the lag in delivery of digital capabilities is the comfort of current relationships. While these relationships served the banking industry well in the past, the financial services industry needs to change our underlying processes to accept these new forms of data, especially in the context of real-time digital processing.

Omnichannel customer engagement should not be a bolt-on product that can simply be added to existing systems to give a little bit more functionality. It needs to take a fresh perspective—wiping the established offline board clean and asking, "How should we be doing this in a digital world?"

Unfortunately, only 23 percent of financial organizations are currently approaching omnichannel customer engagement with a fresh, digital mind-set. Instead, a bolt-on approach is how the majority of retail banks (77 percent) are approaching digital channel engagement, either replicating offline banking capabilities online or adding a small amount of additional functionality (see Figure 4.7). Change is happening, however.

For instance, while 74 percent of banking organizations aren't yet able to facilitate the digital onboarding of customers currently, within the next two years this figure is expected to drop to 24 percent.

Challenge to Digitalization. Why are so many banks and credit unions not yet developing a real-time, digital customer engagement offering when there is an acknowledgment of the importance of this capability? The key challenge lies in legacy systems, with nearly all banks (89 percent) mentioning the challenge of overcoming their legacy systems as a barrier against omnichannel engagement. The high cost of implementation (89 percent) and lack of suitable technology (75 percent) were also seen as hindering efforts to become truly digitized (see Figure 4.8).

Figure 4.7   Banking's Approach to Digital Engagement

Banking approach to digital engagement

Approach to omnichannel customer engagement

19%   23%   58%

New digital approach

Replicate offline capabilities with some extra functionality

Replicate offline

Digital onboarding

24%   26%   50%

Fully digitized onboarding

Plan to fully digitize onboarding in the next two years

No plans to fully digitize onboarding in the next two years

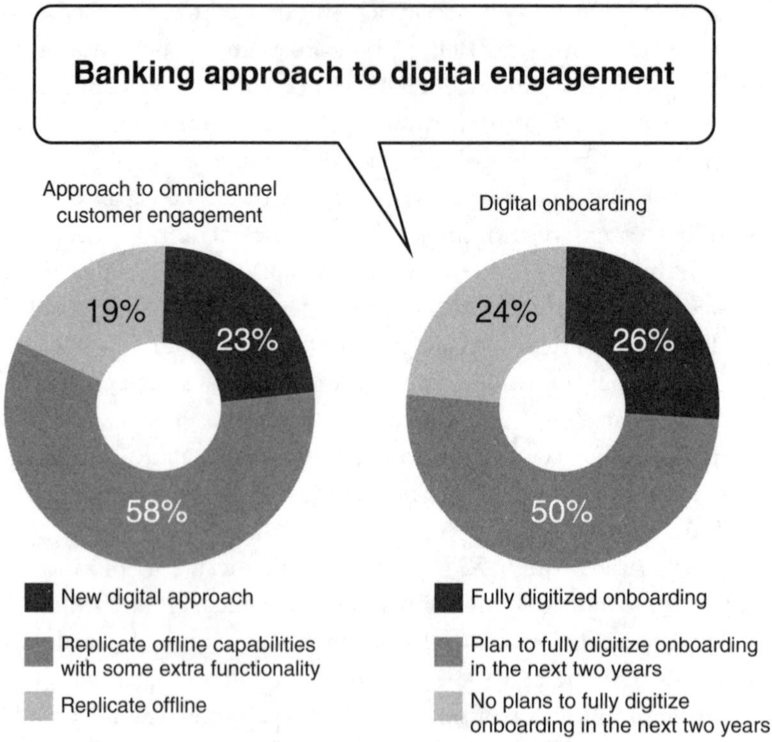

SOURCE: Oracle © November 2015 *The Financial Brand*
Omnichannel engagement might require quite a bit more of an overhaul than banking executives are planning.

Is Delivering the Bank of the Future Possible? The banking model for the future will be customer-centric as opposed to being driven by products and services. This model will enable an information-driven and value-centric relationship as opposed to being based on the bank's needs. While 48 percent of the banks believe that customers in the future will want to use a bank where tasks can be completed in real-time across multiple synchronized digital and offline channels, there is only a limited belief that the industry will be able to live up to this challenge.

Nearly one-third believe that most banks will be operating with disconnected digital channels in five years, with 22 percent believing that most banks will have failed to adopt digital at all. The discrepancy

Figure 4.8 Barriers to Engagement

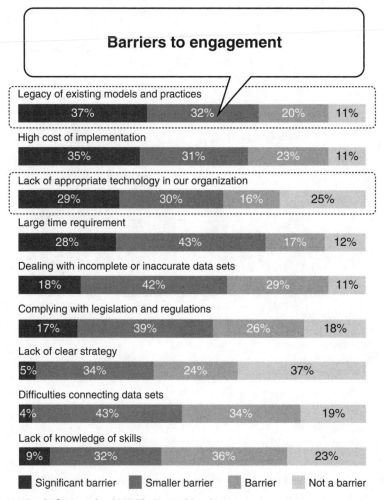

Barriers to engagement

Legacy of existing models and practices
| 37% | 32% | 20% | 11% |

High cost of implementation
| 35% | 31% | 23% | 11% |

Lack of appropriate technology in our organization
| 29% | 30% | 16% | 25% |

Large time requirement
| 28% | 43% | 17% | 12% |

Dealing with incomplete or inaccurate data sets
| 18% | 42% | 29% | 11% |

Complying with legislation and regulations
| 17% | 39% | 26% | 18% |

Lack of clear strategy
| 5% | 34% | 24% | 37% |

Difficulties connecting data sets
| 4% | 43% | 34% | 19% |

Lack of knowledge of skills
| 9% | 32% | 36% | 23% |

■ Significant barrier ■ Smaller barrier ■ Barrier ■ Not a barrier

SOURCE: Oracle © November 2015 *The Financial Brand*
Nearly 90 percent of banking executives site legacy systems as a barrier to omnichannel engagement. A convenient excuse that has run its course with consumers.

between what banks think customers will want and what the market will be able to deliver is greatest in North America and the European markets, but no more than one-third of banks in any region believe that banking will be able to provide truly synchronized, digital omnichannel banking within five years (see Figure 4.9).

Figure 4.9   Omnichannel Banking Models in Five Years

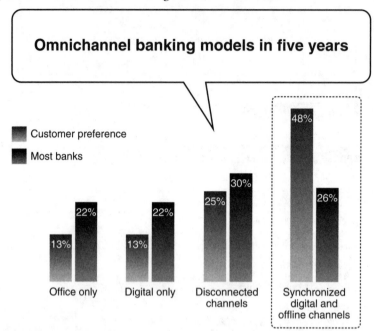

SOURCE: Oracle © November 2015 *The Financial Brand*
Only 26 percent of banking executives believe banks will be able to deliver upon the promise of omnichannel engagement within five years.

According to a study by Oracle, "Failing to meet customers' expectations is dangerous in any industry; it could be lethal in an environment where the competitive landscape is becoming ever-more congested." ("Banking is changing... with or without the banks." Oracle Financial Services Global Business Unit, 2015) While there is clarity of what is expected by the consumer, there is definitely less assuredness if banking will be able to keep pace with expectations, given the level of investment and commitment required.

Your organization's primary benefit in the increasingly competitive banking industry is your breadth of customer relationships. Despite increased competition from banks, startups, and technology companies, you can still position your organization as the principal gatekeeper and facilitator of the overall financial service relationship.

Banking is one of the oldest, largest, and most important of our industries, with most adults having some form of relationship with one or several banking organizations. While transforming over time, the industry's basic purpose has not changed.

The role of banks and credit unions is to make loans and protect depositors' money. Even if the future takes our organizations completely off the street corner, these needs must be served in some manner—by some entity.

But, traditional functions are being contested or commoditized, and emerging competitors are replicating banking functions better and at lower cost. How can legacy banks and credit unions retain the customer relationships we have built over time?

A very viable option is to reposition banks as the principal gatekeeper to your customers, creating an ever-evolving ecosystem of services and experiences provided internally and externally for the benefit of customers. By retaining the foundations of a strong customer experience, today's banks and credit unions can be the best option for most consumers.

Unfortunately, the banking industry isn't doing as well as we think when it comes to customer trust, loyalty, and creating a personalized banking experience. In fact, there are serious gaps between how banking executives believe they are doing, and how our customers really feel. This can negatively impact the ability to be the gatekeeper of financial services in the future for many organizations.

Consumer Experience Perception Gap. While banking can satisfy the most basic customer demands, banking executives are far too optimistic as to how well they meet these basic consumer needs today (see Figure 4.10). While 62 percent of retail banking executives indicate their organizations are able to deliver an excellent customer experience, only 35 percent of retail customers share this view—a 27 percent gap!

For wealth management, the gap was even greater, at 41 percentage points. Fifty-seven percent of wealth-management executives believe they provide an excellent experience, while only 16 percent of wealth-management customers agreed.

Although banking did better than bankers anticipated on capabilities like timelines and consistency, the industry falls short in the key

Figure 4.10　Banking's Overestimation of Customer Satisfaction

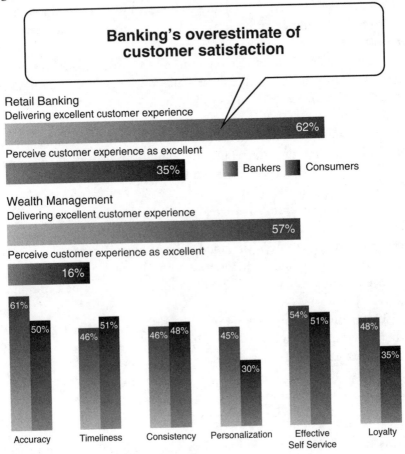

SOURCE: Oracle © November 2015 *The Financial Brand*
Clearly, you aren't as good as you think you are.

areas of creating a personalized customer experience across interactions (45 percent for bankers, 30 percent for customers), and encouraging customer loyalty (48 percent for bankers and 35 percent for customers).

Customer trust is also overestimated by banking executives surveyed. As many as 96 percent of bankers believe their customers trust them more than other nonbank competitors, while only 70 percent of customers agree. Fewer still (67 percent of customers) trust their primary bank compared to other bank competitors.

Unique Opportunity for Enhanced Customer Experiences. These survey results could present challenges for the banking industry as it becomes increasingly dependent on customer loyalty to compete. Alternatively, banks and credit unions can work to position their organizations at the center of rapidly evolving banking ecosystems. While fintech startups are able to leverage new technologies to compete against banks in specific functional activities, they do not yet have the benefit of our customer and member relationships suggests a report from IBM.[6]

From the IBM report, "This is a wake-up call for banks faced with increasing competition. As other industry players including financial technology firms, mobile payments companies and startups begin to replicate banking functions, traditional banks will be forced to find new ways to differentiate themselves," said the study. "For organizations that recognize early on that the value is shifting away from banking services to the deep customer relationships they have carefully built over decades, this could be a time of opportunity as bank ecosystems shift dramatically."[7]

The IBM research believes that banks and credit unions have an opportunity to position themselves at the epicenter of evolving ecosystems, offering a broad range of best-in-class services for the benefit of their customers. By offering these new and existing services under one roof (or as part of one app), banking organizations can retain customer loyalty through lower costs and a wider selection. Relieved of the burden of offering the services themselves, banks and credit unions could focus more heavily on enhancing the customer experience ... reducing the experience gap.

An interesting side benefit is that infrastructure costs could fall as fewer services are offered. Instead, there will be a greater focus on pass-through commissions or markups, allowing margins to increase. The *value add* will be the ability to leverage contextual insights across products to provide highly personalized solutions for consumers.

Omnichannel engagement might require quite a bit more of an over-haul than banking executives are planning.

Five Capabilities Needed for the Future. The survey of banking executives identified five key capabilities required to accelerate the transformation required to be the financial services gatekeeper.

- *Partnering and collaboration*—To be positioned at the center of the consumers' financial ecosystem, banking organizations will need to be able to partner and collaborate with new fintech players. Forty-five percent of global banking executives believe that partnerships and alliances improve their banks' competitiveness.
- *Agility*—Traditional banks will need to have agility similar to the new fintech startups. Only 21 percent of global banking executives believe their organizations have above-average agility compared to fintech peers, reflecting a gap in capabilities.
- *Innovation*—Simplified business processes and openness were thought to enhance and speed up innovation processes. The survey indicated that 48 percent of bankers thought social media will help them innovate in products and services.
- *Analytics*—Actionable insights would allow for personalized interactions and transform customer relationships. Forty-eight percent of bankers say investment in predictive analytics is a key priority.
- *Digitalization*—It was believed that digitalization was imperative for a next generation bank. As a result, 52 percent of global banking executives say that investment in mobile technologies is a key priority.

Banking and Fintech: A Symbiotic Relationship. When you compare the strengths and weaknesses of traditional financial organizations and newer fintech startups, there is a strong correlation between the strengths of existing banks and credit unions and the weaknesses of fintech, and, conversely, the strengths of fintech and the weaknesses of legacy organizations (see Figure 4.11).

The most obvious complementary factor is that fintech firms need the scale of customers that the banking industry already possesses. With a much longer tenure and scale, legacy organizations also have the

Figure 4.11   Banking Strengths vs. Fintech Weakness Self-Assessment

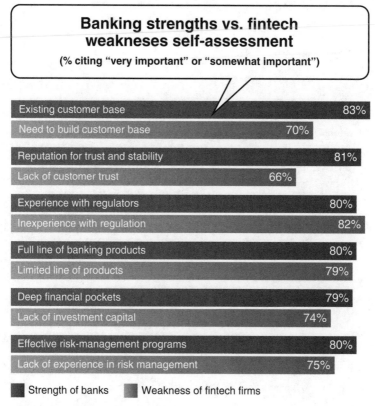

Banking strengths vs. fintech weakneses self-assessment
(% citing "very important" or "somewhat important")

Existing customer base	83%
Need to build customer base	70%
Reputation for trust and stability	81%
Lack of customer trust	66%
Experience with regulators	80%
Inexperience with regulation	82%
Full line of banking products	80%
Limited line of products	79%
Deep financial pockets	79%
Lack of investment capital	74%
Effective risk-management programs	80%
Lack of experience in risk management	75%

■ Strength of banks   ■ Weakness of fintech firms

SOURCE: The Economist Intelligence Unit © November 2015 *The Financial Brand*
A self-assessment of banks and fintech startups shows seemingly complementary strengths and weaknesses.

reputation of stability and trust as well as experience navigating the myriad of regulations and compliance requirements. Lastly, the banking industry has the capital that is the lifeblood of any growing fintech firm.

Focusing on the weakness of banks (and correlated strength of fintech firms), it is clear that today's banking organizations are severely constrained by legacy systems that can stifle innovation and the ability to be agile (see Figure 4.12). Beyond the obvious challenges of working with old systems, this inhibits the ability to recruit the level of technological expertise needed to improve products.

Figure 4.12   Fintech Strengths vs. Banking Weaknesses Self-Assessment

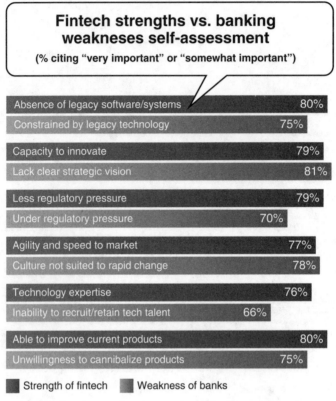

SOURCE: The Economist Intelligence Unit © November 2015 *The Financial Brand*
The "Innovator's Dilemma" is alive and well with incumbent financial institutions.

"If I were a betting person," Phil Heasley, CEO of ACI Worldwide told EIU, "I'd say that some really smart banking organizations are going to survive by merging with some really smart fintech firms." The process could be summed up as "keep two cultures, but integrate the technology back office." This solution can preserve the culture of innovation, marry it to the assets of today's banking firm, and accelerate the combined offering to market.

Your Options for the Future. As fintech startups and innovative banking organizations replicate traditional banking functions with less friction and at lower cost, financial services organizations have three options:

- They can do nothing and wait for the marketplace to overtake their organization.
- They can try to compete in low-margin services, being relegated to a processor role.
- They can leverage the benefit of current customer relationships and build a powerful ecosystem as the relationship gatekeeper.

"Traditional concepts of what a bank does will change fundamentally and permanently," said Likhit Wagle, IBM Global Industry Leader for Banking & Financial Markets. "Bankers will no longer be bankers in the traditional sense. The most successful banks will be focused on collaboration, agility, innovation, analytics, and above all on going beyond digital and transforming into becoming a Cognitive Bank."

Leveraging the deep relationships traditional banking organizations have with customers will allow banks and credit unions to position themselves as the principal gatekeeper to their customers, creating an ecosystem of even better services and experiences. Most importantly, this strategy can be implemented regardless of size or organizational structure.

Scott Mills

I've always been skeptical of public relations folk and their actual knowledge and passion for our industry. Scott is the glaring exception. It's no accident that over the past few decades, his family-run agency has influenced all corners of fintech and banking.

@WMAScott
Scott Mills, APR is president of William Mills Agency, an Atlanta-based integrated communications firm specializing in the financial industry and fintech. Through his work at the agency and on industry boards, Mills has provided communications strategy with hundreds of companies ranging in size from entrepreneurial start-ups to large, publicly traded corporations throughout North America and Europe.

Bankers who have a passion for learning, thinking strategically, and who have a pragmatic view of themselves and the institutions they serve will always be in demand. The reality is that community bankers can't outspend large banks, nor do they have the same resources from which to draw from.

There are a few myths we need to consider:

1. *There is a technology or series of technologies that will level the playing field.* While it is true that some technology is now considered standard or expected by customers, there is no "silver bullet" solution. Today's forward thinking banker needs to prioritize spending and do a better job of rolling out new capabilities internally and externally. For example, what good is a small business mobile solution if you are waiting on the customers to realize you have one?

2. *My customers KNOW us and will always stay with us because of our focus on service.* It is often cited that customers choose community financial institutions because of the familiarity and friendly staff. Moving forward, however, customers will use the branches less, mobile and call center channels more, and ultimately expect a great experience every time. Maybe we should consider it more of an aspirational statement than a myth, but the reality is that if the FI's in-person and remote experiences are not in synch, customers will move banking services elsewhere. It is *not* important to be all things to all people, rather community bankers will continue to be relevant by doing what they do as good or better than the next.

   Have you ever measured your service; and if so, are you as good as you think?

3. *I need an internal team to manage the transformation.* It is true you need talent around you, but the truth is that you need to pick your outside teams wisely. Whether it is a consulting firm, marketing partner, technology provider, or law firm, your institution will benefit from "best practices" within the banking industry when you select the right partners. Don't be timid about using and embracing what works for other FIs. Partners often have seen innovation occur and can bring those experiences with them.

   There is an enormous focus on our industry, from investors to startups who want to carve out a piece of our industry. Most will fail, but the lessons they teach us (good and bad) will make us a better industry in the process.

JP Nicols

Another industry influencer who has his hand in everything. If you have the opportunity to attend one of JP's talks or Next Money events, do it. Then, kidnap him and have him speak to your board.

> ### @JPNicols
> A former senior bank executive, JP Nicols is Managing Director of the FinTech Forge, which provides innovation as a managed service to financial institutions. He was also founder of the Bank Innovators Council which is now a part of Next Money, a global community committed to reinventing financial services through design, innovation and entrepreneurship.

How Community Institutions Can Thrive as We Move from Evolution to Revolution. Let's be honest, bankers don't really like change all that much.

We're wired to measure, mitigate, manage, and minimize risk, and we develop policies and procedures to establish and spread best practices to ensure consistency and predictability.

That's exactly the right way to manage a loan book, but is it the right way to manage your overall business strategy in a rapidly changing world?

Banking Evolution. Evolution is a very long process of adaption to the environment, and that certainly describes most of the banking industry over most of its history. Generations upon generations of bankers have adapted slowly, changing only when forced to for survival.

Physical money and no efficient way to traverse large distances made face-to-face human interaction the banking norm for centuries. Slow adaptations were made over time as increasingly sophisticated electronic means of bookkeeping and transfer created new ways to bridge distances, but the core functions of banking remained intact.

Still, location, location, and location were the three most important things in banking, and most business was still done locally, on paper and within bricks-and-mortar physical locations.

The industry itself provided little impetus for change, as interstate banking and other geopolitically based laws combined with other industry regulations created barriers to entry that still have not fallen away completely.

There is an old joke where one camper tells the other that he didn't have to worry about running faster than a bear that was stalking their campsite. "*I only have to run faster than you,*" is the punch line.

Financial institutions have evolved slowly because they only had to outrun the slowest of their fellow campers—because they only had themselves as competition. They compare themselves to their peer-group and get a false sense of security, because disruption is happening around the edges of the industry, where the game is being changed and the measurement bar is being raised.

Banking Revolution. Every single product and service that institutions offer, and every single line on their income statements, now have nonbank competitors. It's now possible for consumers—and businesses—to conduct their entire financial lives without direct relationships with institutions. FIs may provide the underlying services for many of these new asymmetric competitors, but as an anonymous utility, not as a result of conscious consumer choice.

Many bankers take undue solace in the fact that the banking industry has so far survived the assault of its would-be disruptors, but we are still in the very early stages. Your business owner customer who spends her weekend watching whatever she wants on Netflix and shopping on Amazon from her iPhone in Starbucks probably experiences a major customer experience gap when she is told she has to take time out of her busy day to visit your branch and sign a piece of paper. How long will she stay a customer if that gap is not closed?

I can't imagine a future without some form of "banking" as we know it—gathering deposits, making loans, holding and transferring monetary values—and I can't imagine a future without institutions. But that doesn't mean the industry isn't being disrupted.

Disruption does not necessarily mean that the entire industry and all of its current participants will cease to exist. Disruptive innovation changes the game by creating new markets and new relationships between organizations and individuals, and that is already happening. Banking will survive—but the real $64,000 question is, will *your* institution?

What Does All This Mean? The old ways of providing customers the financial services they need are no longer adequate for a growing group of customers—let alone potential new customers. Community institutions have to rethink their role in the community and how they are going to stand out in this world of revolution.

First, they have to think about not only differentiating themselves from one another or their big bank competitors, but also from a whole new slate of potential *substitutes* to FIs. This is not something we've ever had to deal with before.

Second, they have to think about how they're not only going to satisfy today's customers, but how to find new ones to continue to grow. Henry Ford allegedly said that if he had asked customers what they wanted, they would have said "a faster horse," and I'm sure many community bankers are quite convinced that a paper-based, face-to-face bricks-and-mortar approach is exactly what their customers want.

That is true for some customers, of course. But as digital delivery of more and more things becomes more and more commonplace to more and more people, how are you going to attract new customers when the gap between what they experience in the rest of their life and what you are offering?

Words like *value* and *customer service* have to be defined on the *customers'* terms, not ours, and we have to pay more attention to what they *do* than what they *say*.

Today's banker/camper is advised to look outside the tent and notice that there is now a whole new den of hungry cubs outside. Fintech solutions now exist to compete with every single banking product and service. The disruption is happening.

It's time to adapt and evolve. If you don't like change, you're really going to hate irrelevance.

Suresh Ramamurthi

An enigmatic brain inside of a bull inside of a china shop, Suresh Ramamurthi breaks things to fix them his way. Bankers can learn a lot from how Suresh gets stuff done, which is probably why he, his tiny community bank, and his fintech company continue to pile up the awards.

Suresh Ramamurthi is chairman and CTO of CBW Bank, and the founder and CEO of Yantra Financial Technologies. Suresh was also named Innovator of the Year by *American Banker* and CBW Bank was named Celent Model bank of the Year for Corporate Payments.

A few days after the acquisition of CBW Bank (then Citizen's Bank of Weir), I reached out to the core-processing vendor and met with their representative and I wanted to discuss APIs. He was obviously not the right person to talk to. He flat-out told me that his company would not support. I persisted and even located a brochure on the web that his company had produced indicated that it was possible to connect to the core. He relented, went back to his company and came back and told me that it was not available for the version of the product we had. At that time the Bank had no "online banking," let alone mobile check deposit, online account opening, or even mobile banking.

We switched to another core vendor with a promise of APIs and that promise was addressed in the contract. It is many years later; I still don't have those APIs. In this context, it is quite difficult for small community banks to compete and thrive against larger banks with larger technology budgets.

So we started our own technology initiatives via internal efforts, affiliate entities and partnerships. To achieve our goals, I founded a technology startup that focused on building and supporting a digital banking platform that would allow us to:

a. Open an account online in less than a minute with comprehensive KYC and CIP.
b. Create multiple cards per account with support for multiple types such as debit, gift, incentive, HAS, gas cards.

c. Create customer vertical specific solutions such as gift cards that will only work at certain locations.

d. Access debit rails to send money instantly within the United States.

e. Access bank's payment gateways to end money near instantly (where applicable) globally.

f. Manage risk in near real-time.

g. Ensure compliance with AML regulations as well as BSA.

This allows CBW Bank to address the needs of consumers and corporates. See below for various examples:

1. *Parent–child card*. We can now enable consumers to create multiple debit cards in a given account instantly and even make the card available virtually to their children with limits on them.

2. *Gas card*. A parent or a corporation can now create a gas card that works only at certain gas stations for certain amounts. We are even able to link the card to a device in the car to track the number of miles since last refueled.

3. *Prepaid card*. A consumer can now create a prepaid card with a certain dollar limit on the card that can be used online or even at retail without worrying about card number theft.

4. *Gift card*. A consumer or corporate can create a gift card on demand and send it over to persons or entities that they would like to gift. They can even create rules on where the gift card would work.

5. *HSA card*. A consumer can create a HSA card to subscribe to the HSA program under IRS rules.

6. *Expenses card*. A corporate entity can create an expense card that only works at certain locations for certain amounts.

7. *Mass disbursements*. We can now support corporations that need to send funds to large number of recipients via API as well as file upload and we can distribute the funds via multiple channels including ACH, WIRE, and debit rails.

And so on … Once we built out a flexible platform, we are now able to create different types of products for different types of consumers and corporates. This also allows us to learn the needs of each type of consumer and corporate entity and build a solution that meets their needs. All these solutions are on the payment side.

On the credit side, CBW Bank is collaborating with another entity to launch a lending platform that will cater to the borrowing needs of all these types of customers ranging from credit cards, home mortgages, commercial loans, lines of credit, SBA loans, on-demand consumer retail purchase loans, and so on, leveraging the next generation real-time underwriting technology.

Our platform, simply put, is a platform built by bankers for bankers to meet their customer's needs.

Steven J. Ramirez

Any conversation with customer experience expert Steven Ramirez will leave you with a laundry list of to-dos when you get back to the office. Consider these thoughts a toe-in-the water, and then connect with him on Twitter for more insight.

> **@BeyondTheArc**
> Steven J. Ramirez is the chief executive officer of Beyond the Arc, Inc., an agency recognized as a leader in helping financial institutions transform their customer experiences. Prior to leading Beyond the Arc, Ramirez served as an executive with Time Warner, where he was responsible for creating and successfully implementing marketing and corporate development strategies.

Master the Pivot. Community institutions are facing a difficult landscape. Just to survive, they will need to learn how to pivot. That means exploring *new* ways of doing business, offering *new* products and services, and applying technology to solve problems in *new* ways. All that "new" is enough to frighten any banker. Certain questions inevitably will come to mind. How can we introduce this level of change and not run afoul of compliance concerns? Do we risk alienating our customers because they expect us to operate in a certain way? Can we actually afford the level of investment that this kind of transformation will require? And perhaps the best question of all, do we really have to do all of this?

In Silicon Valley, a short distance from where I'm writing this, we have a language all our own. Borrowing from author Eric Ries in his book *The Lean Startup*, we define a pivot as a "structured course correction designed to test a new fundamental hypothesis about the product, strategy, and engine of growth." In other words, if your previous business model isn't working for you, maybe it's time to try something different. And fast.

There are a number of forces that keep community FIs from developing and testing new ideas quickly—and you need to overcome these challenges to master the pivot.

How Well Do You (Really) Know Your Customer? Community institutions have a deeply held belief that they are close to their customers. Some bankers may even believe that the linkage is stronger than ever with compliance-driven programs that require an institution to *know your customer* (KYC). However, many community FIs lack the customer insights that are crucial to successfully evolving their business models.

Focus on the End-to-End Experience of Customers. Financial institutions are often siloed, tending to look at individual processes without thinking about how they interrelate across products or lines of business. That means their view of the customer is fragmented. It's important to take a holistic view, evaluating the customer experience across all channels and touch points to ensure you really understand how customers view your business.

Often, businesses focus too much energy analyzing processes from an internal perspective.

They ignore important context that can better inform them about the customer experience. For example, when analyzing survey data, a bank may gather customer comments but often neglects to capture the type of accounts a customer has, the length of time they've been a customer, how and where they conduct their banking, and their economic value to the business.

Place Emphasis on High-Value Customers. Some community FIs undertake customer research and collect mountains of data, but relatively few know who their most profitable (not largest) customers are. The fact is that a relatively small number of customers will typically represent the significant proportion of your profit, which means these are the ones you should target first with your innovation efforts.

Start by tracking the customer journey as they interact with your business across touch points, and prioritize improvements to optimize "moments that matter." What are the things that matter most to your customers, and why? Frame your new business strategy, offerings, and communications around what resonates best.

Too often, businesses do what they think is right for customers, but it's based more on what the company can do than what customers said they want. To build stronger relationships, listen and learn through a Voice of the Customer program.

If you don't clearly identify your high-value customers, you'll just wind up paying attention to the people who complain the loudest. *A successful pivot requires customer-obsession and an in-depth knowledge of the customer journey.*

Are You Using Data to Enable New Business Strategies? With advanced analytics, CMOs can gain a much richer picture of their customers, from their purchase and transaction patterns, to their preferences, demographics, behavior across channels, and more. This deeper knowledge increases the effectiveness of cross-sell and upsell, but also opens up a critical opportunity.

By delivering more relevant, personalized experiences and building customer loyalty, FIs can increase the likelihood of achieving that "holy grail" of marketing—creating positive word-of-mouth and brand advocacy across social networks.

Grow Your Way to Success with Data-Fueled Marketing. Community bank CMOs do not need to become data scientists—but when they effectively partner with their CIO and data analysts, they can uncover a wealth of insights to drive highly targeted marketing.

Every bank that collects at least some data about its operations can learn valuable lessons by analyzing that data. For example, our agency has illustrated how predictive analytics could reveal that married couples with a mortgage through the bank, but not a credit card, are more likely to respond to a home equity line of credit offer. Those kinds of insights just aren't possible without successfully applying advanced analytics.

Everyone's Data Is Big (Enough). Smaller institutions have been slow to benefit from advanced (big) data analysis. Tony Pines, a data scientist at Beyond the Arc, notes that, "Leading companies are thinking beyond Big Data, and making the most of the data they have available."

Analytics won't create value unless a bank can take action. CMOs can help to revamp internal marketing processes to capitalize on analytics. For digital campaigns, that might include these five actions:

1. Personalize offers based on predictive analytics.
2. Refine email marketing by only mailing to prospects identified as most likely to purchase.
3. Re-mail to prospects who didn't respond, but should have.
4. Email those least likely to accept the offer less frequently, to minimize opt-outs.
5. Consider incentives for long-standing customers to acknowledge their loyalty.

As numerous bankers, industry analysts, and other thought leaders have argued, community FIs no longer have a choice. Today, there are fewer community institutions than there were 10 years ago, and the survivors have a smaller market share. They either innovate—by mastering the art of the pivot—or they will cease to exist. Some will be absorbed through M&A, others will just close because they are no longer financially viable.

Successfully making the transition to new business models has two pre-requisites. First, community institutions have to take a systematic approach to gaining customer insights and improving customer experience. Second, they will need to harness all of the data at their disposal to wring greater results from their current marketing efforts, and fuel new approaches to products and pricing.

In our view, community FIs make a unique and important contribution to our economy. Unfortunately, that won't be enough to guarantee their future.

Phil Ryan

Bank Innovation has quickly become one of the most respected fintech publications and industry conferences, due in large part, to the work of Phil Ryan. Phil gives us just a few minutes of his time below, but you can always read more from him on BankInnovation.net.

@PhilipGRyan

Phil Ryan is a New York–based writer and editor responsible for the *Bank Innovation* blog and managing Bank Innovation INV, a fintech accelerator. When he is not writing about fintech and the future of financial services—actually, that is all he does.

In 1850, a new bank opened its door in New York City. Called Emigrant Savings Bank, the new institution was formed with a specific goal in mind: serving the waves of Irish immigrants fleeing the potato famine wracking their country. This was the heyday of the Free Banking era, when it was a simple matter to form a bank—the country needed capital to finance its rapid growth—and institutions like Emigrant arose to serve specific needs.

Financial institutions today could rarely say so precisely what need they fill, or who they serve.

The next hundred years saw more and more banks appear, particularly in rural areas, to serve the needs of a wealthy and growing population. According to Paul Schaus, CEO of the consultancy CC Catalyst, the number of banks in the United States peaked at about 22,000 around 1960.

Today there are just over 6,300 (and a similar number of credit unions). In the years to come, this number will drop, perhaps precipitously. What can individual banks do to make sure they are among those that survive, and even flourish?

They can specialize, serving a need like Emigrant, and they can be more "kid-friendly."

Specialization means finding what your institution is good at and doing more of it. A small FI lacks the resources to be all things to all people. Both businesses and politicians are best served by focusing on their core customers or constituents. In the era of digital banking, this is no longer just a matter of geography. It's about staking out an area of expertise or particular strength and going all-in on that.

A few years ago, bankers woke up to the affection customers have for some nonbank brands. "People love Starbucks," a bunch of smart bankers thought, "so let's make our branches like coffee shops." Now, in many cases a branch refresh was sorely needed, so that was helpful, but trying to make a branch into a Starbucks was the wrong message.

Some people go to Starbucks and want to rush through in 10 seconds flat and buzz along on their way, and Starbucks accommodates that with some of the best mobile technology available—"We're a technology company that sells coffee," CEO Howard Schultz said. Other people want to sit and sip coffee and use the free wifi, and Starbucks accommodates that, too. But the foundation of the company's success was selling high-quality coffee in places where the only alternative for coffee to go was gas station coffee or reheated diner coffee. All the cool stuff, the enviable mobile app, flowed from there—Starbucks did one thing well and delighted its customers.

Being kid-friendly doesn't mean free lollipops (though free lollipops are awesome). It means reaching out to young people in meaningful ways, such as having kid-friendly accounts. Parents know most accounts for kids suck, and institutions are strikingly uncreative about how to bring in these youngest customers and engender loyalty in them. Similarly, accounts for young people just out of school and entering the workforce should offer more than the bare bones, even if these customers are not profitable—yet.

Financial institutions fret over wealth management and "discovering" the affluent among their customer base to offer them products before they send their money to an outside brokerage account. Good luck with that. Instead, they should offer more personalized service to new customers, so that when they get some money in their accounts, they naturally look to their bank, to help with investments.

Serving young people also means having top-shelf mobile capabilities, and being involved in social media. The big banks don't own the tech space anymore, and any FI can be a fast follower in mobile, which is perfectly fine. You don't need to keep up with Facebook or Amazon, but you should only allow yourself to fall a few years behind, and always be moving.

It is frustrating and expensive to have to maintain so many channels, but customers have to have options available around the clock. No matter how big you are or where you are, you are there for your customers. Young, demanding customers are coming, and don't worry—you will have young, demanding employees to help you connect with them.

Ron Shevlin

No discussion on fintech and banking would be complete without input from our industry's outspoken, stubborn, opinionated, and, often dead-on accurate realist, Ron Shevlin. It's hard to have a conversation with Ron or read one of his books and not feel that you're losing the mental chess match. He's always thinking several moves ahead, and that is exactly the kind of person you want to guide you into the future.

> ### @RShevlin
> Ron Shevlin has been a management consultant and industry analyst for more than 25 years. Ron is the author of the best-selling book *Smarter Bank,* and has been ranked among the most influential voices in banking by *The Financial Brand, Bank Innovation,* and others. His blog, Snarketing 2.0, is consistently ranked among the top marketing blogs in any industry.

Community Banks and Credit Unions: Busting Through the Strategy Fog. There's little dispute that community banks and credit unions will need to offer more technologies and more services—and offer them through an increasing number of channels or touch points—in the future to survive and thrive in the financial services industry. But to make the right choices of what technologies to invest in, which consumers to design products for, and when and where to do these things, requires a sound business strategy.

This leaves today's community-focused financial institutions in one of two boats. Either: (a) They have a strategy, or (b) They don't have a strategy.

Being in the first boat might not be as good as it sounds.

The *Harvard Business Review* recently reported, "Surveys suggest that 50 percent of employees don't have a clear understanding of their company's strategy. What's worse, that lack of knowledge is even more pronounced for sales and service employees. Withholding information about strategy for competitive reasons often results in greater risk for the business."[8]

This raises an important question: Why do 50 percent of employees NOT have a clear understanding of their company's strategy?

The *HBR* article implies that employees don't have a clear understanding of their firm's strategy because their company intentionally withholds information from employees in fear that competitors will get wind of it. For sure, there are many execs who want to keep their firm's strategy a secret from their competition.

There is another and much more prevalent reason why half of employees don't have a clear understanding of their company's strategy, however: There is no clearly defined, well-articulated strategy.

When asked what their firm's strategy is, there is no shortage of bank and credit union execs who say, "our service." Sometimes they even put the word "superior" in front of "service."

Does that mean: "We fix our mistakes better and faster than the other guy!"? Or "We have friendlier people than they do!"? Does it mean they're more "convenient" than other banks? Can they quantify this alleged service superiority? Oh wait!

In reality, the default strategy for many banks and credit unions is: "We're not them." Where "them" are the mega banks that the CFPB (Civil servants Fixed on Punishing Banks) would have us believe are evil.

Many people believe that Peter Drucker said it best when he said, "Strategy is as much about figuring out what you won't do, as it is about what you will do." Few people, however, seem to like my corollary: "If you don't figure out what you won't do, you'll find yourself in a lot of doo doo."

I bet those 50 percent of employees who don't have a clear understanding of their firm's strategy have no clue what their firm won't do.

■   ■   ■

I remember an incident a few years back when I was a junior IT strategy consultant. The project team and I came back to the home office after interviewing execs and collecting data. The partner in charge asked the team, "So ... what's their IT strategy?" And we unanimously said, "They don't have one."

The partner nearly exploded, "Of course they have an IT strategy! It might suck, it might be poorly formulated, it might be poorly communicated, but damn it, they have an IT strategy! It was your job to figure out what it is!"

■ ■ ■

It's not an employee's job to figure out the firm's strategy. Unless, of course, that employee is the CEO. The CEO's job is to figure out what the strategy is, figure out if it's the right strategy, and if it isn't, to correct it and develop a new one, then communicate it, and execute on it.

Actually, that's just one of the CEO's jobs. What a sucky job that is, eh?

Did you catch all the pieces? Let's go through them again:

1. Current strategy definition (what is our current strategy?)
2. Current strategy assessment (is our current strategy working?)
3. New strategy formulation and planning (what should our new strategy be, how will it be different from the current one, and what will we actually do?)
4. New strategy communication (how do we communicate the new strategy and avoid mass mutiny?)
5. New strategy execution (or, as Shia LaBeouf would say, "JUST DO IT!!!!")

■ ■ ■

Regarding a firm's strategy, the *HBR* article said: "What's worse, that lack of knowledge (of the firm's strategy), is even more pronounced for sales and service employees." This is a misinterpretation of the data.

The problem isn't that sales and service employees don't know their firms' strategies. The problem is that they feel the pain of a poorly defined strategy more so than bean counters sitting in headquarters.

It's the sales and service folks who have to tell customers "no" because their bosses tell them to, because their incentives are structured in such a way that they personally profit by not giving customers what they want, or because their company has inferior products or services for a particular client or prospect. And, in the back of their minds, while telling the customer "no," they hear that little voice reminding them what their company's alleged strategy is. What a sucky job they have, eh?

■ ■ ■

So here we are at a certain point in time. And you either: (a) Have a clearly defined, well-articulated strategy, or (b) You don't have a clearly defined, well-articulated strategy.

But at some previous point in time—namely, that point in time when the last strategy formulation effort took place—it's a good bet that then-current strategy wasn't defined and adequately assessed. And after the then-new strategy was formulated, it's a good bet that the then-new strategy wasn't clearly communicated, nor has it been perfectly executed.

And so the sins of the past hurt efforts to determine the strategy of the future, because few firms take the time, and expend the effort, to clarify their current strategy, assess it, and figure out if it was design or execution that is causing the under-delivery of promised results.

As a result, the senior exec team may think it knows what the company's strategy is, but in reality, it isn't what the plan created last year—or two or three years ago—says it is.

This leaves many companies in what can best be described as a *strategy fog*: A state of being in which an organization is unable to clearly see where it is, how it got there, where it's going, and/or where it should go.

■ ■ ■

At the start of the annual planning season, many community banks and credit unions will repeat the sins of the past, and ignore steps #1 and #2 (define and assess current strategy) of the five easy pieces to strategy. With better clarity regarding the current strategy—and an understanding of why (and to what extent) it is and isn't working—developing and communicating a new strategy (and how it will be different) becomes a lot easier.

But that still leaves an important question unanswered: How well will the firm execute on the new strategy?

If your organization wasn't particularly good at executing on the previously defined strategy, what makes you think it will be good at executing on the new strategy? If you don't do an honest assessment of capabilities—in the context of the firm's strategy—you cannot answer the question I just posed.

Bottom line: Strategy formulation is a contextual exercise. That is, it happens within the context of a firm's current strategy. Without clarity of the current strategy, future strategy development is bound to be flawed. Without this clarity, you may be stuck in a strategy fog.

■ ■ ■

But enough about the strategy formulation process; let's get back to strategy content, and the contention of so many community banks and credit unions that their competitive advantage is their superior service.

I mentioned to a friend of mine—a senior executive at a mid-sized credit union—that many banks and credit unions deceive themselves when they say their competitive advantage is their superior level of service.

My friend said, "You don't get it. We do have superior service. It comes down to knowing our members better than any mega bank could ever know them."

I looked at him and said, "You, my friend, don't know JACK! Or Jill, Jim, Jerry, or Jeannie, or any of your other members whose names start with the other 25 letters of the alphabet."

I explained to him that his credit union knows just a thin layer of who its members are: "Sure, when a member walks into a branch, employees know that it's Jack Jones, that his wife's name is Jane, and that they have two wonderful kids, Jenny and Jeffry, who attend Jefferson College.

"But your credit union doesn't know:

1. *How much money Jack has.* You only know how much he has with you. And if he's got any money, it's a good bet he doesn't have much of it, let alone all of it, with you. So you really don't know his investment needs or risk tolerance.
2. *What Jack's financial goals are.* Oh sure, you have a PFM app that has a goal-tracking capability. But PFM users account for what, 10 percent of your overall member base? What's the chance that Jack is one of those members AND uses the goal-tracking feature?

3. *How Jack makes his money.* You might know how much he makes because you can see that direct deposit coming in every month, but you don't know if that stream of income is safe and stable, or if Jack works in an industry that is on the decline. You definitely don't know if he's got an Etsy business raking thousands of dollars into a PayPal account.

4. *How Jack spends his money.* You've got a small percentage of your member base using your online bill pay platform, and it's a good bet you didn't issue all the credit cards he has, so you really don't know where the money is going. And worse, you're not even doing anything to analyze the debit card spend data you do have."

Not wanting to lose a friend, I eased off the gas pedal and said, "So you see, you don't know Jack. And as I look around the industry, it's the mega banks and fintech startups—not the community banks and credit unions—that are doing something about it."

■ ■ ■

If community banks and credit unions don't have the right data about their members/customers, aren't capturing the right data about them, and don't or can't analyze the data to figure out what the right data is and make assumptions and judgments about them, then: (1) those FIs can't say they know their members/customers better than any mega bank could, and (2) their self-professed competitive advantage isn't much of a competitive advantage.

■ ■ ■

Back in the late 1990s, a couple of really smart consultants wrote a book called *The Discipline of Market Leaders* in which they asserted that market leaders excelled on one of three competitive dimensions, while maintaining reasonable levels of performance on the other two. Those dimensions were: (1) operational excellence, (2) product leadership, and (3) customer intimacy.[9]

The reaction of many firms was predictable:

1. *"We don't want to compete on price and be the low-cost provider."* Which completely misinterpreted what dimension #1 was all about.

2. *"We're in a commodity business, so there is no opportunity to compete on product leadership."* Which completely missed the opportunity to decommoditize a commodity business.

3. *"We compete on customer intimacy, and knowing our customers better than our customers."* Which completely overlooked what intimacy really meant, and what investments were required to achieve and maintain that intimacy.

■ ■ ■

Mega banks have the scope and scale to compete on product leadership and operational excellence. Competing on customer intimacy is difficult for mega banks because of the complexity involved with defining discrete customer segments and developing custom solutions for those segments.

The path to success in the future of the banking industry for community banks and credit unions is competing on customer intimacy. But what does that really mean? It doesn't mean knowing who your customers/members are when they walk in the door or log on. It means putting that intimacy to work by providing advice and guidance that other FIs can't because they don't know your customers/members as well as you do.

Scarlett Sieber

I have yet to find a banker on this planet who hasn't closely watched BBVA's acquisition of fintech darling Simple, and BBVA's pursuit into opening APIs for fintech providers. If you want to meet the driving force behind the future of these endeavors, you'll need to get it in gear, as Scarlett Sieber isn't going to hit the brakes for you to catch up.

> **@ScarlettSieber**
> Scarlett Sieber is SVP of global business development under the New Digital Business team. In this role, Scarlett leverages BBVA's assets (including Simple, BBVA API Market, etc.) to secure the right partnerships and opportunities within the ecosystem.

With the world shifting and technology's role in this future, no one wants to be left behind, and there is no reason the smaller banks and credit unions have to be.

Being small has its advantages. The smaller players can act more quickly and iterate in ways that larger players don't have the freedom to do. Structure your teams so that you have at least one group who is constantly testing, and more importantly failing, as you can learn more from what doesn't work than what does. This process doesn't have to be expensive and you don't have to risk your brand reputation or current customer loyalty to do it.

Be creative—make a dummy Twitter account and a landing page with the tech you are offering and go after your target users, see if they go to your website and sign up to hear more or and put up a new product on Kickstarter to see if it gains traction. It is also important to create balance and make sure that the entire institution is not focused on innovative initiatives, keep part of the team dedicated to doing what you already do well and focusing on your current customers.

Next, accept the fact that the role of a financial institution is changing, and to stay relevant, you will need to transition with it. Start making these changes now and put being a digital only or digital mostly institution as a high priority in your strategy meetings. Being a digital FI means focusing on the customer experience.

Most FIs say they put the customer first, but try to identify what this really means. If you want to appeal to millennials, make sure that you have millennials within your organization actively participate in the strategy, product, customer acquisition, etc., conversations. Research and data are great, but having the people who live and breathe this stuff every day is a whole other ball game.

Startups have a saying, "get out of the building." The idea here is to spend time talking with your current customers or future customers and listening to what they want and need, not thinking you have the answer, as oftentimes, you will be surprised. Focusing on digital means delivering a terrific mobile experience (maybe this will be wearables in the future, maybe something else), it means being simple, engaging, and transparent. Invest all you can in making banking an experience people love.

Lastly, make strong partnerships. We have seen competition and disruption taking over the financial services world, and with that, startups are shifting from taking out the banks to partnering with them.

This is a great opportunity.

Look for startups that have backing to stay around awhile (12 months or more) and find ways to work together. We are watching a shift of the *unbundling of banking,* so find a niche (a key demographic or vertical) that you excel in, and own that niche. It doesn't hurt to look at other industries outside of banking who are going through similar transformations and learn from them, both what worked well and what didn't work.

Take advantage of the age that we live in and access to information, there are so many possible partners from both within and outside of this industry.

Shari Storm

I first met Shari Storm when she was busy getting her credit union named "Innovator of the Decade" by Online Banking Report in 2010. A long-time credit union executive, Shari knows what it means to transform banking organizations for future success, and has an extraordinary track record for creating effective marketing programs.

> ### @ShariStorm
> Author, speaker, consultant, and agent, Shari Storm, spent 16 years as an executive at a Seattle-area credit union. She now owns her own consulting company and speakers' bureau called Category 6.

Shifts in Marketing. The shifts in marketing pose a significant problem for bank executives. For almost five decades marketing and advertising was basically pretty straightforward. Your marketing department would create newspaper, television, radio, billboard, or a direct mail piece. You could see them out in the community, as did your friends, and you had a basic understanding and appreciation for them.

Now, your CMO is probably coming to you with reports like, "We had 30,000 hits on our Vine." Or, "We just made the front page of Reddit." Chances are, you have little to no idea what they are talking about and no way to get a personal understanding or appreciation for these accomplishments.

The days of the whole family sitting down to watch the same TV show and see the same cereal commercial are long gone. Marketing today is far more fragmented and dispersed. If a family is watching the same show, they are probably not watching it at the same time or in the same place or from the same device. Dad may be watching in the den on the big screen, while brother is watching from his phone in his room, and sister is watching on Hulu on her laptop.

The good thing about today's marketing landscape is that it is far easier to pinpoint the type of consumer your institute wants to message. Today the amount of information we can get about a consumer is growing exponentially. We can tell where they are in the buying cycle. We can see how much they comparison shop. We know if they ask for referrals on a product or service. We can even surmise how price sensitive they are.

A smart online marketing campaign can analyze a host of facts about a person's online activities and target those people who are most likely to want to buy your product or service.

Back in the early 1900s John Wanamaker famously quipped, "Half of my advertising dollars are wasted. I just don't know which half." Those days are also gone. Now, with smart analytics, your marketing team can tell who clicked on a link, where they went on your website, and ultimately what they ended up buying.

Because marketing is now more targeted online, it is not likely that you'll ever see the bulk of your advertising because it is published in places you don't visit, nor do your friends.

So how do you keep up? I jokingly tell my clients to befriend young people. But in all honesty, having a generational consultant is a good idea. Even better, bring together a whole group of them. An advisory group of people ages 15 to 22 can be a tremendous help in understanding up and coming trends in everything from marketing to technology to work and spending habits.

Several years ago, I was at a mobile banking conference and I sat next to a young man who was 23 years old. I remember he was the first person to tell me about Bitcoin. At the end of the conference, I asked him if he would be my friend. He thought it was a strange request but he was game. A few weeks later, I sent him and email and asked, "What is Snapchat?" A long and helpful (for me) friendship followed.

Marketing to Moms. I've never understood why banks and credit unions don't make more of a concerted effort to win the business of moms. After all, moms make 83 percent of all household spending decisions, they are the biggest influence of where their children will do their banking as young adults and they have a tremendous referral network, both online and in real life.

But let's take a step back and look at what makes a good target market. A good target market should have a strong sense of affiliation, a certain degree of homogeneity, and a high degree of influence.

Breaking these three things down:

1. *Strong sense of affiliation*: When looking for a target segment, you want to be sure that your audience identifies with that segment. For example, if you are targeting affluent people, it is difficult to know with certainty who considers themselves rich. You'll always have some folks with nothing in the bank who think they are players and you'll have just as many with high net worth that don't believe they can afford luxury items. I've seen plenty of people training to run a half marathon who do not consider themselves runners. With the category of moms, it is a safe assumption that someone who is a mom knows with certainty that they fall into the parent category. Additionally, they often identify strongly with this category.

2. *A certain degree of homogeneity*: A target market has strength if you can predict with some reasonableness how that group will react to a product or message. It is easier to make those predictions if the group thinks and acts similarly. Moms have a lot of similarities. They view themselves as caregivers. They view themselves as overworked and underappreciated. They care deeply for the welfare of their children. They respond positively to things like the sound of children laughing, images of happy children, stories that embrace the betterment of the world.

3. *Influence*: Moms control where their household will do their banking and often where their friends and extended family do their banking. This is an important distinction of this demographic and should not be underestimated in its importance.

Parents are the number one indicator of where their children will do their banking. A recent study by The Money Advice Service asked over

1,000 teenagers about their financial habits. When it comes to taking advice on money matters, 15-17 year olds have a clear hierarchy of who they turn to. Over three quarters (77 percent) of those surveyed said they find their parents' financial advice most helpful. I have long contended that financial institutions' focus on teens and consumers in their early twenties is misguided. By the time a consumer is in their teens, they have made their banking decisions. FIs that want to earn the business of teens must win their business when they are in elementary school.[10]

Another reason moms make such a good target market is their online behavior. Moms were one of the first groups to embrace blogging, Facebook, Pinterest, and Instagram in their early stages. The blogosphere is inundated with mom blogs. According to a 2012 Mashable article, there are 3.9 million mom bloggers in the United States. Moms congregate online. That is nice for a marketer, because you know where to find moms. But what makes it good for a strategist is how moms use social medium forums. Mom actively ask for, give, and act on referrals. If you want to see this in action, go to Facebook, type in your town's name plus the word moms and see how many groups come up and how many people belong to those groups.

I often tell the story of a focus group we held with 12 local area moms. We were in the midst of changing the name of our checking account and wanted to test some of the names we were considering. A funny thing happened. The first mom answered the first question, then the second mom answered the first question. The first mom blurted, "I like her answer better! Can I change my answer to hers?" This happened time and again, leading one of the men watching the focus group to ask, "Do these women ever make a decision without consulting each other?!" To which I replied, "That's why, as a marketer, I love them!"

When I worked at Verity Credit Union, one strategy was to focus on the mom market. Here are some of the things that we did:

1. *Family-friendly branches*: We wanted kids to love visiting the credit union. We wanted to win the hearts and minds of kids long before they became teenagers. To that end, we built childrens' corners, had a multitude of giveaways and contests. Santa comes, the Easter Bunny

comes, we built huge statues out of Peeps in the spring, we period-
ically have cookies and hot cocoa on cold days. We are always the
place that gives out stickers, suckers, coins, anything to make kids
love visiting the credit union.

2. *We renamed our checking account Cartwheel Checking*: All of our creative centers around parents watching their kids play, the sound of
   children laughing, radio spots that say things like, "remember when
   the toughest thing you had to worry about was perfecting your
   cartwheel" (cue to sound of children laughing).

3. *Focusing on convenience services*: Services like mobile, mobile deposit
   capture, and PFM became more important to us because we understood how critical easy-to-use services are to this demographic. Our
   checking account refunded ATM fees (once certain criteria were
   met). We didn't want moms to have to worry about searching for a
   hard-to-find free ATM (see Figure 4.13).

Figure 4.13   ATM Surcharge Fees

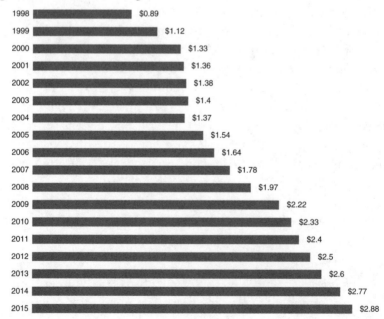

SOURCE: Bankrate
The average ATM surcharge fee has increased quite a bit since the 1990s.

Some of the ways we measured the success of Verity's mom initiative included the number of new checking accounts opened, the number of young members joining the credit union, and the number of people following the Verity Mom spokesperson on social media. We are happy to report that the number of new checking accounts increased each year since the implementation of the program. The average age of new members decreased by three years and the Verity Mom spokesperson counts thousands of followers in various mediums.

It's not just credit unions who are paying new attention to the mom market.

Warner Bro's Studio, the motion picture company, launched a website called MomLogic in 2008 with the main objective to reach the mom market. To date, that site gets hundreds of thousands of visitors each month.

When Sienna released its online Swagger Wagon videos in 2011, Toyota hit their Sienna sales goal in just nine months, during a time when car sales were flat or declining.[11]

Sauza Tequila decided to focus on the woman and mom market by launching their "Make It With a Fireman" campaign. Although the company won't say more than the campaign was a great success, we do know that the videos had over 10 million views and landed a spot on YouTube's Most Watched Ad list.

I've had a few people mention to me that the mom market seems too small of a segment for serious focus. To that worry, I point to USAA. USAA, which has an asset size of over $45 billion focuses unapologetically on current and past military members and their families. Of which, there are 61 million in the United States. Compare that to the 84 million moms that are currently in the United States.

In short, moms make up an incredibly powerful market that is often overlooked. I urge financial institutions to rethink that stance. When you earn a mom's business, you often earn her family, her friends, and her community.

Lee Wetherington

Years ago, an elderly banker told me that I was Lee Wetherington, and that he did not like my presentation because I was too loud and too southern. I tried to tell the banker that even though I, too, am loud and southern, and that I also spoke at the same conference, that I was not Lee. I further evidenced this with the huge name badge around my neck. He still did not believe me. I did not know Lee at the time, but quickly found him to be a dynamic thinker, engaging speaker, and, yes, loud and southern. Here, he gives you what his top 10 moves over the next 10 years would be if he led a community financial institution. Oh, and feel free to confuse me with Lee any time.

@LeeWetherington
Lee Wetherington is director of strategic insight for Jack Henry & Associates (JKHY: NASDAQ). He directs the development of actionable insights and strategy for the financial services industry at large.

My Top 10 For The Next 10
1. Grow FI to at least $1 billion in assets.
2. Do that by combination of acquisition(s) and strong organic customer growth in markets served.
3. Achieve organic growth by explicitly and strategically committing to UX (User eXperience) across all channels as the primary driver of both revenue generation and cost reduction, that is, vow never to intentionally diminish UX to make a buck (e.g., pushing signature debit that slows POS and exposes customers to higher incidences of fraud vs. PIN just so FI can make more interchange).
4. Smartly divest resources from branch channel to invest into digital channels.
5. Use those digital investments to simplify UI and bolster UX via contextual, conversational, advisory nudges and notifications that materially help customers spend less, save more, and track/achieve milestone financial goals.
6. Integrate emotion-as-a-service (e.g., Affectiva API) to track and measure in real time whether and how well you are taking customers

from negative to positive money emotions across digital channels—and revise/evolve those channels accordingly over time.

7. Streamline branch so that remaining staff are not just "universal" in knowledge but have the highest-caliber soft skills (because, as transactions diminish, branch interactions that remain become more emotionally fraught—that is, people who continue to come in will be doing so because they have problems, are angry, anxious, or ignorant of what to do next. Even as branches become smaller and smarter, they must also become much better at UX. In fact, I think branch UX must be your best UX going forward because of the qualitative change in the nature of branch visits over time and the fact that these interactions will be higher stakes.

8. Master *the via negativa*, the art of subtraction, the courage to take away feature/function clutter to create clean, coherent user experiences.

9. Leverage compelling card rewards to improve your cards' chances of being the default card-on-file as payments sublimate (Uber, Apple Pay, et al.) over the next five years.

10. Eventually build or integrate both shopping and mobile POS payments into your own native mobile banking app so that you can provide meaningful funds-availability and cash-flow context to purchase decisions in real time (hopefully with integrated merchant rewards/couponing, too).

Notes

1. For example, Bank of America currently offers 1 basis point interest on kids' accounts, which means your child's $1,500 average balance earns 1 cent per month!

2. Social Money, owner of SmartyPig, was acquired by Q2 Holdings in December of 2015.

3. BECU offers a similar boost for the first $500 of over-18 members as well, but the rate is only 4 percent.

4. Matthew Dixon and Brent Adamson, The Challenger Sale, Portfolio (2011).

5. Herbert V. Prochnow and Roy A. Foulke, *Practical Bank Credit* (Prentice-Hall, 1939).

6. Jim Brill, Nicholas Drury, Anthony Lipp, Anthony Marshall, and Likhit Wagle, "Banking Redefined," IBM Corporation (2015).

7. Ibid.

8. Frank V. Cespedes, "Aligning Strategy and Sales." *International Journal of Sales Transformation* 1, no. 1 (April 2015): 52–54.

9. Fred Wiersema and Michael Treacy, *The Discipline of Market Leaders* (Addison-Wesley, 1995).

10. Money Advice Service, "The Financial Capability of 15-17 year olds" (2013).

11. http://thedojohouse.com/Toyota-Swagger-Wagon.

Chapter 5

Finishing Move

An Introduction to the End

Tomorrow is yesterday. That's clear.

As we approach the disruption black hole, our bubble of a ship gives passengers a crystal-clear view of the lab's latest creation: a gravy-lathered and room-temperature time melt. Thin is the bubble's skin—parallax error-free—where the slow and cozy inside ends and its blurry outside begins is anyone's guess.

Some bulkhead and others exit-row seated, the never-enough-connected passengers are seduced by both ends of time simultaneously connecting and repelling itself.

Inside the bubble, giants figure. Startups raise. Networks writhe. Investors scramble. Millennials age. Institutions stutter. Analysts wax semantic.

It's still today. And the discussion is still here. And the uneasy panel of fortuneteller professors are still attempting to elucidate "disruption."

Pseudo-intellectual drivel or MBA-inspired rant—they are one and the same. Volumes to learn, see, and buy from skewed-research salesmen and skewered-research dreamers.

Who doesn't have an answer? Who hasn't a theory to elucidate?

Perhaps it's a bit more difficult than it sounds. Their cerebella as axels wrapped in dissonance. As if asymmetrical concordance might help all us chickens rationalize an antidote.

"The sky is falling!" ... "Define 'is.'"

The graffitied walls of this echo chamber, patented by payments trolls and overhyped by investors. Simultaneously soothsaid and daily reality, some can't shake the feeling of a long-lost mammal in a Darwin-inspired *Far Side* comic.

No doubt at some mid-evolution point, a prehistoric thing wondered if he too might spurt that evolutionary trait to mark his existence on this planet relevant. Perhaps he also quickly became too distracted/comforted/fooled by his present to see his future.

Innovator's Dilemma as it were, and as it is. You can't change a human, but you can alter his environment and his experience.

Years and years ago, we were concerned that small banks would go away and big banks would replace them. That change in power was scary. Local decisions moving to big central offices, causing small businesses to stagnate in their funding needs ... crunch.

It's more clear than ever, though, that that fear may not materialize as expected.

In the United States today, I can replicate every retail and commercial banking service without enduring the nostalgia of a bank or credit union. And the services are provided faster, lighter, kinder, cheaper, and more tailored to my preferences than anything coming from trained humans, arcane buildings, and rigid silos.

We Expect More with Each Passing Day

My bank knows everything about me—what I buy, where I eat, which places I visit most often—but it wants me to fill out a captcha, wait for a text to my mobile phone, and then answer an automated phone call to login in to mobile banking.

My pretty little thermostat knows me better than my bank.

What a paradox.

Twenty years ago, when I would visit your branch each week, you knew the topical things about me. I would dress up before walking into your lobby, so you would think I was more responsible. You would greet me and shake my hand when I walked in, and I would look you in the eye so you would trust me. You knew my kids' and pets' names, and anything else I wanted you to think about my life.

You knew the part of me that I wanted to show you at that time.

Confounding as it may be, now that you can see and qualify nearly any piece of data about me, you don't. So you know even less about me than I wanted you to know 20 years ago.

And that's what the bankruption is all about. It's not about a mobile wallet or a rebundling of banking services. It's teaching the establishment a lesson. Anarchy against knuckle-drag. Nothing personal.

But it absolutely is personal, and that's why we are where we are.

The Future of Retail Banking Will Be Optimized

"Banks and credit unions should focus on building mobile apps that engage customers and prospects in the processes that lead to selling opportunities. The financial institutions with superior mobile marketing capabilities will be the winners over the next five years."[1]

—Ron Shevlin
Director of Research at Cornerstone Advisors, Inc.

Twenty grackles crackle and fly into the walls of my skull. An ocean of lacrimal fluid pools the eyes that wander, no matter how hard I oversteer. Numb gums play poor host to my nervous, now weightless teeth.

Thursday morning regrets follow a Wednesday night soaked by Old Cubans and lit Cubans. Going out like I came in: hungover, sleepy, and pissed off. Here goes everything...

There Is No Doubt: Modern Retail Banking Is Dreadful

For the entire history of retail banking, humans have endured pain related to finances.

Humans are terrible at math, profoundly impatient, and forgetful. Modern banking gave humans a check register and a pat on the back—reminding consumers to "carry the one" in their arithmetic. This setup was nearly comedic as humans bounced checks, swiped cards past their limit, and made many other mistakes that, while not the institution's fault, banking providers took advantage of via penalties and fees.

And so, banking became an incessant, agonizing reminder that we suck at math, and we will never be as good at money management as we thought we would be when we were kids.

Which is why our industry is nearly criminal. The very fact that for one to successfully manage his finances he must be good at math, store data, and recall it instantaneously and flawlessly, intake incongruent and unformatted data from a variety of incompatible electronic and nonelectronic systems, and forecast future money movement is a crime against humanity.

Each of those chores is a machine task, not a human task.

If banking were medicine, we are all self-certified doctors with day jobs regularly performing self-administered meatball surgery. I can hold a scalpel, but that doesn't mean I should use it.

Likewise, I can lock up my money in a CD for five years, but should I? What rate should I get? What are my other options for my money? Why do I have to think about this—can't some app do this for me?

If I Have to Think about My Banking, You're Doing It Wrong

"Engagement banking" may just ring as the last desperate cry of those who believe in a failed model—delusions of humans actually wanting to bank (or to pay or to manage their money).

While retail banking accountholders want to be paid for their deposits and rewarded for loyalty, they don't really want to know or be regularly involved with their debit or savings provider.

We're all too busy for that. We don't have time to be engaged with each other, much less our money. Whether it is on their phone, on their wrist, in glasses, with Alexa, via VR, or any other technology, few people on this Earth relish managing their money. Otherwise, we'd all call it "playing money."

The real future of retail banking is one where everything happens automatically, for us, without us ever having to think about banking or its underlying vaults.

Let's make it more tangible.

If people didn't have to do so, they would prefer to avoid:

- Knowing the difference between a credit union and a bank
- Searching for the best auto rate
- Downloading and agreeing to disclosures
- Setting up a mobile wallet
- Setting a savings goal
- Appending receipts to transaction line items
- Seeing a pie chart of their spending
- Shopping for a mortgage
- Getting alerts for overspending
- Taking a photo of their utility bill to save entry on bill pay
- Applying for anything
- Being told how little money they will have in the future

The problem with retail banking is not green-screened monolithic computer antiquities, expensive physical branch footprints, town depopulation, or expensive regulation. The real problem with retail banking today is the requirement of human engagement.

And, from a consumer's perspective, we all know our lethargy with our banking is costing us money.

As an Accountholder, I Know I'm Getting Messed Over with My Money—Somewhere

Am I getting the absolute best car loan, credit card, checking account, CD, HELOC, or mortgage rates? Really? Out of 12,000 other financial institutions, and 150,000 different rate-driven products, I happen to have perfectly optimized my financial life with the flippant, set-it-and-forget-it banking decisions I made?

That can't be possible. Even if I made the best choices when I opened the accounts, as rates change and my credit score changes, I'm losing somewhere. I get an auto loan over here for 1.70 percent, the next month I see a billboard over there for 1.50 percent. (I could refi my auto loan, but how does that refi fee factor into the lifetime savings?)

What about that junk mail from the megabank offering $500 to move $5,000 money into a savings account for six months? Or the credit card offer I got to move my balance over from another card at 0 percent for 18 months?

It sure seems like if I took advantage of some of these offers, I could make better use of my money. But I'm too busy. What if there were a system looking out for my banking with as much vigor and expertise as today's robo-advisers?

Today, changing financial institutions is a lot like changing batteries. No one thinks, "Boy, I really need to swap this Duracell out with an Energizer." They wait until they really feel the pain—until the toy stops working and their kid is crying—before they take action. And even then, the action is often as "engaged" as digging in the battery box for anything that fits.

The Year Is 2030, and No One Thinks about Banking

By the year 2030, thousands of the diffused 11,000 community-based financial institutions of today will form to act more like one large shopping mall, with co-op'ed products, technologies, and marketing, yet distinct rates and offers at the individual FI level (see Figure 5.1).

Figure 5.1   Forecast—Total US Financial Institutions to 2030

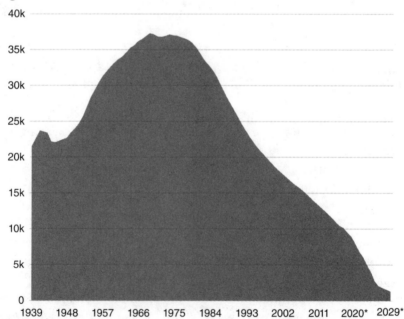

Source: CUNA & FDIC; Post-2015 Forecast by Author
The landscape of financial institutions in the United States will change even more considerably the next 10 years.

This network will allow for efficient placing of deposits, transactional data reconciliation, and so on across a previously heterogeneous data set. It would require a phenomenal amount of cooperation between all participating community banking partners, free integration between technical components, and an agreement between the parties to essentially kill retail "relationship-oriented" banking in favor of utilitarian banking.

In addition to this one big community institution network, the United States will have about 40 very large banks (all of which are global banks) with 5 of those distinguished as retail-only institutions.

Each of these 40 banks, as well as the aforementioned independent-banking shopping network, have uniform, simple, secure points of interaction and data transfer available to explicit systems (presumably, working across distributed ledgers). One of these connected systems is the Banking Optimization System (BOS)—an open-standards, rules-based optimization engine for retail banking.

A few overarching points on BOS:

- BOS will be a continuously informed and learning system that receives bids and incentive offers from financial institutions.
- BOS will have power of attorney to create accounts, move money, and perform various other banking activities on your behalf.
- BOS will negotiate, continuously with all financial institutions on your behalf, optimizing for the best rate on every cent across your accounts.
- BOS will not be owned by any financial institution, and its guidelines will be implemented entirely by a rule-making governmental body.
- BOS will have a set of APIs that allow any number of registered third-party firms to develop "interfaces" for an otherwise faceless system.
- BOS will have a data store with a variety of sharing, learning, and rules-implementing permissions. This will be accessible to you at any time, in any of the robust cloud-storage systems, such as Google, Amazon, Facebook, Ant Financial, and Microsoft.
- BOS will improve the affordability of banking for those currently forced to use suboptimal banking alternatives (i.e., the "under-banked" or "unbanked" person), and will concurrently improve the position of any existing banking user.

Some nontechnical, evolutionary roadblocks to BOS:

- *Humans will need to trust code over humans.* This will be less of a concern as Internet of Things continues to improve our world, and as natural attrition related to generational shift continues in the United States.
- *Community institutions will need to find a way to work together and share resources.* There is an example of this coopetition-framed network right now (e.g., Kasasa), but it is currently focused on developing the relationship between the consumer and the institution. BOS is specifically focused on killing that relationship; BOS wants to turn FIs into utilities.

  The network of community institutions is imperative to the BOS working successfully for a few reasons: helps avoid a banking monopoly by allowing for access to a variety of banking products across competitive FIs, and smaller FIs may (for a time) make much better offers—making BOS more interesting to early adopters.
- *Community institutions will need to give up their consumer relationships.* This will be the most difficult chasm to cross, and will, ultimately lead to the very slow death of most community banking institutions.
- *Regulations, CFPB(?), FDIC, etc. will need a slew of updates.* While a benefit if regulation updates concurrently, there are ways to make BOS work without too many changes in the existing protocol. If the regulations don't evolve with BOS, the biggest concern to community institutions would be those with geographic market requirements. Again, there are any numbers of ways to solve for this problem.

It seems natural that a PFM company might want to become the BOS itself. They already see transactions and balances for millions of accounts across thousands of financial providers. The channel problem is a heck of a blocker to this, however, as soon as any partner FI who does not want to become a utility sees what their PFM vendor is doing.

There's at Least a Decade until 2030

BOS could be an exciting evolution that levels the playing field by improving the affordability of banking for all, while simultaneously removing the pain and friction of optimizing your money. Or, BOS could be interpreted as a dystopian future where personal choice and relationship give way to the almighty rate—where relationship-driven financial outposts are converted to ones and zeroes utilities. Or, BOS could be seen as just plain silly. All valid.

Hey, BOS is just one of many ideas on how the future of retail banking might evolve, and what do I know? I dropped my crystal ball years ago, as it was obviously defective (see what I did there?).

This takes us back to where we began: not 2030, but today and tomorrow.

The most important thing community financial institutions can do today is to start planning their tomorrow. Think strategy, then tactics. Take a glance at Figure 5.2 for inspiration.

Figure 5.2 Payphones in United States

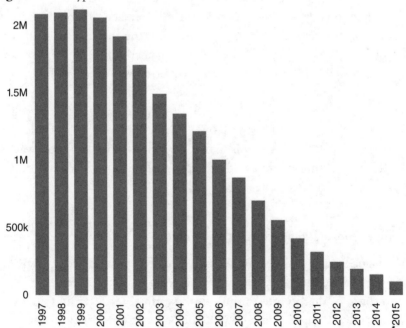

SOURCE: Federal Communications Commission; * = estimated
Remember when payphones were everywhere?

Here's the Tough List

Still want to remain a universal institution for all? Here's some thought starters. If you can't or don't want to do the hard work and answer these, sell your institution now to someone who does:

- Create a plan to onboard users beyond your current geographical footprint. This may involve changes to charters, internal processes, or simply change in mind-set. You may not need it today, but you will need it soon.
- Who at your institution owns the outreach to your examiners to discuss digital acquisition and future innovative ideas? Name her/him.
- Which branches are you going to cut? Name them.
- How much total expense will you cut out of your remaining branches? Specify a dollar amount and a deadline for the reduction.
- Which expert partners will you align with to help you? You will need the scale of experts—for almost all you do.
- Which board member(s) do you need to replace? Think of them. ☺
- Write the steps needed to apply for, and the number of actual days before hearing a decision on a checking account, personal loan, auto loan, credit card, mortgage, and small business loan. Cry. Then make it fully digital, and fast.
- Create a schedule for the above list—work back from the rollout date until you get to tomorrow. If there are gaps in your planning because you don't know if there's a vendor to do what you want to do, just assume there's 5 (there's probably 50), and do the research after your brain dump.

I Hope That's Enough to Get You Started

After trudging through some history to discover the present, analyzing a few opportunities for community banking, and considering the ideas from some of the brightest minds in the industry, you should now have at least a few things to discuss with your executive team and board.

If you haven't gone to the Bankruption website, now is the time to do it. I've built over 100 charts and graphs and made them available for you to use in your personal presentations and on social media. I just ask that you keep the images intact with the sourcing information and the copyright notice on the image.

Also, if you haven't done it yet, follow me on Twitter, and become my LinkedIn pal. Don't forget to go to bankruption.com to see where your institution sits on the Bankruption Index, and, please, come say hi to me at the conferences, and share with me what's on your mind.

And in case I didn't say it yet, thank you for all you do.

Now, let's get to work.

Note

1. *Digital Banking Report*, Financial Marketing Trends 2016.

About the Author

J ohn Waupsh is a renowned speaker at top fintech and banking conferences. With one hand in community banking and the other in
fintech, he is well-regarded for balancing straight-talk consultation
with research-backed ideation.

John is Chief Innovation Officer at Kasasa®, the company formerly
known as BancVue®. Waupsh has pioneered integrated fintech and
financial marketing solutions for over a decade, including Kasasa, the
first national brand of financial products offered exclusively at hundreds
of community financial institutions around the United States.

John is Austin Chapter Lead of Next Money, a global fintech
networking organization, and a mentor with Bank Innovation's global
fintech accelerator, INV.

His work has helped Kasasa grab three Finovate "Best of Show"
titles, recognition in *Fast Company*'s "10 Most Innovative Companies in
Finance," standing in the FinTech Top 100, as well as numerous Mar-
Com Awards.

In his spare time, Waupsh runs a music conservancy called *The Preser-
vation Project*, which discovers, restores, and releases previously unpublished music from the 1920s through the 1970s. He lives in Austin, Texas,
with his wife and two children.

About the Companion Website

This book includes a companion website, which can be found at www.wiley.com/go/waupsh. Enter the password: bankruption17. This website includes the charts and figures in this book as well as many additional charts to support the bankruption story.

Index

Page references followed by f indicate an illustrated figure; followed by t indicate a table.

Virtual session, 182
Voice America, 209
Voice response system, 127
Voluntary attrition rates.
   See United States
Voluntary closures, 16–18

W

Wachovia, impact, 34
Wagle, Likhit, 227
Wall Street & Technology, 186
Wal-Mart, 192
Wanamaker, John, 249
Washington Mutual (WaMu),
   impact, 34
Wealthfront, 68
Wealth management, 221
   worry, 239
WeBank, 62–63
Website, market area, 9
WeChat, 63
Wells Fargo, 202
Westpac, implementation, 67

Wetherington, Lee, 253–255
"We Want You" PowerPoints,
   117
White Label
   delivery, 66–67
   fintech providers, 114
   point solutions, 118
William Mills Agency, 227
Women-owned businesses, 114
Word-of-mouth, creation, 236
World Council of Credit Unions,
   51
WV United Federal Credit Union
   (Element FCU), 58

X

Xanga, 179

Y

Yantra Financial Technologies, 232
Y Combinator fintech startup, 124
Youth banking products/services,
   165t–170t